Teaching Nabokov's *Lolita* in the #MeToo Era

Teaching Nabokov's *Lolita* in the #MeToo Era

Edited and with an Introduction by
Eléna Rakhimova-Sommers

LEXINGTON BOOKS
Lanham • Boulder • New York • London

Published by Lexington Books
An imprint of The Rowman & Littlefield Publishing Group, Inc.
4501 Forbes Boulevard, Suite 200, Lanham, Maryland 20706
www.rowman.com

6 Tinworth Street, London SE11 5AL, United Kingdom

Copyright © 2021 by The Rowman & Littlefield Publishing Group, Inc.

Cover art © "Peeling Back the Silence" by Graciella Delgado

All rights reserved. No part of this book may be reproduced in any form or by any electronic or mechanical means, including information storage and retrieval systems, without written permission from the publisher, except by a reviewer who may quote passages in a review.

British Library Cataloguing in Publication Information Available

Library of Congress Cataloging-in-Publication Data

Names: Rakhimova-Sommers, Elena, editor.
Title: Teaching Nabokov's Lolita in the #metoo era / edited by Eléna Rakhimova-Sommers.
Description: Lanham : Lexington Books, [2021] | Includes bibliographical references and index.
Identifiers: LCCN 2020054234 (print) | LCCN 2020054235 (ebook) | ISBN 9781793628381 (cloth) | ISBN 9781793628398 (epub) | ISBN 9781793628404 (pbk)
Subjects: LCSH: Nabokov, Vladimir Vladimirovich, 1899-1977. Lolita. | Nabokov, Vladimir Vladi-
    mirovich, 1899-1977--Study and teaching. | MeToo movement.
Classification: LCC PS3527.A15 L6374 2021 (print) | LCC PS3527.A15 (ebook) | DDC 814/.54--
    dc23
LC record available at https://lccn.loc.gov/2020054234
LC ebook record available at https://lccn.loc.gov/2020054235

To the Courage, Beauty, and Resilience

of the Girls and Women

of #MeToo

Contents

Acknowledgments	ix
Introduction: The Anxiety of Teaching Nabokov's "Tale of Non-Consent" Eléna Rakhimova-Sommers	1

I: Asking the Question: Why Teach *Lolita*? — 9

1. (How) Should a Feminist Teach *Lolita* in the Wake of #MeToo? — 11
   Marilyn Edelstein
2. Why I Teach *Lolita* — 31
   Anne Dwyer

II: Offering Suggestions: How to Teach *Lolita* — 43

3. Students' *Lolita* Jury Duty: Teaching with Reader-Response Theory — 45
   Eléna Rakhimova-Sommers
4. A *Requiem* for Dolores: Teaching *Lolita* in a Russian Prison Literature Course — 57
   José Vergara
5. Teaching *Lolita* in the Department of Drama — 73
   Alisa Zhulina
6. Three *Lolita*s: The Evolution of a Cultural Icon in Fiction and Film — 93
   Julian W. Connolly
7. Dolores Haze: Author — 109
   Charles Byrd

8 Nabokov and #MeToo: Consent, Close Reading, and the
   Sexualized Workplace   125
   Eric Naiman

9 Resisting Humbert's Rhetorical Appeals: A Reevaluation of
   Lolita's Ethics   151
   Lisa Ryoko Wakamiya

10 Reading *Lolita* as a Teenage Girl   167
   Francesca McDonnell Capossela

Index   181

About the Editor   183

About the Contributors   185

Acknowledgments

The finishing stages of the work on this volume took place during the first winter and spring of the 2020 pandemic. As we polished our essays, we taught online, led programs and colleges through the first months of COVID-19 reality, socially distanced, quarantined, helped "flatten the curve," and took care of our children and parents. We compared notes, read each other's work, and maintained positive energy. I want to thank all of my contributors/fellow Nabokovians for their dedication to scholarship and the craft of teaching. Warm words of gratitude go out to John Givens, Anne Dwyer, and my daughter, Rachel Valentina Sommers, for their valuable feedback on my drafts. It has been a pleasure to work with all of you as we created *Teaching Nabokov's* Lolita *in the #MeToo Era* together.

Introduction

The Anxiety of Teaching Nabokov's "Tale of Non-Consent"

Eléna Rakhimova-Sommers

This volume seeks to describe, develop upon, and critique Nabokov's *Lolita* from the standpoint of its teachability to undergraduate and graduate students in the twenty-first century.[1] The #MeToo movement has spurred a reassessment of what constitutes appropriate professional and sexual relations, a reassessment that has challenged how we teach our students, especially when we are teaching controversial works. The time has come to ask—in the #MeToo era and beyond, how do we approach Nabokov's inflammatory masterpiece, *Lolita*? This volume offers practical and specific answers to this question and includes suggestions for teaching the novel in conventional and online modalities. The volume is divided into two parts: part I, "Asking the Question: Why Teach *Lolita*?" and part II, "Offering Suggestions: How to Teach *Lolita*." Essays by distinguished Nabokov scholars explore the multilayered nature of Nabokov's *Lolita* by sharing

- innovative assignments and creative writing exercises, which give students an outlet to engage with and reimagine the novel through face-to-face and online methods of instruction
- teaching approaches to especially challenging parts of the text
- methodologies of teaching the novel through different mediums, from film to theatre
- new critical analyses and interpretations

Teaching Nabokov's Lolita *in the #MeToo Era* is student-focused in its approach and appropriately concludes with an essay by a recent student of a *Lolita* class who offers new ways of accessing the novel's lasting and evolving impact on the reader.

Lolita requires intellectual commitment and, given the degree of emotional labor involved, a certain additional level of trust between faculty members and their students. After teaching Nabokov for decades, a great number of faculty have witnessed (and continue to witness) a fascinating shift in student responses to the novel. Such responses range from questioning *Lolita*'s established place on the syllabus to embracing it as a groundbreaking textbook on predatory rhetoric and its dismantling, as I discuss in my essay, "Students' *Lolita* Jury Duty: Teaching with Reader-Response Theory." Student feedback parallels global conversations generated by the #MeToo movement. Contributors to this volume demonstrate that studying *Lolita* with our students now entails examining not only the context that gave rise to it, but the context in which it is read, and this makes *Teaching Nabokov's* Lolita *in the #MeToo Era* timely, culturally relevant, and pedagogically urgent.

Part I opens with Marilyn Edelstein, who asks, "(How) Should a Feminist Teach *Lolita* in the Wake of #MeToo"? Edelstein begins by discussing some of the most compelling feminist literary criticism on *Lolita* (Kauffman, Herbold, and Patnoe) as well as public debates about the novel's teachability. She argues that the cultural, political, and social climate in which we teach the novel dramatically changed between 1955 and 2020, and that faculty, including Nabokovians, can no longer ignore the impact of feminist literary criticism or the realities of child sexual abuse and rape. For Edelstein, *Lolita* is at its most basic level a novel "about" pedophilia, incest, and child sexual abuse, even if it is also "about" many other things—including the complex relations among aesthetics, ethics, and gender, and the problematics of empathy. The challenge is to "balance analysis of its brilliant language and its aesthetic complexity with due attention to—including feminist analyses of—its troubling content." Edelstein cautions against traumatizing (or re-traumatizing) students and urges faculty to frame the novel "with awareness of the complex relations between its fictional world and our real world." The essay discusses "trigger warnings," the issue of "anxious students" opting out of reading the novel, and the practice of nurturing "more skillful and more empathetic readers." Edelstein explores these questions and discusses issues facing faculty—especially feminist faculty—in considering whether and how to teach *Lolita*.

Anne Dwyer's "Why I Teach *Lolita*" tackles a real-life scenario in which her students declined to read the novel in a single-author seminar devoted to Nabokov's work.[2] Dwyer's students wondered—how can she justify teaching *Lolita*? Is she not "perpetuating rape culture"? In her lecture-response, Dwyer defends reading *Lolita* on three grounds and frames her answer with questions that lend themselves to engaging class discussions. She begins by pointing out that *Lolita* makes us think about *"what literature can do and why we read books."* She argues that Nabokov "both tells us *not* to identify and manipulates us *into* identifying with characters"—two very uncomfortable options, which need to be explored. Her essay goes on to suggest that we ought to approach *Lolita* historically and consider what values are shaping our reading here and now (in elite American liberal arts colleges in the twenty-first century), and how these values and assumptions may or may not differ from other historical periods invoked in the novel. Dwyer concludes by raising the question of (self) censorship that looms over this book—"we should think about what it means to decide *not* to read something." She reminds us that Nabokov's essay "On a Book Entitled *Lolita*" identifies race, sex, and religion as the three taboos of American culture—and that the author pokes at all three in *Lolita*. Dwyer concludes by saying that "it's hard to consider *Lolita* a book that should be consigned to oblivion—even if it means we must read *Lolita* differently now than we once did." She imagines future iterations of the class and ways that faculty can adjust their pedagogy in the #MeToo era.

Part II, "Offering Suggestions," opens with Eléna Rakhimova-Sommers' essay "Students' *Lolita* Jury Duty: Teaching with Reader-Response Theory." This study, framed by Wolfgang Iser's approach to decoding the mysteries of the author-text-reader dynamic, is designed as a "view from within," incorporating both faculty and student perspective. While reflecting on ten years of teaching *Lolita* in her "Dangerous Texts" course, she focuses on her classroom experiences throughout 2018 and 2019, when "the tsunami of #MeToo cleared the way for a national conversation about the nature of sexual coercion and the dynamics of victim silencing." Rakhimova-Sommers stresses the need for innovative pedagogy that allows students to engage with and intervene in the novel to help alleviate the commonly reported "helpless bystander" syndrome. She provides samples of assignments that give the class a "creative pause" by allowing for a redirection from close reading to visual analysis and creative writing. These assignments are designed to fit both conventional and online modes of teaching. Selected passages from students' award-winning essays create a multi-voiced conversation and demonstrate how her classes have journeyed through the *Lolita* experience, facing its challenges and reaping its rewards.

José Vergara continues this pedagogical thread by offering his thoughts on including *Lolita* in a "Prison Literature" course such as "Crime or Punishment: Russian Narratives of Incarceration and Captivity." He argues that aspects of the novel are thrown into greater relief when read alongside a range of seminal texts. The reading list ranges widely and includes nineteenth- and twentieth-century Russian classics, Anna Akhmatova's "Requiem," Susan Sontag's *Regarding the Pain of Others*, Elaine Scarry's *The*

Body in Pain, as well as Mikhail Khodorkovsky's *My Fellow Prisoners,* and *The Prison Letters of Nadya* [Tolokonnikova] *and Slavoj* [Zizek]. This approach lends itself well to #MeToo-inspired discussions on topics including guilt and power relations. As a text composed in prison by Humbert and as a work that chronicles a young girl's experience being held against her will, *Lolita* is read through the "dual and conflicting prisoner perspective. . . ." Vergara draws students' attention to the fact that "Humbert's calculated method of hijacking Dolores's narrative . . . generates a second-level captivity echoing the #MeToo era scenarios." Joining other volume contributors, Vergara points out that reading *Lolita* feels all the more pertinent to students during the #MeToo era, when numerous accounts and defenses of illicit behavior regularly fill news streams. The students are both better equipped to read through Humbert's justifications for his actions and, in certain cases, more reticent to appreciate the text as art(ifice).

In "Teaching *Lolita* in the Department of Drama," Alisa Zhulina offers another fascinating avenue for teaching the novel in courses on "Dramatic Literature," in the context of a school of the arts. She reminds us that "from John Barry and Alan Jay Lerner's failed musical *Lolita, My Love* (1971) to contemporary experimental productions of Edward Albee's lambasted *Lolita* (1981), the history of *Lolita*'s theatrical adaptations is a string of failures." According to Zhulina, these very failures, however, present an opportunity: "Thinking about the challenges that Nabokov's controversial novel continues to pose to stage and screen adaptations encourages students to explore issues of embodiment, the aesthetic representation of women's bodies in art, and the need for more stories told from women's perspectives." In the #MeToo era, discussing with the students the problems and possibilities of adapting the novel into a performative medium has proven to be a dynamic site for asking questions about the relationship between the artist and the art. Zhulina asks, "[s]hould we take John Ray's advice and be 'entranced with the book while abhorring its author'"? Thinking about how to translate the novel to performance inevitably makes students think about the visibility of Dolly's body and the importance of her voice.

Zhulina illustrates the possibilities of new interpretations of the novel by citing the example of the 2019 York Theatre workshop production of the musical *Lolita, My Love* which told the story from a woman's perspective. This time around, *Lolita, My Love* was staged as Humbert Humbert's confession to a female therapist, named June Ray, who offers a corrective commentary on his thoughts and actions. Dialoguing with Linda Hutcheon's *A Theory of Adaptation*, Zhulina asks the following questions: what are the dangers of adapting *Lolita* into other media? And how can thinking about adaptation with students shed light on the relationship between text and performance?

Julian W. Connolly's "Three *Lolitas*: The Evolution of a Cultural Icon in Fiction and Film" offers a comparative approach to the teaching of the novel by incorporating two film versions, Stanley Kubrick's *Lolita* of 1962 and Adrian Lyne's *Lolita* of 1997. The point of this method is "to cast Nabokov's distinctive treatment of Dolly Haze's relationship to Humbert Humbert into sharp relief by making students aware of the particular cultural contexts in which these artistic works were conceived and made, and subsequently, of the students' own position in a specific cultural moment—the present day." Students in a course designed along these lines consider several different aspects of the literary and film versions. Among these are point of view. Nabokov's use of a first-person narrative mode is a key feature of his novel. Kubrick's film diminishes that mode, while Lyne's film goes a long way toward restoring it. Connolly argues that awareness of the potential of a first-person narrator to manipulate an audience is crucial to understanding the creator's purpose and its effect on audience reception. Another feature to examine is the representation of Dolly's age, from twelve to fourteen in the original novel, to mid or late teens in Kubrick's film, and back to a younger age in Lyne's film. Students consider what the novelist and filmmakers convey to us about the child's reaction to Humbert's attentions (curiosity, excitement, boredom, disdain?) as well as about Charlotte Haze's own interest in Humbert. Connolly wants students to learn about the contemporary critical and popular reaction to the three *Lolita*s, focusing on the way these reactions have evolved over the course of time. Finally, and perhaps most importantly, Connolly wants students to evaluate their own reactions to the novel after concluding their comparative analysis: has their view of Nabokov's creation changed from their initial conception, and if so, how and why?

Charles Byrd's essay grants Dolores authorial rights, a reevaluation inspired by Dr. Christine Blasey Ford's 2018 testimony against Brett Kavanaugh's Supreme Court Judicial Nomination. Byrd reevaluates the two letters Dolores pens in the novel, the letters that have been eclipsed by "Humbert Humbert's verbal pyrotechnics and sick sense of misogynistic humor." The first note, written by a twelve-year-old Lolita from camp, invites closer interpretation as it contains the suggestive line "I [crossed out and re-written again] I lost my new sweater in the woods" (81). Byrd explores the significance of the "lost sweater/lost virginity" metonym and draws our attention to the fact that "this is the only passage in the novel which is explicitly stated to have been 'crossed out,' and thus, it differentiates the voice of its humble, hesitating author from the confident, honey-tongued loquaciousness of the prose belonging to Humbert." Lolita's second letter is much longer, and contains two of the novel's most memorable lines: "You can't see the morons for the smog [referring to the town of Coalmont]," and the beautifully understated "I have been through much sadness and hardship" (266). Byrd argues that the latter suggests the mature ownership and overcoming of trauma celebrated by the #MeToo movement and prompts extended reflection on Humbert's failure to own the anguish of his mother's death.

Eric Naiman argues that the #MeToo movement and *Lolita* can coexist without tension if we accept the fact that "literature and life are conceptually and morally distinct" and should be treated "as separate realms with separate rules." He suggests that inclusion of the #MeToo movement into class discussion should not make the teaching of *Lolita* "apologetic, but rather, more interesting." The reader, he hopes, "can believe survivors, practicing empathy and building solidarity, while disbelieving—along with Nabokov—in the truth of his created world . . ." He hopes for the "harmonious compatibility" of Nabokov's good readers and the #MeToo movement, "two groups ostensibly committed to the importance of a rigid line between fiction and fact." This relationship, he suggests, offers potential for analyzing how principles of interpretation and concepts of predation central to the #MeToo movement function differently in a work of art. Naiman juxtaposes *Pnin* with *Lolita*, two books about the misuse of authority and consent—"parental authority and sexual consent" in one and "narrative authority and mental consent" in the other. The essay then proceeds to examine two stories, "A Nursery Tale" and "The Vane Sisters," as parables that explore the affinity between failure at close reading and sexual predation. The third part of Naiman's essay looks at the potential for reading *Lolita* as either a hostile or an empowering experience for the female reader. The final section offers several pedagogic approaches to *Lolita* that can build upon and put to use insights from the preceding discussion.

Lisa Ryoko Wakamiya begins her essay, "Resisting Humbert's Rhetorical Appeals: A Reevaluation of *Lolita*'s Ethics," by acknowledging that since her 2008 study in *Approaches to Teaching Nabokov's Lolita*,[3] her methodology has changed. She explains that "[she] has changed, as have the students and the climate in which they encounter the novel." Echoing other contributors to this volume, she argues that students' responses to *Lolita* are an integral part of its pedagogy as they instantly recognize the novel's relevance to the present. Ryoko Wakamiya draws our attention to that fact that fauxpologies—non-apologetic, damage control–seeking, PR-driven statements issued by public figures to explain away actions that they claim to regret—inevitably color students' responses to Humbert's narrative: "If my students twelve years ago wondered how they should read *Lolita*, with some eventually ascribing agency to the briefly glimpsed, married and pregnant Mrs. Dolly Schiller, my students in 2018 struggled to read as they evoked the apologias of Harvey Weinstein, Kevin Spacey, and others that emerged in the wake of #MeToo." She observes that student responses reveal their distrust of a form they associated with high-profile sexual predators who seek to defend their public reputations and argues that Humbert's literary allusions, "as references that assume a shared body of knowledge between the implied author and reader, are just as suspect as the transcendent values public apologists invoke when they appeal to our common humanity and understanding."

Ryoko Wakamiya also points out that anxiety over the changing reception of *Lolita* "bespeaks the unsettled relations between the novel and the ethical situations encountered in our daily lives." The essay examines the emergence of the apologia as a public genre, recent reassessment of past literary classics, and the notion that current events and daily life have replaced literature as the field in which we explore ethical questions. Her discussion of a student's #MeToo paper demonstrates that while "shared enjoyment of *Lolita* as Great Art" does not extend to all readers, value in reading it can be found in unexpected places during a time of rhetorical and social instability.

It is symbolic and deliberate that this volume's conversation concludes with an essay by a recent student of a *Lolita* class. Now a creative writer herself, Francesca McDonnell Capossela looks back on her *Lolita* experiences and offers new ideas about how to best approach the text. Capossela's essay is unique as it offers three distinct layers of experience of reading *Lolita*—as a "dizzyingly in love with it" fourteen-year-old girl, as an "angry" college student pushing against the text's violation at a time of growing consciousness around sexual assault in 2016, and finally as a creative writer during the #MeToo and #TimesUp era. She asks: "How do we approach a text in which the narrator—and seemingly the novel itself—is oppressive? And doesn't any novel, simply by having a narrator, introduce some hierarchy of power, some kind of oppression?" Due to the fact that even the relationship between narrator and reader in *Lolita* can feel predatory, some authors, like Sarah Weinman, have responded by attempting to resurrect the titular character. Discussing Weinman's *The Real Lolita,* which details a real-life kidnapping of Sally Horner that may have inspired Nabokov, McDonnell Capossela argues that although the author "introduces extraneous content in order to remedy the damage done by *Lolita*, she ultimately fails to locate the character of Lolita." She contrasts Weinman's method with her own in order to make an argument about how we should study *Lolita*, and how that methodology can help us decide what role morality and identity should play in studying literature.

For McDonnell Capossela, the novel's aesthetic merit is determined by whether *Lolita*, like Humbert, silenced Lolita. To answer this question, she embarks on a project of locating Lolita within the text by highlighting every sentence of her speech. She catalogues her interests: fast food, dance, acting, and bike-riding. This method of reading convinced her that "Lolita takes linguistic and imagistic control of the novel." She argues that "Nabokov buries the evidence of Lolita's agency, but once excavated, it is undeniable." "The apparent hierarchy of the novel—in which Humbert has agency and Lolita does not—is undercut by Lolita's metafictional objections to the narrative, her attempts to rewrite Humbert's story, and her relationship to the physical objects around her, which at times act in defense of her." McDonnell Capossela concludes that *Lolita* is a novel about a female subject who wrestles away control of the very text the tyrannical male narrator has created. She considers it to be a uniquely Nabokovian feat that can teach us about how to read democratically, in order to realize the possibilities of narrative.

BY WAY OF CONCLUSION

After sending out a call for papers and in the process of working on this volume, I was honored to receive a multitude of responses and inquiries from across the United States, as well as from Russia, England, and India. These messages arrived and continue to arrive from a cross-section of faculty: from seasoned instructors teaching *Lolita* to undergraduates and graduates (and even prisoners in rehabilitation programs), and from new faculty about to teach the novel, a bit apprehensive, and in need of advice. Together with this volume's contributors, I want to thank everyone for engaging in an important conversation on the evolving nature of teaching *Lolita*. We hope this volume answered some of your questions and helped shape a successful course.

Trust yourself. Trust your students. Explore *Lolita*. *She* is worth it.

WORKS CITED

Approaches to Teaching Nabokov's Lolita, eds, Zoran Kuzmanovich and Galya Diment. New York: The Modern Language Association of America, 2008, pp. 141-47.

Mendelsund, Peter. "Fictions." In *Lolita—The Story of a Cover Girl: Vladimir Nabokov's Novel in Art and Design*. Blue Ash, OH: Print Books, 2013, p. 29.

NOTES

1. I borrow the term "non-consent" in the title of this introduction from Peter Mendelsund, "Fictions." *Lolita—The Story of a Cover Girl*, 29.
2. The essay is a new and expanded version of the 2018 *Inside Higher Ed* opinion piece. https://www.insidehighered.com/views/2018/05/14/teaching-lolita-still-appropriate-opinion.
3. "Humbert's 'Gendered' Appeals to the Jury Not of His Peers."

I

Asking the Question: Why Teach *Lolita*?

Chapter One

(How) Should a Feminist Teach *Lolita* in the Wake of #MeToo?

Marilyn Edelstein

Feminist analyses of Vladimir Nabokov's novel *Lolita* only began to appear in the mid-1980s—more than thirty years after the initial 1955 Olympia Press publication of *Lolita* in France and more than a decade after the emergence in the United States. in the 1970s of what Elaine Showalter calls "feminist critique"—feminist readings of literature by male writers, who even in the 1970s still dominated the literary canon. Jenefer Shute (a literary scholar as well as the author of four novels, including one called *Sex Crimes*) published a proto-feminist essay in 1985 on the male gaze and the female body in Nabokov's *Ada* and *Lolita*.[1] But it was Linda Kauffman's influential and explicitly feminist 1989 essay "Framing Lolita: Is There a Woman in the Text?" (first published in the aptly named edited collection *Refiguring the Father: New Feminist Readings of Patriarchy*) that opened up feminist critical conversations on Nabokov's problematic novel.

Subsequent feminist work on *Lolita* in the late 1980s and the 1990s by Elizabeth Patnoe, Sarah Herbold, and others helped shift some of the later critical conversation away from the dominant concerns of much earlier *Lolita* criticism: Humbert's tragic, romantic, and/or obsessive quest to re-create his lost childhood love; Nabokov's critiques of American culture; both Humbert's and Nabokov's linguistic and literary games and/or creation of "aesthetic bliss." Some scholars had focused on ethical issues in the novel, in spite of Nabokov's frequent warnings against and mockery of such readings and his claim, in *Lolita*'s Afterword, that he has "no moral in tow" in the novel. But rarely had non-feminist critics foregrounded gender issues, which link ethics and politics, or provided a sympathetic reading of Lolita's character (in both senses of the word). Yet the emergence of feminist analyses of

Lolita shifted much of the critical focus to Lolita "herself" and Humbert's treatment of her. In spite of decades now of feminist analyses (both positive and negative) of *Lolita*—a novel by a writer who was clearly not a feminist (and in whose literary and other texts some of us find at least traces of sexism and even misogyny)[2]—the question remains whether *Lolita* can—or should—be taught by feminist faculty, especially in the wake (or midst) of the #MeToo movement.

At the most basic level, *Lolita* is, after all, a novel "about" pedophilia, or what some psychiatrists and psychologists—including forensic psychologists—call "hebephilia," since Humbert is sexually attracted to pubescent (or almost pubescent) girls rather than exclusively pre-pubescent ones, as a "true" pedophile is. But Humbert's paraphilia exists on the border between pedophilia and hebephilia, since nymphets are those "chosen creatures" among girls between the ages of nine and fourteen, whose "nymphic (that is, demoniac)" nature is perceptible only by "bewitched travelers" at least twice their age (16). But if the novel is about pedophilia/hebephilia, quasi-incest (or what Humbert refers to as a "parody of incest" [287]), and child sexual abuse, it is also "about" many other things, as countless literary critics and reviewers have noted over the decades since its publication. As I will discuss in the rest of this essay, we can also view *Lolita* as illuminating the complex relations between fictional worlds and the "real world," between (male) writers and (female) readers, and between aesthetics and ethics, including the ethics of teaching.

Whereas few readers when the novel was first published—especially male readers and critics—would have been aware of the prevalence of child sexual abuse, incest, rape, and other forms of sexual violence (and the effects of these on their predominantly female victims),[3] such problems have become much more widely acknowledged and decried in recent decades. Even before the emergence of the #MeToo movement, and perhaps due to the "internet revolution" itself, many Americans and Europeans were becoming increasingly aware of the prevalence of pedophilia and child sexual abuse. What many of us think of as the "origin" of the #MeToo movement, when white actresses like Alyssa Milano and Ashley Judd started publicly using the #MeToo hashtag in 2017 to accuse influential film producer Harvey Weinstein of sexual assault, also had its (initially unacknowledged) precursor. Civil rights and feminist activist Tarana Burke had "founded" the MeToo movement in 2006 (before the origin of hashtags themselves in 2007) in response to hearing a thirteen-year-old African American girl's disclosure of her sexual abuse at the hands of her mother's boyfriend—a situation much like that of "Lolita" herself.

Yet in spite of persistent cover-ups of child sexual abuse as a systemic problem, it has been widely exposed in recent years by traditional mass media (through investigative reporting in newspapers and magazines, on television, in books and films) and via social media. Americans have learned about infamous child predators who molested girls for many years, like former USA Gymnastics and Michigan State University team doctor Larry Nassar and, more recently, high-society financier (and sex trafficker) Jeffrey Epstein—both of whom were eventually convicted and put in prison, where Epstein soon committed suicide. Over the last twenty years or so, we have also learned more than most of us want to know about widespread, systemic abuse of children and teenagers not only by members of global pedophile (and child pornography) rings but also, even more disturbingly, by many Catholic priests, who, when found out, have often been merely shuttled from parish to parish. According to data from the organization From Darkness to Light, "about one in seven girls and one in 25 boys will be sexually abused before they turn 18."[4] According to recent federal data gathered by RAINN (Rape, Abuse & Incest National Network), about 11 percent of girls under eighteen have experienced sexual abuse or assault by an adult (most often, a parent); two out of three victims of child sexual abuse are, like Lolita, between the ages of twelve and seventeen.

Awareness of the prevalence of pedophilia (and of the increasing sexual objectification of children, especially girls) was much greater in 1997 (one year after the killing of six-year-old child "beauty queen" JonBenét Ramsey—an unsolved murder which quickly became a media spectacle), when Adrian Lyne's film of *Lolita* was completed, than it had been in 1962, when Stanley Kubrick's film of the novel was released, or in 1958, when the novel itself was first published in the United States. When Lyne's film, which treats the novel as Humbert's tragic love story and Lolita (played by the fourteen-year-old Dominique Swain) as almost a *femme fatale*, was completed in 1997, no American company would release the film then due to the strong likelihood of protests by victims' rights groups and feminists—which did occur when it was released in Europe. In the United States, the film was finally shown in 1998 on Showtime and then, in limited release, in theaters, where it was a financial failure, in spite of some positive reviews. Americans and Europeans in the late 1990s had little taste for a film "about" pedophilia.[5] So, even though Nabokov often proclaimed that literature (especially his own) does not reflect—or comment on—society, culture, or politics, it is clear that cultural and social contexts strongly affect the reception of both literary and cinematic works.

Public awareness of the prevalence of all forms of sexual assault—including on college campuses—has also increased greatly in the last few decades, in part through recent #MeToo "hashtivism" but also because of decades of work by earlier feminist scholars and activists. Like *Lolita* and Lolita herself, the #MeToo movement had a precursor—in particular, second-wave feminist activism and writings on rape and sexual harassment, from the beginnings of the women's liberation movement in the United States in the late 1960s and early 1970s (e.g., with such influential texts as Susan Brownmiller's 1975 book *Against Our Will: Men, Women, and Rape*). On college campuses, beginning in the late 1960s and continuing today, student activists—most of them feminists, including male feminists—have helped create rape-prevention programs, organized "Take Back the Night" marches, and lobbied colleges to create better means of both preventing and dealing with sexual assault.[6]

As college students, faculty, staff, and administrators work on preventing and responding to sexual assault and sexual harassment on campus, the #MeToo movement has added a renewed sense of urgency and visibility to these issues, including the ways in which they intersect with curriculum. Many faculty now wonder whether we should remove from our syllabi the work of writers credibly accused of sexual harassment or even assault. Two widely taught, award-winning American writers—Sherman Alexie and Junót Diaz—have, in the last several years, been publicly accused, by multiple women students and writers, of sexually inappropriate and/or abusive behavior—behavior both writers have publicly acknowledged, to varying degrees. Should faculty continue to support these writers' works by including them in syllabi and thus affirming both their literary and cultural value and also increasing book sales? Many feminists have argued that Diaz's and/or Alexie's fiction is itself at least sexist if not misogynist—even if it is also, I believe, brilliant as well as anti-racist—so assigning this work is problematic on multiple levels.

But the issues confronting faculty now considering whether and how to teach Nabokov's most (in)famous novel are quite different from those regarding whether or not to teach Alexie or Diaz, since there have been no accusations against Nabokov himself of sexually abusive behavior. So the issue some of us may have is not with the author but rather with the plot and characters in *Lolita*, especially Nabokov's "creature" and first-person narrator Humbert, whose sexual proclivities, attitudes, and behaviors (if not verbal style) seem quite distant from those of the "real" Nabokov, as we discern him from biographies, interviews, letters, his autobiography, and his paratexts.[7]

If we do choose to teach *Lolita*, we now do so with awareness that there's a high probability that some of the women in our classes (and possibly some of the men) have been or will become victims/survivors of sexual assault, including child sexual abuse. Some studies suggest that as many as one in three or four female college students have been or will become victims/survivors of sexual assault during their time in college.[8] So, if we do continue to teach *Lolita*, should our syllabi include "trigger warnings"—the subject of intense national debates pro and con in higher education circles, starting around 2013–2014—to avoid re-traumatizing those students who have already been traumatized by sexual abuse? And, if not, should we at least warn students or potential students about the novel's subject matter? Should we let concerned students opt out of reading the novel? If we decide to teach *Lolita*, how do we balance analysis of its brilliant language and aesthetic complexity with due attention to—including feminist analysis of—its troubling content?

What does it mean to read—and/or teach—*Lolita* as a woman or, specifically, as a feminist? *Being* a woman does not necessarily mean "reading as a woman." As Judith Fetterley argued in her 1978 book *The Resisting Reader* (a feminist reader-response analysis of canonical male American writers, from Hawthorne to Mailer), "as readers, teachers, and scholars, women are taught to read as men, to identify with a male point of view, and to accept as normal and legitimate a male system of values, one of whose principles is misogyny." Fetterley calls this process the "immasculation" of women readers (xx), and the alternative she demonstrates in her own readings and recommends to other women is to learn to become a "resisting reader" and thus more conscious of a male-authored text's "impalpable" designs on its women readers (xxii). Feminist reader-response critic Patrocinio Schweickart agrees with Fetterley that feminists must learn to become resisting readers of androcentric texts and an androcentric culture, since "a feminist cannot simply refuse to read patriarchal texts, for they are everywhere, and they condition her participation in the literary and critical enterprise" (Schweickart 50).[9]

Although one could argue that this process of acculturating (or indoctrinating) girls and women into male values and norms—through literature, education, culture—is weaker and less coherent in 2021 than it was in 1978 when Fetterley published her book (or in 1955, when *Lolita* was published), it still occurs whenever female readers (including college students) are discouraged from expressing feminist responses to or interpretations of literary texts (or films, etc.) by men or mocked as "feminist killjoys" who "kill other people's joy by pointing out moments of sexism" (Ahmed 65) or who "ruin" some readers' pleasure by pointing out that *Lolita* is centrally rather than peripherally "about" child sexual abuse.[10] The first few decades of *Lolita* criticism were dominated by male critics, some of whom rather blindly took what they inferred to be Humbert's and/or Nabokov's point(s) of view as determinative in interpreting the novel. Of course, there were important exceptions to the male-dominated Nabokovian critical terrain in its earliest decades, in the work of women scholars (not all or always feminist) like Julia Bader, Ellen Pifer, and Leona Toker in the 1970s and 1980s.

Not all women read *as* women, and certainly not all women read, write, or teach as feminists. Nor does one have to be a woman to be a feminist.[11] Robyn R. Warhol and Diane Price Herndl provide a useful working definition of what it means to be a feminist literary critic: "Feminist critics generally agree that the oppression of women is a fact of life, that gender leaves its traces in literary texts and on literary history, and that feminist literary criticism plays a worthwhile part in the struggle to end oppression in the world outside of texts" (xiii). Of course, a major concern in analyzing any of

Nabokov's texts (including paratexts), as it is for much deconstructive literary theory, is whether there *is* a "world outside of texts"—or, more appropriately, outside of (or prior to) language and textuality, even if our experience and knowledge of this world is mediated by language.

It is precisely the relationship between the created, imagined, fictional world of a novel and "our" reality that concerns feminist scholars and teachers considering whether or not to teach *Lolita*. Decades before the emergence of both poststructuralist and feminist literary and cultural theories in the 1960s and 1970s, and perhaps in response to Modernism itself, New Critics had proclaimed the separation of literary texts, seen as "verbal icons," from history, social and political contexts, their authors, and their readers. Even earlier, in the first few decades of the twentieth century, Russian formalists (with whose work it appears that Nabokov was familiar)[12] had also focused on the formal devices and language—the "literariness"—of a literary text and its differences from everyday language and separation from "everyday reality." Later, during the dominance of "high theory" in the 1970s through the 1990s, many critics (with the exception of most Marxists and most feminists) also assumed that literature did not and could not reflect or shape reality, even though their theoretical premises and forebears differed radically from those of New Critics. But then we saw the emergence of New Historicism and the (re-)emergence of "the ethical turn" in literary studies in the 1980s, along with the rapid growth of interdisciplinary fields like cultural studies, body studies, affect theory, and trauma studies—approaches in which feminists and gender theorists have played a pivotal role. As such approaches have become more prominent, many critics have begun to rethink the complex, dynamic relations between literature and "reality" (although some of us who have read a lot of Nabokov still use the word "reality" in quotation marks).

Virtually all feminist teachers believe that our teaching can and should play "a worthwhile part in the struggle to end oppression in the world outside of texts" (Warhol and Herndl xiii). Most faculty engaged in any form of critical pedagogy share this belief, as do many other faculty who believe that teaching literature can help our students become not only better readers and writers but also better critical thinkers—skilled in analyzing and using language, able to connect texts to their historical and cultural contexts, and attentive to both texts' nuances and their larger implications. But feminist teachers are also committed to helping our students (both female and male) understand and analyze the ways sex and gender shape both literary texts and the cultures in which they are produced and read, and be able to imagine more egalitarian and humane ways to live in and act on the world. As Schweickart puts it, "the feminist story stresses that patriarchal constructs have objective as well as subjective reality; they are inside and outside the text, inside and outside the reader" (50).

One especially important issue for many feminist scholars, many girls and women (including undergraduates), and some men is the sexual objectification of women and, even more disturbing, of girls that has become so common in our culture and which has played a large part in creating and reinforcing what feminists call "rape culture." Feminists have been critiquing such sexual objectification of women and girls—in not only pornography but also advertising, film, social media, the internet, and literature—and its cultural effects for decades. In a 1995 essay that drew on earlier feminist work on sexual objectification (e.g., by Andrea Dworkin and Catharine MacKinnon in the 1970s and 1980s) as well as on literary texts and ethical theory, influential philosopher Martha Nussbaum outlined seven characteristics of objectification of others, three of which are especially applicable to *Lolita* and to Humbert's treatment of Lolita: "*instrumentality:* the objectifier treats the object as a tool of his or her purposes," "*denial of autonomy*: the objectifier treats the object as lacking in autonomy and self-determination," and "*denial of subjectivity*: the objectifier treats the object as something whose experience and feelings (if any) need not be taken into account" (257). In "Feminist Perspectives on Objectification," Evangelia Papadaki summarizes three more features of specifically *sexual* objectification that feminist philosopher Rae Langton added to Nussbaum's list, which I think are also clearly instantiated in *Lolita*: "*reduction to body*: the treatment of a person as identified with their body, or body parts; *reduction to appearance*: the treatment of a person primarily in terms of how they look, or how they appear to the senses; *silencing*: the treatment of a person as if they are silent, lacking the capacity to speak" (Langton 228–29; cited in Papadaki). As Linda Kauffman puts it in her feminist analysis of *Lolita*, "Lolita is as much the object consumed by Humbert as she is the product of her culture" (141).

Young women in the United States are especially susceptible to—even if some of them become aware of and try to resist—this "reduction [of women and girls] to appearance," which is a critical issue in much feminist cultural studies, including work in body studies (e.g., in Susan Bordo's pivotal *Unbearable Weight*), as it has been in feminist theoretical work on the "male gaze." In *Lolita*, we often see Humbert reduce Lolita to her appearance, and even to her body parts—a kind of fetishization we also frequently see in popular culture. While Humbert frequently rhapsodizes about Lolita's body, he also acknowledges, late in the novel, that "I did not know a thing about my darling's mind" (284). And while Lolita often speaks (and sobs) and Humbert reports (and often criticizes) her words, he never seems to care about what she says (and does not change his behavior in spite of her sobs), and thereby he silences her even while he rhapsodizes about her body.

Humbert's obsession with Dolores Haze begins when he first sees her immature twelve-year-old body on the Haze house's "piazza," and notes her "frail, honey-hued shoulders . . . silky, supple bare back . . . [and] juvenile breasts" (39). Soon after, but still before Humbert marries Charlotte Haze in order to gain access to Dolores, he admires Dolores' "pre-adolescently in-curved back" (67).[13] Although Dolores—who he soon rechristens "Lolita"—seems to Humbert, at least initially, to be the reincarnation of his lost childhood love Annabel—with whom he shared intellectual and spiritual interests as well as unconsummated passion—it is Lolita's body and not her mind that he desires to "know." Anika Susan Quayle makes a similar point, noting that "Humbert objectifies her [Lolita] . . . reducing her to the physical body." Quayle devotes most of her essay to critiquing those scholars who argue that Humbert ignores, aestheticizes, or idealizes Lolita, since Quayle believes that Humbert is "well aware of Lolita's true character, emotions and desires." Although I think Quayle overstates the case for Humbert actually understanding the "real" Lolita, I agree with her that Humbert does not really care about Lolita's "character, emotion and desires." In this regard, his relationship with Lolita is radically different than his relationship with Annabel had been, and not only because of the huge age and power differences between Humbert and Lolita. Whereas the young Humbert and the similarly young Annabel were "madly . . . in love *with each other*" (*Annotated Lolita* 12; my emphasis) and were brought together by shared backgrounds and interests as well as youthful passion, it is clear—even to Humbert—that Lolita never loves him, so the reciprocity and mutuality of the Humbert-Annabel relationship is absent.

And, as many recent critics have also argued, it is quite possible to doubt Humbert's claims—even in the final scenes of the novel—that he ever "really" loved or knew (rather than was obsessed by) the "real" Lolita. Upon his final meeting with the still teenaged but also married and pregnant Lolita, before he murders Quilty (the one man Lolita seemed actually to love), Humbert says, "I loved her. It was love at first sight, at last sight, at ever and ever sight" (270). But his phrasing here, with its focus on sight, suggests that Humbert only and always "knew" Lolita as an object of his vision, of his male gaze.[14] Quayle joins other critics in arguing that the novel, through "showing the harm caused to Lolita by Humbert's treatment of her . . . constitutes a comment on the dangers of, and the moral turpitude of, objectification."[15] A feminist teaching *Lolita* might be able to open up fruitful classroom discussion of the ways in which Humbert's extreme (and fictional) "case" can help illuminate patriarchal culture's sexual objectification of women (especially young women) and girls, which contributes to the continuing problems of not only sexual harassment but also sexual abuse, including the sexual abuse of children.

In Linda Kauffman's influential feminist analysis of *Lolita,* she argues that most previous critics (especially male critics) have elided the incest at the center of the novel (as, she says, John Ray, Jr. also does in his Foreword), and thus elided the girl Dolores Haze, thereby contributing to her silencing and objectification and reflecting "utter disregard for Lolita's suffering" (142). Some of these critics blamed and shamed Lolita for her ostensible pre-Humbertian sexual experience—for which we have only the word of Humbert, our unreliable, frequently institutionalized narrator, who claims that it was Lolita who seduced him [*Lolita* 132]), as support—and her "wantonness" (Kauffman 149).[16] Other critics have focused almost exclusively on Humbert's and Nabokov's creation of "aesthetic bliss" through language. Kauffman argues that the Humbert-Lolita relationship demonstrates clinical features of real-life father-daughter incest. Yet, Humbert is not actually Lolita's father (even though he has implied—falsely—to the Farlows and others that he might be) and has only been her stepfather briefly before he has sex with (or rapes) Lolita at the Enchanted Hunters Hotel. Humbert's violations of Lolita are, in many ways, more like those of real-life child predators who kidnap and rape girls they do not know (as with Frank LaSalle's 1948 kidnapping of Sally Horner, a real-world case mentioned briefly in the novel) than to those violations of longstanding trust and affection when a father or even long-time stepfather commits incest with his daughter or stepdaughter.

In her analysis of *Lolita* and Lolita, Kauffman tries to walk a middle ground between what she calls "the representational fallacy"—treating characters as if they are real people (which was anathema to Nabokov)—versus treating a novel as purely a verbal artifact with no obvious relationship to our real world. She argues that "feminist theory must . . . focus on language and signification, not just what is being represented" and on "the mechanisms of representation." But she stresses that while "the textual body is *fabricated*," a feminist critic "can inscribe Lolita's viewpoint and simultaneously stress its *verisimilitude*—as opposed to its *veracity*" (149). Finally, Kauffman argues that *Lolita* and Lolita are "framed unsettlingly between the horror of incest and aesthetic jouissance, between material reality and postrepresentation" (150). Yet, in his critique of those Nabokov scholars (including feminists and ethical critics) who attempt to connect *Lolita* to "the real world" instead of focusing primarily if not exclusively on aesthetics and artifice, Eric Naiman claims that in her "attempt to reinscribe Lolita's body" into the text, Kauffman "rewrite[s] herself as a positivist" (154)—an accusation that Kauffman would dispute and I find troubling. No matter what recent critics like Naiman and earlier critics like Page Stegner and Julia Bader, who focus on aesthetics and artifice in Nabokov's fiction, may argue, readers *do* and, I think, should make connections between fictional worlds and their own world, between fictive characters and real-world people even if they should not be conflated. If students and other readers are dissuaded, by teachers or critics using purely aestheticist or formalist approaches to *Lolita* (which I consider at least a semi-realist novel), from finding or imagining such connections, then is there any point in studying literature, apart from becoming more attentive to language and literary techniques? The challenge, as we can see in Kauffman's analysis and in our teaching, is to pay due attention to language, structure, style—that is, literariness—*and* also to the ways in which fictional texts draw from and can also affect "reality." For example, Nabokov frequently discussed reading many real-life case histories of pedophiles and researching facts about young girls (about whom he claimed to know nothing, having only been a father to a son) while he was writing *Lolita*. Even if we assume this research was intended merely to "inject a modicum of average 'reality' . . . into the brew of individual fancy," as Nabokov puts it in *Lolita*'s afterword (312), he also refers there to "pale, pregnant, beloved, irretrievable Dolly Schiller [Lolita] dying in Gray Star" (316) as one of the "subliminal co-ordinates" of the book, as if there is *real* pathos in her (fictional) life and death. And even though Nabokov claimed, in his essay on "Good Readers and Good Writers," that "the work of art is invariably the creation of a new world . . . having no obvious connection to the worlds we already know," he goes on to say that once we have carefully studied that new, fictional world, we can "examine its links with other worlds, with other branches of knowledge" (*Lectures on Literature* 1).

For feminists committed to changing and improving the world, including through our pedagogy, these links between words and world are always important. One important issue in some recent feminist work on *Lolita* and on various iterations of the Lolita theme (e.g., in popular culture, as explored by M. Gigi Durham, and in recent feminist novels that can be seen as responses to *Lolita*, as discussed by Michele Meek) is whether feminists like Kauffman and others who stress Lolita's victimization thus deny both Lolita's and real girls' sexual pleasure and sexual agency. I would argue that both Humbert and the novel itself deny Lolita almost any form of agency other than, occasionally, the power of resisting or of, reactively, manipulating Humbert, especially given that she winds up as an object of exchange between men (Humbert and Quilty), as Kauffman also notes (146). But I am wary of feminist analyses that want us to focus too much on the sexual pleasure and sexual agency of twelve year olds in a world in which child sexual abuse is far too common and girls and young women often have far too little choice of when and with whom to have sex or even marry.

Is it possible to teach *Lolita* in a feminist way and without further traumatizing those of our students who may be survivors of sexual violation? As Elizabeth Patnoe argues, too few critics focus on "the trauma Humbert inflicts on Lolita, and none contend with the trauma the book inflicts on readers" (87). Clearly, some critics, primarily feminists, have begun to analyze the traumas inflicted on Lolita, and more and more teachers (and students) are becoming aware of the potential for readerly traumas, especially when and if *Lolita* is required course reading.

I last taught *Lolita* in 2015, in my "Ethics and Literature" course—before the widespread public emergence of the #MeToo movement. We read a number of theoretical and philosophical essays about the relations among literature (primarily fiction), aesthetics, and ethics. I included both *Lolita* and, later in the quarter, Barbara Kingsolver's novel *The Bean Trees*, which also deals with child sexual abuse (of a toddler, in this case, but which occurs, for the most part, "off-stage" and outside the present action of the novel). Although in Kingsolver's novel there are, as in *Lolita*, two pivotal road trips, lots of humor, and major characters displaced from their countries of origin, in most other ways, the two novels could not be more different. With its spunky female first-person narrator (barely out of adolescence herself when the novel begins), casual and conversational style, and themes of women's friendships, the need to find or build both family and community, and the capacity for healing from trauma, *The Bean Trees* is a tender-hearted, reader-friendly novel brimming with compassion. I thought that since both novels explore ethical issues, *The Bean Trees* would provide a welcome counterbalance to *Lolita*.

In this class, I had a female student who at first told me she simply wouldn't be able to read *Lolita* because, based on what she had heard about the novel's subject matter, she thought it would be too painful for her, given her own experience with sexual abuse. However, as we talked about the novel in class (since she had chosen to keep attending regularly), she decided to read it after all. In our class discussions, I had opened up the possibility of imagining the novel from Lolita's point of view, even though her perspective is difficult to discern through the screen of Humbert's first-person narration. It is also possible that seeing the novel from the perspective of Lolita might make reading it even more painful, especially for survivors. We also discussed the ways in which Nabokov, both as implied author and as extratextual author, evokes readers' sympathy for Lolita and both implicitly and explicitly critiques Humbert's solipsism and egocentrism. We also read Linda Kauffman's feminist analysis of *Lolita*, which this student and most others found quite illuminating. Yet, my students, like many previous readers and critics, realized how difficult it is for readers not to be seduced, at least to some degree, by Humbert's brilliant rhetorical strategies, which are directed at readers as/and his "jury."[17] Students discussed how they felt compelled to interrogate their own responses—affective, aesthetic, ethical—to the novel, since many (but not all) of them felt both sympathy for Humbert (especially given that he is the first-person narrator, even if an often unreliable one) and increasing revulsion at his behavior, and also increasing sympathy for Lolita. We had to ask ourselves what it means for some (but certainly not all) readers to "enjoy" or even "love" a novel about pedophilia. Reading and using feminist approaches to the novel and foregrounding gender issues may help students "understand why and how the same text can be so pleasurable for some and so traumatic for others," as Elizabeth Patnoe suggests (85). Through their own reading and our discussions in class, some of my students (both male and female) were able to be or become "resisting" readers of Humbert's rhetoric and point of view, while also appreciating Nabokov's daring and literary skill in writing a compelling, artistic novel "by" and about a pedophile.[18]

I believe that faculty—especially feminist faculty—considering whether or not to teach *Lolita* should consider students' potential intellectual as well as affective responses to reading the novel in a college course, which also means attending to what I will call "the illusion of affect" in the novel itself, that is, the author's evocation of the characters' feelings. Perhaps because I now feel more sympathy for Lolita each time I re-read the novel, I find that my students also often feel sympathy while reading—for both Lolita and perhaps, more problematically, for Humbert. Nabokov himself often expresses sympathy and compassion for Lolita, as when he refers to her as "my poor little girl" (although he also says all his characters are "galley slaves") (*Strong Opinions* 94–95) and when he says "I pity her" (*Think, Write, Speak* 274). Nabokov's best reader (other than himself), his beloved wife Véra, made an unsurprisingly similar point when she wrote, in a 1966 letter, that most critics up until then had ignored the novel's "beauty and pathos," so she called their attention to the novel's "tender description of the child's helplessness, her monstrous dependence on monstrous HH, and her heartrending courage all along" (qtd. in Schiff 236).

Nabokov contradicts the claim in his Afterword that Lolita has no "moral in tow" when he says, in a 1959 interview, that *Lolita* "is an indictment of all the things it expresses. It is a pathetic book dealing with the plight of a child, a very ordinary little girl, caught up by a disgusting and cruel man" (*Think, Write, Speak* 255). In 1956, Nabokov wrote to his then-friend Edmund Wilson that "when you do read *Lolita,* please mark that it is a highly moral affair" (*Nabokov-Wilson Letters* 298). Perhaps prophetically, Nabokov suggested in *Strong Opinions* that in the future a "reappraiser will come and declare that, far from having been a frivolous firebird, I was a rigid moralist kicking sin, cuffing stupidity, ridiculing the vulgar and cruel—and assigning sovereign power to tenderness, talent, and pride" (193). And in a 1964 interview, Nabokov said "I don't think *Lolita* is a religious book [!], but I do think it is a moral one. And I do think that Humbert in his last stage is a moral man because he realizes that he loves Lolita as any woman should be loved. But it is too late; he has destroyed her childhood" (*Think, Write, Speak* 337). Even though we can debate how seriously to take Nabokov's assertion that Humbert is or becomes moral or truly loved the "real" Lolita (who is **not** a woman but rather a girl), Nabokov sounds more like he is discussing real people rather than artificial "eidolons" (*Strong Opinions* 94) or "galley slaves." Here and elsewhere in his writings and interviews, Nabokov seems to hedge on the relationships between fiction and reality, between literary characters and real human beings.

One of the most famous and oft-quoted passages in the Afterword to *Lolita* is Nabokov's claim that "for me, a work of fiction exists only insofar as it affords me what I shall bluntly call aesthetic bliss, that is a sense of being somehow, somewhere, connected with other states of being where art (curiosity, tenderness, kindness, ecstasy) is the norm" (314–15). Yet note how Nabokov associates "aesthetic bliss" not only with ecstasy—which might suggest the aesthetic sublime or *jouissance*—but also with tenderness and kindness, which are ethical practices toward others. As other critics have also noted, and in spite of his own frequent protestations, Nabokov does seem concerned with ethics and with "so-called 'reality'" as well as with aesthetics.

Would I teach *Lolita* again? The decision for me is perhaps less complicated than it would be if I were to teach a course focused on Nabokov's work or even one on the twentieth-century American novel (given how often *Lolita* appears on lists of the greatest twentieth-century American novels). These days, I usually teach courses on multicultural American fiction, or American women writers, or feminist literary and cultural theory—courses where the absence of *Lolita* is insignificant. I have, at least temporarily, stopped including fiction by Sherman Alexie and Junót Diaz in my courses, given the compelling accounts by women (including writers who had admired them and even students) who have reported being sexually harassed or molested by these writers. I might teach *Lolita* again if I were to teach the "Ethics and Literature" course in which I last taught the novel. I probably would not include an "official" trigger warning on my syllabus, just as I don't when I frequently teach Toni Morrison's heartbreaking novel *The Bluest Eye*, which also deals, in large part, with child sexual abuse (and includes one brief and graphic scene of a father's incestuous rape of his child). But I would tell students in advance about *Lolita*'s subject matter (in case some of them are not aware of it) and probably provide alternatives to reading the novel (and offer to talk to students privately about their concerns).[19] I would also consider pairing the novel with *The Bean Trees* again, or perhaps with *The Bluest Eye*, which also has a first-person female narrator who is able to resist patriarchal as well as racist norms and narratives. But perhaps a better choice would be a novel *not* about child sexual abuse. And I would definitely frame the discussion of *Lolita* with two or three feminist analyses of the novel, like Kauffman's, and, perhaps, too, discuss real-world facts about real-life problems of child sexual abuse, incest, rape, and other forms of sexual violence. It also seems important to discuss not only the #MeToo movement but also feminist scholarship and activism, from the late 1960s through the present, aimed at ameliorating these problems. Of course, discussing these real-world problems might have the same triggering effect that reading *Lolita* could have for those students who are survivors of any kind of sexual violence, so discussing stories (real or fictional) of survival and healing would also provide beneficial counterpoints to the novel.

Feminist teachers—like many other teachers—usually try to make the classroom a place of mutual respect, genuine dialogue, and, sometimes, productive discomfort (rather than disempowering trauma). I think there are ways to include *Lolita* on a syllabus—with advance notice to students about its content, perhaps an opt-out provision, careful framing with both feminist criticism and a feminist novel or two, and sensitive pedagogy attentive to student affective as well as intellectual responses. But another part of me— the feminist scholar and teacher rather than the Nabokov devotee—thinks that there are so many other wonderful American novels—by both male and female writers—from the past one hundred years to choose from that it would be quite possible to choose great novels that neither foreground sexual abuse of girls or women nor are written by men who have sexually abused women. With our increasing awareness (in part but not only through the #MeToo movement) of just how widespread sexual abuse (including child sexual abuse) is, all of us who teach—whether or not we consider ourselves to be feminists—do need to consider whether requiring our students to read *Lolita* might traumatize or re-traumatize some of them. If we decide the benefits of teaching *Lolita*—whether in providing students an opportunity to explore the complex relations between ethics and aesthetics in the novel and in the real world, to analyze their own responses and positionalities as readers, to become better users and consumers of rhetoric, and/or to understand and resist misogyny and the sexual objectification of women and girls— outweigh the risks, we must figure out for ourselves, based on our pedagogical as well as real-world values, how best to teach it.

WORKS CITED

Ahmed, Sara. *The Promise of Happiness*. Duke University Press, 2010.
Amis, Martin. "Divine Levity." *The Times Literary Supplement*, December 23, 2011, pp. 3–5.
Bader, Julia. *Crystal Land: Artifice in Nabokov's English Novels*. Berkeley: University of California Press, 1972.
Berger, John, et al. *Ways of Seeing*. 1972. BBC. Penguin, 1973.
Bordo, Susan. "The Moral Content of Nabokov's *Lolita*." In *Aesthetic Subjects*, edited by Pamela R. Matthews and David McWhirter. University of Minnesota Press, 2003, pp. 125–52.
———. *Unbearable Weight: Feminism, Western Culture, and the Body*. Second edition. University of California Press, 2004.
Brownmiller, Susan. *Against Our Will: Men, Women, and Rape*. Simon and Schuster, 1975.
Cantor, David, et al. "Report on the AAU Campus Climate Survey on Sexual Assault and Misconduct." American Association of Universities, October 2019. https://www.aau.edu/sites/default/files/AAU-Files/Key-Issues/Campus-Safety/FULL_2019_Campus_Climate_Survey.pdf.
Centerwall, Brandon S. "Hiding in Plain Sight: Nabokov and Pedophilia." *Texas Studies in Literature and Language* 32 (1990): pp. 468–84.

Culler, Jonathan. *On Deconstruction: Theory and Criticism after Structuralism*. Cornell University Press, 1982.

Delage-Toriel, Lara. "Women." In *Vladimir Nabokov in Context*, edited by David Bethea and Siggy Frank. Cambridge University Press, 2018, pp. 35–42.

Doak, Melissa J. *Child Abuse and Domestic Violence*. Gale, 2011. Information Plus Reference Series. *Gale eBooks*, https://link-gale-com.libproxy.scu.edu/apps/pub/3BMX/GVRL?u=sant38536&sid=GVRL.

Durham, M. Gigi. *The Lolita Effect: The Media Sexualization of Young Girls and What We Can Do about It*. Overlook Press, 2009.

Dworkin, Andrea. *Woman Hating*. Dutton, 1974.

Edelstein, Marilyn. "Before the Beginning: Nabokov and the Rhetoric of the Preface." In *Narrative Beginnings: Theories and Practices*, edited by Brian Richardson. University of Nebraska Press, 2008, pp. 29–43.

———. "Teaching *Lolita* in a Course on Ethics and Literature." In *Approaches to Teaching Nabokov's Lolita*, edited by Zoran Kuzmanovich and Galya Diment. Modern Language Association, 2008, pp. 43–48.

Fallon, Claire. "Let's All Calm Down: Trigger Warnings for Books Are Not Like Censorship." *HuffPost*, May 23, 2014, https://www.huffpost.com/entry/lets-all-calm-down-trigge_n_5368319.

Farley, Lin. *Sexual Shakedown: The Sexual Harassment of Women on the Job*. Mc-Graw Hill, 1978.

Fetterley, Judith. *The Resisting Reader: A Feminist Approach to American Fiction*. Indiana University Press, 1978.

Freedman, Estelle. "Uncontrollable Desires: The Response to the Sexual Psychopath, 1920–1960." *Journal of American History* 74 (1987): pp. 83–106.

Glynn, Michael. *Vladimir Nabokov: Bergsonian and Russian Formalist Influences in His Novels*. Palgrave Macmillan, 2007.

Goldman, Eric. "Can You Hear Me Now?: Monologue, Dialogue, and the Other Voices in *Lolita*'s Sexual History." *Nabokov Studies* 14 (2016): pp. 79–110.

———. "'Knowing' Lolita: Sexual Deviance and Normality in Nabokov's *Lolita*." *Nabokov Studies* 8 (2004): pp. 87–104.

Griffin, Susan. "Rape: The All-American Crime." *Ramparts Magazine*, September 1971, pp. 26–35.

Hamrit, Jacqueline. *Authorship in Nabokov's Prefaces*. Cambridge Scholars Publishing, 2014.

Herbold, Sarah. "'Dolorès Disparue': Reading Misogyny in *Lolita*." In *Approaches to Teaching Nabokov's Lolita*, edited by Zoran Kuzmanovich and Galya Diment. Modern Language Association, 2008, pp. 134–40.

———. "'(I Have Camouflaged Everything, My Love)': *Lolita* and the Woman Reader." *Nabokov Studies* 5 (1998): pp. 71–98.

Hillstrom, Laurie Collier. *The #MeToo Movement*. 21st Century Turning Points. ABC-CLIO, 2019.

Kang, Jay Caspian. "Trigger Warnings and the Novelist's Mind." Newyorker.com, May 21, 2014. https://www.newyorker.com/books/page-turner/trigger-warnings-and-the-novelists-mind.

Kauffman, Linda. "Framing Lolita: Is There a Woman in the Text?" In *Refiguring the Father: New Feminist Readings of Patriarchy*, edited by Patricia Yaeger et al. Southern Illinois University Press, 1989, pp. 131–52.

Kingsolver, Barbara. *The Bean Trees*. Harper, 1988.

Langton, Rae. *Sexual Solipsism: Philosophical Essays on Pornography and Objectification*. Oxford University Press, 2009.

MacKinnon, Catharine A. *Feminism Unmodified: Discourses on Life and Law*. Harvard University Press, 1987.

———. *Sexual Harassment of Working Women: A Case of Sex Discrimination*. Yale University Press, 1978.

McNeely, Trevor. "'Lo' and Behold: Solving the *Lolita* Riddle." *Studies in the Novel* 21, no. 2 (1989): pp. 182–99.

Moore, Tony. "Seeing through Humbert: Focussing on the Feminist Sympathy in *Lolita*." In *Discourse and Ideology in Nabokov's Prose*, edited by David H. J. Larmour. Routledge, 2002, pp. 91–110.

Mulvey, Laura. "Visual Pleasure and Narrative Cinema." *Screen* 16, no. 3 (Autumn 1975): pp. 6–18.

Nabokov, Vladimir. *The Annotated Lolita*, edited by Alfred Appel, Jr. Viking, 1991.

———. *Lectures on Literature*, edited by Fredson Bowers. Harvest/HBJ, 1982.

———. *Strong Opinions*. McGraw-Hill, 1973.

———. *The Nabokov-Wilson Letters: Correspondence between Vladimir Nabokov and Edmund Wilson, 1940–1971*, edited by Simon Karlinsky. Harper and Row, 1979.

———. *Think, Write, Speak: Uncollected Essays, Reviews, Interviews, and Letters to the Editor*, edited by Brian Boyd and Anastasia Tolstoy. Knopf, 2019.

Nussbaum, Martha. "Objectification." *Philosophy and Public Affairs* 24, no. 4 (1995): pp. 249–91.

Papadaki, Evangelia (Lina). "Feminist Perspectives on Objectification." *The Stanford Encyclopedia of Philosophy* (Summer 2018 Edition), edited by Edward N. Zalta. https://plato.stanford.edu/archives/sum2018/entries/feminism-objectification/.

Patnoe, Elizabeth. "Lolita Misrepresented, Lolita Reclaimed: Disclosing the Doubles." *College Literature* 22, no. 2 (June 1995): pp. 81–104.

Pifer, Ellen. *Nabokov and the Novel*. Cambridge, MA: Harvard University Press, 1980.

Quayle, Anika Susan. "Lolita *Is* Dolores Haze: The 'Real' Child and the 'Real' Body in *Lolita*." *Nabokov Online Journal* 3 (2009): n.p. http://www.nabokovonline.com/uploads/2/3/7/7/23779748/v3_07_quayle.pdf.

Schiff, Stacy. *Véra (Mrs. Vladimir Nabokov)*. Random House, 1999.

Schweickart, Patrocinio. "Reading Ourselves: Toward a Feminist Theory of Reading." In *Gender and Reading: Essays on Readers, Texts, and Contexts*, edited by Patrocinio Schweickart and Elizabeth Flynn. Johns Hopkins University Press, 1986, pp. 31–62.

Showalter, Elaine. "Feminist Criticism in the Wilderness." *Critical Inquiry* 8, no. 2 (1981): pp. 179–205.

Shute, Jenefer P. "'So Nakedly Dressed': The Text of the Female Body in Nabokov's Novels." *Amerikastudien/American Studies* 30, no. 4 (1985): pp. 537–43. Rpt. In *Vladimir Nabokov's* Lolita*: A Casebook*, edited by Ellen Pifer. Oxford University Press, 2003, pp. 111–20.

Stegner, Page. *Escape into Aesthetics: The Art of Vladimir Nabokov*. Morrow, 1966.

Tamir-Ghez, Nomi. "The Art of Persuasion in Nabokov's *Lolita*." *Poetics Today* 1, no. 1–2 (1979): pp. 65–83.

Toker, Leona. *Nabokov: The Mystery of Literary Structures*. Cornell University Press, 1989.

Warhol, Robyn R., and Diane Price Herndl. "About *Feminisms*." In *Feminisms Redux: An Anthology of Literary Theory and Criticism*, edited by Robyn R. Warhol and Diane Price Herndl. Rutgers University Press, 2009, pp. ix–xvii.

Weinman, Sarah. *The Real Lolita: The Kidnapping of Sally Horner and the Novel that Scandalized the World*. Harper, 2018.

Whiting, Frederick. "'The Strange Particularity of the Lover's Preference': Pedophilia, Pornography, and the Anatomy of Monstrosity in *Lolita*." *American Literature* 70, no. 4 (December 1998): pp. 833–62.

Wunker, Erin. *Notes from a Feminist Killjoy: Essays on Everyday Life*. Book*hug Press, 2016.

NOTES

1. Shute's 1985 essay on the female body in Nabokov's *Ada* and *Lolita*, while not explicitly feminist and not citing any feminist scholars, does use implicitly feminist ideas, including art historian John Berger's influential concept of the "male gaze" (first used in his 1972 BBC-TV series and book *Ways of Seeing*), which would be more fully theorized and applied by feminist film theorist Laura Mulvey in her classic 1975 essay "Visual Pleasure and Narrative Cinema" and then by countless other feminist film, literature, and cultural studies critics and theorists.

2. See, for example, Nabokov's comment in the new collection *Think, Write, Speak*: "I regard 'Women's Liberation' as a joke" (475). Many Nabokov scholars have commented on Nabokov's infrequent but often negative comments on and/or inattention to women writers. Nabokov also has made frequent negative comments in interviews about any public protest movements, including student anti-war protests occurring in the United States during the years he lived in Montreux. See *Think, Write, Speak*. For further analysis of the "real" Vladimir Nabokov's views of women—including women writers and translators as well as women in his own life—and what seem to be the views of Nabokov as implied author of his novels, as interviewee, as critic, and as lecturer on literature, see Lara Delage-Toriel. For an analysis of misogyny in *Lolita*, see Herbold's "'Dolorès Disparue.'"

3. But cf. Frederick Whiting, who argues, citing (among others) feminist historian Estelle Freedman, that there were well-publicized "sex crime panics" in the United States during the period when Nabokov was writing *Lolita*. He quotes Freedman: "Each of the two major sex crime panics—roughly from 1937 to 1940 and from 1949 to 1955—originated when, after a series of brutal and apparently sexually motivated child murders, major urban newspapers expanded and, in some cases, sensationalized their coverage of child molestation and rape" (qtd. in Whiting 836). Whiting sees cultural anxieties about both pedophilia and pornography (both set against the backdrop of the Cold War) as pivotal to the cultural context in which Nabokov wrote *Lolita* (although Whiting does not discuss increasing anxieties among US women about gender roles and norms in the postwar period). One of the most highly publicized child kidnapping and rape cases in this period is mentioned briefly in *Lolita:* that of Sally Horner, who was kidnapped by Frank LaSalle in 1948 and finally escaped almost two years later (but died soon after in a car accident). Sarah Weinman argues, not very persuasively, that the Sally Horner case was the "inspiration" for *Lolita* (even though Nabokov had drafted a rather similar but much shorter tale of an older man and a girl in his 1939 novella *The Enchanter*—before he moved to the United States in 1940, well before the Sally Horner case).

4. Melissa Doak noted in 2011 that "many experts accept the estimate that one out of five (20 percent) American women and one out of 10 (10 percent) American men have experienced some form of childhood sexual abuse (CSA)" (63). Like other researchers, Doak notes the major problem of under-reporting.

5. Fans of Nabokov's *Lolita* and of Kubrick's earlier film of it were also skeptical that a film made by Adrian Lyne, director of such sexually charged, "non-art" films as *Nine ½ Weeks, Fatal Attraction*, and *Flashdance,* could come close to capturing the verbal brilliance or the ethical complexities of Nabokov's novel.

6. Second-wave feminists were also the first to call attention to the sexual harassment of women—a central issue in much of #MeToo activism. See, for example, Catharine MacKinnon's influential 1978 book *Sexual Harassment of Working Women: A Case of Sex Discrimination*. Lin Farley has been credited with coining the term "sexual harassment" in 1975 (Hillstrom 15). And see Farley's 1978 book *Sexual Shakedown: The Sexual Harassment of Women on the Job*. I find it interesting that in spite of second-wave feminist work on rape and other forms of sexual violence, it took a hashtag and social media to bring rape and sexual harassment to widespread public awareness. Second-wave feminists had been highlighting the problem of sexual violence, rape in particular, since the early 1970s, with such influential works as Susan Griffin's 1971 essay "Rape: The All-American Crime," published even before Brownmiller's *Against Our Will*. See above regarding Nabokov's dismissal of the "women's liberation" movement and student activism (*Think, Write, Speak*). For a detailed timeline of legal and cultural predecessors of the #MeToo movement—those related both to sexual harassment and sexual violence (which, as is too often the case, wind up being virtually conflated), going back to Title VII of the 1964 Civil Rights Act—see Hillstrom.

7. For further discussion of the problematics of Nabokov's paratexts—especially Ray's Foreword and Nabokov's Afterword to *Lolita*—see Edelstein "Before the Beginning." See also Jacqueline Hamrit. Some critics and reviewers—e.g., Brandon S. Centerwall—have argued that Nabokov's frequent use of the theme of "older man lusting after young girl" suggests that Nabokov was at least a "closet pedophile," but there is no concrete biographical evidence to support these inferences. However, it is noteworthy, as Martin Amis points out, that of Nabo-

kov's "nineteen fictions, no fewer than six wholly or partly concern themselves with the sexuality of prepubescent girls" (5).

8. According to a new study by the American Association of Universities (AAU), published in October 2019, based on surveys at thirty-three US universities, "the rate of nonconsensual sexual contact by physical force or inability to consent for undergraduate women ranged from 14 to 32 percent across the 33 schools" (Cantor xl). Among undergraduate women, the rate was almost 26 percent (Cantor lx). About half of these cases involved the perpetrator using physical force, while half were the result of the woman's inability to give consent (usually related to alcohol consumption). First-year students are more likely to be victims of such nonconsensual sexual contact than women in their second, third, or fourth years of college. However, the report acknowledges the persistent problem of under-reporting on most campuses. Given this recent data, as well as national data (also strongly affected by under-reporting) on the prevalence of sexual violence, rape, and incest, it is quite likely that some or even many of the female undergraduates we teach have been the victims of at least one form of sexual violence or are friends or relatives of those who have.

9. See Jonathan Culler's section on "Reading as a Woman" in his book *On Deconstruction* for a more detailed analysis of the problematics of reading *as* a woman even if one *is* biologically a woman.

10. On the figure of "the feminist killjoy," see also Wunker. For a male writer's claim that a feminist teacher "ruined" his pleasure in reading *Lolita*, see Jay Caspian Kang. Claire Fallon discusses Kang's 2014 article in which he complains about a (presumably feminist) graduate school professor who told students, "'When you read 'Lolita,' keep in mind that what you're reading about is the systematic rape of a young girl.'" Kang argues that he could not get this announcement (which he compares to the trigger warnings coming into vogue at that time) "out of my head," implying that seeing the novel this way "ruins" the reading experience. Both Kang and Fallon share *Feministing* editor Alexandra Brodsky's pointed response to Kang: "'What a delight it must be to read a book full of graphic accounts of sexual violence and still have the book not be about sexual violence to you! Why is the depersonalized, apolitical reading the one we should fight for?'" (qtd. in Fallon). Fallon argues that "sexual violence is central to the book—Nabokov himself would not have wished for readers to elide that reality" (although see Kauffman on this latter point).

11. See, for example, male critics' "feminist" readings of Lolita—most arguing, not very persuasively, that *Lolita* itself **is** feminist—including those by Tony Moore, Trevor McNeely, and Eric Goldman ("'Knowing Lolita,'" although in his later essay "Can You Hear Me Now?" Goldman more or less retracts his earlier essay's claim that the novel is feminist).

12. See, for example, Michael Glynn.

13. It is also clear, especially from Humbert's negative descriptions of Valeria, his first wife, and Charlotte, his second, that he finds adult women and their "ripe" flesh repulsive, much preferring the "fruit vert" (60) of young girls.

14. I do not have space here to discuss the dubious "sincerity" of Humbert's various expressions of remorse and even of self-loathing for his crimes against Lolita, although these are important issues in understanding some of the ethical complexities of the novel.

15. However, Quayle also asserts that "it is through Humbert's awareness of the 'real' Lolita that Nabokov advances his 'moral message' on pedophilia." As I have argued elsewhere, even if we do not accept Nabokov's claim, in *Lolita*'s Afterword as well as elsewhere, that the novel has "no moral message in tow" (*Annotated Lolita* 314), it seems clear to me that any possible "moral message" we might find in the novel would not be as simple—or unnecessary for the overwhelming majority of its readers—as "don't have sex with children." See Edelstein, "Teaching Lolita" (47–48).

16. I think there are homologies between the attitudes of some critics who claim Lolita is sexually wanton and those people—usually men—who, in real life, including court cases, blame rape and other sexual assault victims for such things as dressing "provocatively," being out "too late," or drinking too much and thus being responsible for being victimized. Given the respective ages of Lolita and Humbert—twelve and almost forty at the start of the novel—and the huge power differential between them, there is no ethical or legal possibility of theirs being a consensual relationship—as the young Humbert's romantic and almost consummated sexual

relationship with Annabel would have been. Even if a reader believes Humbert's re-telling of Lolita's tale that she had sex previously with Charlie, a boy her own age, at camp, Lolita does not and legally cannot provide informed consent to have sex with Humbert, who at the very least engages in statutory rape of her.

17. For a persuasive analysis of Humbert's rhetoric and manipulation of his "audience," see Tamir-Ghez.

18. We also discussed the significance of Nabokov's remarks in the Afterword that pedophilia (and/or incest) was only one theme American readers and publishers found taboo—the other two being a happy interracial marriage or the long and happy life of an avowed atheist. We can discern in these comments Nabokov's social/political critiques of racism—in spite of his frequent protestations that he has no political or social commentaries to make—and of Americans' often superficial or hypocritical religiosity.

19. I include a statement like the following on most of my syllabi: "Since this class will deal with complex, challenging, and sometimes controversial issues and texts, it is important that we create, collectively, a classroom atmosphere of mutual respect, attentive listening, and open-mindedness to others' ideas." If/when I next teach *Lolita* or *The Bluest Eye*, I might add a statement that the novels deal with child sexual abuse—which, I suppose, would be equivalent to a trigger warning. I find Fallon's 2014 article "Let's All Calm Down: Trigger Warnings for Books Are Not like Censorship" persuasive. As I have been arguing, I am concerned about how best to accommodate those students, especially survivors of sexual violence, who may find such novels (re-)traumatizing.

Chapter Two

Why I Teach *Lolita*

Anne Dwyer

This chapter requires a preamble. In 2018 I published a short op-ed in *Inside Higher Ed* recounting my recent experience of teaching *Lolita*.[1] I am a Russianist and comparativist (a scholar of Russian Formalism and of imperial literary production in Russia and Austria-Hungary) at an elite liberal arts institution, housed in a department of German and Russian. Like many of us, I must be a generalist in my teaching. I am not a "Nabokovian" with a deeply reverential attitude to the author, yet Nabokov is one of my very favorite authors to teach—precisely because of the strong responses that he elicits from his readers.

Over the years, I have found that my course on Nabokov draws a highly motivated audience into Russian literature. I get language-loving and often mathematically-minded students I might otherwise never see in my classes. From the outset I explain that I personally have something of a love-hate relationship to Nabokov. I adore Nabokov's writing for the beauty and intricacy of its language and linguistic puzzles, for its ability to transcend national literary canons. I admire Nabokov for succeeding both as a "Russian" and an "American" author. At times I feel frustration over the arrogance he displays toward his readers and for his high modernist sensibilities (which, at other times, I enjoy). Nabokov becomes an impetus to teach "close reading" and to think, as a group, about how language and art work in our world. My students learn Nabokov's invaluable "rules" for reading, which promote the kind of close attention and re-reading that is otherwise challenging to elicit from undergraduates (student papers in this class are above average), but we also question the underlying assumptions and occasional rigidity of these same "strong opinions."

The text that follows is an account of an experience I had with students who enrolled in my single-author seminar on the "Novels of Vladimir Nabokov" in early 2018. I reflect briefly on the afterlife of this Nabokov "intervention," on responses I received from students, and on ways to keep *Lolita* interesting and relevant to students in an age that, for good reason, responds to this particular text in a distinctly negative fashion.

I've taught an undergraduate seminar on Vladimir Nabokov since 2008, repeating it about every other year. In each iteration I've addressed the challenges of reading *Lolita*—a novel whose plot (the *fabula*, to speak in Russian Formalist terms) is about the abduction and ongoing sexual abuse of a child, but whose structures and devices (the *siuzhet*) point everywhere else. The first three or four iterations went smoothly. Then, in 2016, students debated whether I should have included a "trigger warning" on the syllabus. In the 2018 iteration, I added a few words to the syllabus requesting students to inform themselves about the plot of *Lolita* before committing to the class. I asked them to consider what it means that Nabokov treats "a range of human experience in a highly artful, and even artificial, way." But that was not enough.

In 2018, about one week into discussing *Lolita*, I assigned feminist readings of the novel, including Elizabeth Patnoe's 2002 essay on trauma.[2] Because this is a writing-intensive seminar, full of peer editing and discussions of writing (anathema, I fear, to Nabokov's notions of the ideal reader and resistance to collective work), I also assigned a term paper by a former student, Francesca Capossela, whose undergraduate essay successfully located "Dolly's" signature in *Lolita*.[3] (Capossela uses "Dolly" in her essay because this is the name which Lolita uses herself, neither her given name, nor the moniker assigned by Humbert Humbert.) I also read out loud a sexual passage (the frottage scene on the "davenport," when Humbert Humbert announces that Lolita has been "safely solipsized"). After some uncomfortable discussion, my students issued a polite, but concerted challenge: How could I justify teaching a book that inflicted trauma and even perpetuated rape culture? Could I not convey the essence of Nabokov's art without teaching *Lolita*? Was I not excluding some students simply by teaching the text? I felt like a deer caught in the headlights. While I was more or less prepared to talk about rape, I wasn't at all ready to talk about the possibility of not teaching a book I love.

This all happened on a Tuesday afternoon. On Thursday, I gave a lecture entitled "Why I Teach Lolita." Afterward students voted anonymously on whether they'd like to add an extra day to our discussion of *Lolita*. Each student had veto power, since the syllabus "contract" did not include an extra day of *Lolita* instruction. Twelve of fifteen students voted to add a day to discuss the text. No one exercised their veto. What follows is an abridged and redacted version of my lecture.

LECTURE: WHY I TEACH *LOLITA*

Dear students, I was surprised by your suggestion that I NOT teach *Lolita* in a college seminar on the novels of Vladimir Nabokov, whose reputation and fame—at least as an American writer—rests largely on this one novel.

I was *not* surprised by the vehemence of your response to the book, but by the suggestion that we should perhaps not read it at all. That by assigning *Lolita* I am perpetuating trauma and may even be perpetuating rape culture. This last suggestion runs so counter to my own beliefs about what literature does that I found it hard to parry your challenges.

Let me try to explain myself now and make a case for why I will continue to teach *Lolita* this semester and in the future. I'd also like to suggest that what happened in class—if we are able now to process our discussion—is learning at its best. Thank you for speaking your mind. Thank you also for being thoughtful and polite as you did so.

THE UBIQUITY OF SEXUAL ASSAULT

Before I launch my defense, I wish to acknowledge where I went amiss. When I teach this book, I always keep in mind that, in all likelihood, several people in this room have experienced sexual assault. The numbers are staggeringly high; some studies suggest that as many as one in five children experience sexual abuse. Many of the perpetrators are trusted adults.

I accept your point from yesterday that I might have started our discussion of this book differently. Earlier in the semester, I nodded to the emotional and intellectual challenges of reading *Lolita*. However, I never acknowledged that the act of reading three hundred-plus pages is different than knowing the subject matter. The next time I teach *Lolita* I will make sure to address the emotional and intellectual challenges of reading from the outset.

I will also announce loudly and clearly that students may choose not to read the book.

That said, I would urge you—in this class and in other classes—to opt out only when you are experiencing emotions or reliving events that are detrimental to your health and *not* because you are feeling uncomfortable, queasy, disgusted, or morally offended. Your health needs to be protected. But these other responses are ones we should learn to inhabit and process, including by discussing books like *Lolita*.

NO *LOLITA* IN A COURSE ON NABOKOV?

You asked whether I could do justice to Nabokov's art without teaching *Lolita*. The answer is "no."

Not teaching *Lolita* in an English-language seminar devoted to Nabokov would amount to a breach of contract. (A course on the "Russian Nabokov" would be a different matter.) If I don't teach *Lolita*, I am denying you the opportunity to read—in the hopefully productive and relatively safe environment of the classroom—the book that established Nabokov's reputation as an English-language author. *Lolita* is the reason Nabokov's Russian works have been translated into English and why I can attract students to this course. I would not be doing my professional duty as a professor and literary scholar if I side-stepped this difficult but interesting novel. You agreed to this contract when you stayed in this course after reading my syllabus.

The world of *Lolita*, though related to Nabokov's other novelistic worlds, marks a significant shift in Nabokov's oeuvre. "It had taken me some forty years to invent Russia and Western Europe, and now I was faced by the task of inventing America."[4] The Russian novels we've read remain at a distance that allows for safe intellectual contemplation. *Lolita* is likely the first Nabokov novel that touches you—young people living in America who are not much older than Lolita—in a visceral way.

This provocative streak is not new for Nabokov. Both the Russian-language novel *Invitation to a Beheading* and the early English-language novel *Bend Sinister* turn totalitarianism into farce. In *Bend Sinister* horrific scenes of child torture are rendered through Shakespearean allusions run amok. Consider how you might feel reading that book if you knew someone who had died in a Stalinist gulag or Nazi concentration camp?

Lolita is not the first novel where Nabokov turns horrific events into linguistic play. But it's the first time he does it in a deeply *American* book that touches us today at such a deep core of, yes, trauma. *Lolita* captures something that is wrong with the time and place in which we live. Without *Lolita*, we lose a sense of the provocative nature of Nabokov's writing and lose an opportunity to reflect on the transition from Nabokov, the *Russian* writer, to Nabokov, the *American* writer.

LOLITA AS AN EXTREME CASE OF NABOKOV'S POETICS

In class we've discussed the relationship between author, reader, and characters in Nabokov. One student suggested that we return to the essay "Good Readers and Good Writers" to think through the impasse at which we find ourselves when thinking about Humbert Humbert and Lolita.[5] Nabokov tells, nay, orders us not to identify with a book's hero or heroine. Look what happens in *Lolita* if you don't follow the rule! Either you slip into identification with HH and find yourself in the subject position of a child molester. Or, if you identify with Lolita, you feel abused and traumatized!

I'm not saying that we should avoid identifying with characters. To my mind, that is one of those (slightly bullying) Nabokovian instructions that has to be taken with a grain of salt. Identification is deeply wired in the human psyche. This is how we engage with narrative. But Nabokov is challenging us to read differently. And part of his program means that either possibility for identification in *Lolita* is very uncomfortable indeed. This dilemma is interesting. Nabokov both tells us *not* to identify and manipulates us *into* identifying.

You may be angry and mad about this. Even offended. But I would argue that this manipulation is itself a reason to read this book and not to let it rot on the shelf.

THE SPECTER OF CRUELTY

Whether Nabokov is "cruel" to his characters and readers is another important and contentious issue. Nabokov speaks of the author as a demiurge. He dismisses the notion that a character could ever take on a life of her own outside of the author's control.

There is a recurring scenario in Nabokov's fiction when characters become aware of their status as characters. In *The Luzhin Defense* the chess master Luzhin jumps out of the window when he intuits that some outside force is in control of his life, only to find another chessboard spread out "inexorably" before him. The finale of *Invitation to a Beheading* seems to bring the hero, Cincinnatus C., a kind of extratextual freedom—he escapes his dystopian world to join the other "voices" akin to him.

In *Lolita* we see, especially in the "authorial" relation to the heroine, both sides of this coin. On the one hand we have the naked level of "plot" where Lolita is abused. But we also intuit authorial empathy. On the level of metafiction (but not in "real" life), Humbert gets his come-uppance. Lolita is, the novel suggests, smarter than HH, and plays her cards as well as she can.

Nabokov can also be cruel toward his reader. In *Strong Opinions*, for example, Nabokov offers a scathing review of one critic's Freudian interpretative efforts, ordering him unceremoniously "to remove his belongings."[6] Eric Naiman writes about the "hermeneutic performance anxiety" Nabokov provokes among his readers—we experience intense desire to prove ourselves as "good readers" and to outperform our readerly rivals.[7] Even as Nabokov makes many of us feel stupid or inadequate, we may also experience a Pavlovian reward or intense pleasure when we get the writer's erudite joke. Public conversations about Nabokov are prone to turn into interpretative jousting matches, with a fair amount of collateral damage. How can an author have such power over his audience even beyond the grave? And how does cultural gatekeeping work in other contexts? This question is worth class discussion.

DOES LANGUAGE TRUMP ALL ELSE?

Nabokov called *Lolita* his "love affair with the English language." But are we able (and should we be willing) to set the "plot" aside and delve into the novel's linguistic pyrotechnics? *Lolita* offers an important challenge to the genre of the social novel and to our accustomed modes of reading. Nabokov's novels resist didactic interpretations and obvious social criticism. To think creatively and openly about the power of *language* and its relationship to social realities and competing truth claims is one of the provocations of the novel, as much in our current era as in any other. If we accept this challenge, we learn much about ourselves. But to do so we do need to move beyond the immediate plot and make an effort to untangle the verbal layers of the text.

"ALWAYS HISTORICIZE!"

We need to think more historically.[8] One issue at the core of our current difficulty with *Lolita*—and at the heart of the book itself—is a clash of historic and national sensibilities. In *Lolita*, we are dealing with at least four layers of history (which coincide loosely to particular subject positions). First, we need to think of Nabokov as a member of the turn-of-the-century European elite. Second, Nabokov is an immigrant in 1950s America, offering us an outsider's perspective on postwar American life and culture in the McCarthy era. Third, Nabokov offers us layers of literary allusion to past centuries, most prominently Elizabethan England, seventeenth- and eighteenth-century France, and nineteenth-century America. Finally, we need to reflect on our own American moment now, and especially our attitudes toward culture, politics, and sex.

We must acknowledge that our attitudes toward sex are historically constructed. In Nabokov's novels, sex is dangerous, revealing, and also hilarious. In 1950s America, polite society pretended sex didn't exist even as popular culture oozed sensuality, and men traded sexually explicit jokes in private. Since 2018, we have had a president with a dubious track record toward women, have become invested in the #MeToo movement, and have come to think that sex should be healthy, consensual, and (probably) serious. The thought of gay sex no longer disturbs many of us (unlike in Oscar Wilde's England); BDSM is acceptable as long as there is a safe word (though we might not know that the "S" refers to the Marquis de Sade, and the "M" to Leopold von Sacher-Masoch). But sex between a child and an adult is so taboo we have trouble even starting a conversation about childhood sexuality; Freud's readers at the turn of the twentieth century may have had an easier time with than we do today.

In "On a Book Entitled Lolita," Nabokov wrote that there were three taboos that American publishers refused to tackle. The first concerns *Lolita* (he never names the exact taboo); the second is "a Negro-White marriage which is a complete and glorious success resulting in lots of children and grandchildren." The third is "the total atheist who lives a happy and useful life, and dies in his sleep at the age of 106." Let us abstract these concepts: sex, race, religion. Are these not the accursed questions of our lives in America today? ("Accursed questions," by the way, is a term taken from the Russian nineteenth century.)[9]

(SELF-)CENSORSHIP

Finally, there is the question of censorship. Nabokov was not published in the Soviet Union. Soviet proscriptions on ideological form and content prohibited his elitist form of aestheticism. One commonplace in Communist Party discussions of forbidden books was, "I haven't read it, but . . ." Nabokov—a Russian émigré, who fled Berlin with his Jewish wife in 1937—knew about censorship and persecution. In writing *Lolita*, he pushes Americans, with their (our?) expressed ideology of "freedom," to notice where they (we?) enact censorship, too.

Professors need to assign, and students need to read, difficult books. The challenges we face are not new. Our students are not "coddled" (a discourse which I abhor). But we need to read and discuss and come to our own conclusions. Even if that conclusion is that Nabokov contributed to a "Lolita myth" that has at times had horrific resonance in our culture. (Jeffrey Epstein's "Lolita Express" is only one recent iteration of this phenomenon.)

CLASSROOM POSTSCRIPT

After I published my lecture, readers asked me in person and online what my students' reactions had been. At least one student was emphatically not convinced. While she did not veto the extra class discussion of *Lolita,* she stayed away the day of our follow-up discussion. But a letter from an international student moved me deeply—perhaps especially because I had felt challenged by him in class; he seemed to want a more traditionally (European? male?) authoritative voice from his professor than I cared to offer. In the letter he apologized for his attitude and expressed his admiration that I had held my ground and offered a well-considered defense of the novel that did not belittle the students' concerns: "I want to thank you for showing me how this sort of conversation (or self-expression) ought to be handled in an empathetic yet effective manner."

The context of the student's letter replays some of the challenges of teaching *Lolita,* pitting one (European) intellectual tradition against another (American) college setting. The international student told me he had begun to keep his non-US perspective on social issues under wraps because he found it hard to represent minority opinions in conversations on campus. *Lolita* allows us to investigate the power of cultural expectations and stereotypes and to explore the potential and danger of cross-cultural encounters. I suspect that my lecture showed my international student that to embrace an open-ended discussion format in a literature class does not equal intellectual laziness or an absence of "strong opinions"; I hope that some of my other students thought harder about the historical specificity of our own current discourse around gender and sexuality and began to appreciate the value of accessing other, including older, attitudes and worldviews.

My own takeaway is to remember that people *feel* when they read; and that *Lolita* makes many readers feel angry, disgusted, or hurt. It's my job both to acknowledge this effect of literature and to push students to read in a variety of ways so that they may come to their own, informed conclusions about the book. I need also to reflect on my own embeddedness in a particular set of social and cultural paradigms. As a professor, scholar, and university administrator who is herself transnational and multilingual, I emphatically wish to reach across differences and promote a sense of belonging for students who might feel left out of the university classroom. I grew up in Vienna, Austria, so an interest in modernism, emigration, and multilingualism is part of my cultural DNA. But I also know that European canons (which include the "American" *Lolita*) must be supplemented by cultural artifacts from radically different traditions—including those that argue for supplanting books like *Lolita* altogether. *Lolita* must not stand alone.

LOOKING AHEAD

I wish I could offer a postscript here outlining a new, wildly successful, inclusive, and aesthetically satisfying approach to teaching *Lolita* in the era of #MeToo. But I have not yet had a chance to teach the course again. What I do know from experience is that when the question of sexual assault becomes the absolute forefront of classroom conversation, many other aspects of Nabokov's immensely rich text receive second billing or go by completely unnoticed. When this happens, the text itself loses its literary and pedagogical value, for important conversations about the possibilities and limitations of aesthetic and ethical reading cannot occur.

Perhaps most urgent in my re-thinking of how next to teach *Lolita* is to update my scholarly toolbox—I am looking forward to reading the contributions to this very volume. I am quite certain, for example, that I will not teach Elizabeth Patnoe's essay next time—what was once an important feminist intervention in the reading of *Lolita* strikes me today as reinforcing a by now dominant ideological discourse without opening significant new access points into the novel. New, more nuanced, feminist readings are needed, as provided by my own student Francesca Cappossella, for example, looking for traces of Dolly's writing, or by Eléna Rakhimova-Sommers, who investigates the epistemological dilemma of Nabokov's women as "passportless wanderers," privileged readers and muses who remain mostly voiceless and who represent the "ultimate challenge to knowability."[10]

Among the previous generation of criticism, I appreciate close textual analysis that asks difficult questions about gender, form, and desire. Sarah Herbold investigates female desire in *Lolita*, while Elizabeth Freeman places *Lolita* within a long American literary tradition of child brides crossing the great American expanse as part of the doctrine of Manifest Destiny.[11] Rachel Bowlby's attention to *Lolita* in the broader context of advertising is also illuminating.[12] Undoubtedly there are many more recent contributions of this ilk that I have not yet investigated. In the past I have taught Nafisi's *Reading Lolita in Tehran*, which I suspect misunderstands *Lolita* as a novel, but which nonetheless shows how the text can be read as a sign of liberation, rather than as one of oppression, and allows students to look beyond their own historical and social context to a different group of readers.[13]

Teaching *Lolita* successfully in the era of #MeToo demands close reading—of the text, of the students, of our historical moment. But it also means teaching the art of distance, of what the Russian Formalists called *ostranenie* or defamiliarization. Child molestation is all too familiar. My assignment as a professor includes acknowledging the affective, emotional toll the novel takes on some of its readers; I must be able to lead a serious and compassionate discussion around this question. But I must also give students tools to access at least some of the text's other layers—Quilty games, erotic poetry, Shakespeare, advertisement from the 1950s, American road novels, religious and legal confession, etc., etc., etc. Without access to these details, students will be unable to make an informed decision about where they stand in relation to such a challenging and problematic text. Thinking about *Lolita* should help students reflect on what the role of books and art is in our lives today—and what they think it should be.

WORKS CITED

Bowlby, Rachel. "Lolita and the Poetry of Advertising." In *Vladimir Nabokov's* Lolita: *A Casebook*, edited by Ellen Pifer, 155–79. Oxford: Oxford University Press, 2003.

Capossela, Francesca. "Alive in a Magic Democracy: On 'The Real Lolita.'" *LA Review of Books*, September 12, 2018. https://lareviewofbooks.org/article/alive-in-a-magic-democracy-on-the-real-lolita/.

Dwyer, Anne. "Teaching 'Lolita' Is Still Appropriate (Opinion)." *Inside Higher Ed*. https://www.insidehighered.com/views/2018/05/14/teaching-lolita-still-appropriate-opinion.

Freeman, Elizabeth. *The Wedding Complex: Forms of Belonging in Modern American Culture*. Series Q. Durham: Duke University Press, 2002. http://doi.org/10.1215/9780822384007.

Herbold, Sarah. "'(I Have Camouflaged Everything, My Love)': Lolita and the Woman Reader." *Nabokov Studies* 5, no. 99 (1998): 71–98. https://doi.org/10.1353/nab.2011.0023.

Jameson, Fredric. *The Political Unconscious: Narrative as a Socially Symbolic Act*. Ithaca, NY: Cornell University Press, 1981.

Nabokov, Vladimir. "Good Readers and Good Writers." In *Lectures on Literature*, edited by Fredson Bowers, 1–6. San Diego: Harcourt, 1980.

———. "On a Book Entitled Lolita." In *The Annotated Lolita*, edited by Alfred Jr. Appel, Revised ed., 311–17. New York: Vintage International, 1991.

———. "Rowe's Symbols." In *Strong Opinions*, 304–7. New York: Vintage International, 1990.

Nafisi, Azar. *Reading Lolita in Tehran: A Memoir in Books*. New York: Random House, 2004.

Naiman, Eric. "Hermophobia (On Sexual Orientation and Reading Nabokov)." *Representations* 101 (2008): 116–43.

Patnoe, Elizabeth. "Discourse, Ideology, and Hegemony: The Double Dramas in and around Lolita." In *Discourse and Ideology in Nabokov's Prose*, edited by David H. J. Larmour, 111–36. London: Routledge, 2002.

Rakhimova-Sommers, Elena, ed. "Introduction—Nabokov's Passportless Wanderer: A Study of Nabokov's Woman." In *Nabokov's Women: The Silent Sisterhood of Textual Nomads*, xv–xxxi. Lanham: Lexington Books, 2017.

NOTES

1. Anne Dwyer, "Teaching 'Lolita' Is Still Appropriate (Opinion)," *Inside Higher Ed*, accessed May 11, 2020, https://www.insidehighered.com/views/2018/05/14/teaching-lolita-still-appropriate-opinion. Permission to republish granted.

2. Elizabeth Patnoe, "Discourse, Ideology, and Hegemony: The Double Dramas in and around *Lolita*," in *Discourse and Ideology in Nabokov's Prose*, ed. David H. J. Larmour (London: Routledge, 2002), 111–36.

3. Later Capossela included an expanded and more sophisticated version of the essay in her senior thesis. She also published an excellent review essay, "Alive in a Magic Democracy: On 'The Real Lolita,'" *LA Review of Books*, September 12, 2018, https://lareviewofbooks.org/article/alive-in-a-magic-democracy-on-the-real-lolita/.

4. Vladimir Nabokov, "On a Book Entitled Lolita," in *The Annotated Lolita*, ed. Alfred Jr. Appel, revised ed. (New York: Vintage International, 1991), 311–17.

5. Vladimir Nabokov, "Good Readers and Good Writers," in *Lectures on Literature*, ed. Fredson Bowers (San Diego: Harcourt, 1980), 1–6.

6. Vladimir Nabokov, "Rowe's Symbols," in *Strong Opinions* (New York: Vintage International, 1990), 304–7.

7. Eric Naiman, "Hermophobia (On Sexual Orientation and Reading Nabokov)," *Representations* 101 (2008): 116–43.

8. Fredric Jameson, *The Political Unconscious: Narrative as a Socially Symbolic Act* (Ithaca, NY: Cornell University Press, 1981).

9. Nabokov, "On a Book Entitled *Lolita*," 312.

10. Eléna Rakhimova-Sommers, ed., "Introduction—Nabokov's Passportless Wanderer: A Study of Nabokov's Woman," in *Nabokov's Women: The Silent Sisterhood of Textual Nomads* (Lanham: Lexington Books, 2017), xv–xxxi.

11. Sarah Herbold, "'(I Have Camouflaged Everything, My Love)': *Lolita* and the Woman Reader," *Nabokov Studies* 5, no. 99 (1998): 71–98, https://doi.org/10.1353/nab.2011.0023;

Elizabeth Freeman, *The Wedding Complex: Forms of Belonging in Modern American Culture*, Series Q (Durham: Duke University Press, 2002), http://doi.org/10.1215/9780822384007.

12. Rachel Bowlby, "Lolita and the Poetry of Advertising," in *Vladimir Nabokov's Lolita: A Casebook*, ed. Ellen Pifer (Oxford: Oxford University Press, 2003), 155–79.

13. Azar Nafisi, *Reading Lolita in Tehran: A Memoir in Books* (New York: Random House, 2004).

II

Offering Suggestions: How to Teach *Lolita*

Chapter Three

Students' *Lolita* Jury Duty

Teaching with Reader-Response Theory

Eléna Rakhimova-Sommers

Question: Is *Lolita amoral*?
Nabokov: On the contrary. It has a very moral moral: don't harm children.
(Nabokov, Interview with Anne Guerin for *L'Express*, 1961)[1]

INTRODUCTION

This chapter is designed to provide a view from within. I reflect on my experience of teaching *Lolita* in the immediate post #MeToo years of 2018 and 2019, share examples of innovative assignments, and showcase students' work. Selected passages from students' essays create a multi-voiced conversation and demonstrate how my classes have journeyed through the *Lolita* experience, facing its challenges and reaping its rewards.[2] In the span of the past ten years, I have taught *Lolita* in my "Nabokov-heavy" undergraduate, honors-level "Dangerous Texts" course to a predominantly "techie" student audience of engineering, computer science, and game design majors. Each class concludes with an anonymous course evaluation titled "My Intellectual Journey: What, if anything, I learned in *Dangerous Texts*." This opportunity encourages students to engage in much needed end-of-semester introspection, and they often use it to share their thoughts on close reading *Lolita*.

Lolita can be studied from a variety of perspectives, but given that fact that Nabokov sets up his novel as a diary of a redemption-seeking child molester, addressed to the "gentlewomen of the jury," reading it will always lend itself to the process of judging Humbert. This becomes especially true during the #MeToo era, when the novel faces its own "trial" by a new generation that is sixty-five years removed from Nabokov's imagined "good reader" in 1955. These new readers seek to carve out new roles for themselves to critically and creatively engage with the text in the production of meaning.

Before I analyze the dynamics of my students' evolving relationship with *Lolita*, I want to frame my discussion with Wolfgang Iser's reader-response theory that focuses on the interactive and even collaborative nature of text interpretation. Iser insists that readers play a larger role in the interpretive reconstruction of a novel's meaning than previously acknowledged. In "Interaction Between Text and Reader," Iser argues that "[c]entral to the reading of every literary work is the interaction between its structure and its recipient" and that "the study of a literary work should concern not only the actual text but also, and in equal measure, the actions involved in responding to that text" (1673). More importantly, Iser demonstrates that the author-text-reader-dynamic is an evolving process where the reader continuously readjusts and sometimes rejects the expectations that the text establishes as she modifies her interpretation. Iser stresses that the text and the reader are partners in the communication process as the reader creates meaning out of "gaps" in the text. "Whenever the reader bridges the gaps," Iser argues, "communication begins":

> What is said only appears to take on significance as a reference to what is not said; it is the implications and not the statements that give shape and weight to the meaning. But as the unsaid comes to life in the reader's imagination, so the said "expands" to take on greater significance than might have been supposed: even trivial scenes can seem surprisingly profound. (1676)

Equally important is Iser's notion of "virtual text," which positions the interpreted novel in the interactive space between the text and the reader:

> The work itself (the novel itself) cannot be identical with the text or with its actualization but must be situated somewhere between the two. It must be virtual in character, as it cannot be reduced to the reality of the text or to the subjectivity of the reader, and it is from this virtuality that it derives its dynamism. As the reader passes through the various perspectives offered by the text, and relates the different views and patterns to one another, he sets the work in motion, and so sets himself in motion, too. If the virtual position of the work is between text and reader, its actualization is clearly the result of an interaction between the two. (1674)

If we follow Iser's theory, and specifically the notion of the "virtual text," we have to acknowledge that each act of reading *Lolita* represents a yet unrealized interpretive potential. It is a promise and a hope of discovery. Nabokov in a sense invites the reader to engage in a creative partnership by offering her a set of typed up and bound pages, promising that the bundle is worth her time and attention. If the invitation is accepted, the movement from text to novel might begin. *Lolita* the novel is what happens if and when the text and reader collaborate in the creation of meaning.

READER AS WITNESS AND JUROR

In her study titled "Whether Judgements, Sentences, and Executions Satisfy the Moral Sense in Nabokov," Susan Elizabeth Sweeney draws our attention to Nabokov's fascination with crime, specifically the subject of ineffectual or illegitimate judicial and penal institutions, responsible for but failing to punish such acts as blackmail, kidnapping, torture, molestation, rape, and murder (*Nabokov and the Question of Morality*). It is true that all Nabokov readers are frequent, if reluctant, witnesses to unpunished, unresolved, and unatonable pain, especially children's pain, caused either by criminal or simply absent-minded adults.[3] Some examples include: the chilling end of *Bend Sinister*'s "accidentally" tortured and decapitated eight-year-old David, the death of the ignored and broken-hearted eleven-year-old Irma in *Laughter in the Dark*, multiple scenarios of Mira Belochkin's murder in a Nazi concentration camp in *Pnin*, and, of course, the tragic death of seventeen-year-old Dolores and her stillborn baby girl in *Lolita*.

Sweeney appropriately asks: "why does Nabokov emphasize the need to address wrongdoing, . . . yet fails to show those actions being legitimately carried out?" (167). In answering this question in regard to *Lolita*, Sweeney introduces the notion of "rhetorical justice," the kind of justice where the perpetrator gets the privilege to act as his own judge and jury. However, continues Sweeney, since "it's impossible to come before oneself, let alone to exonerate, convict, sentence, or punish oneself, this reinforces the need for someone to render a decision about this case." And that "someone," is, of course, the reader:

> Nabokov emphasizes the suffering of individual characters, especially those who are defenseless, abandoned, or misunderstood; he presents the judicial and penal systems within his fictional worlds as either illegitimate or irrelevant; he describes criminals' misguided efforts to settle their own cases; and he often depicts his protagonists as dying before justice can be determined, thus poignantly underscoring the need to judge, convict, acquit, sentence, punish, rehabilitate, avenge, or redeem them. Because Nabokov's novels deliberately withhold such a resolution, however—even after anticipating, rehearsing, predicting, and demanding it—his readers must provide it instead. (169)

Sweeney seems to echo Iser's reader-response theory when she argues that in Nabokov, the job of determining the nature of the crime, the guilty party, mitigating circumstances, and "the exact degree of forgiveness or condemnation" (169) falls on the readers' shoulders. The job is, indeed, a challenging one, and the burden can feel heavy at times. While we cannot be sure that *Lolita* prepares all of its readers to take on such a task, most who choose it rise to the challenge. The following study explores my students' experience as they took responsibility for "the last word."

CLASSROOM EXPERIENCE: WATCHING FROM BEHIND YELLOW TAPE

As I studied my students' responses to a variety of *Lolita*-related assignments during the 2019 fall semester, a line caught my eye: "This class has given a greater meaning to learning, making it about the pursuit of truth . . . it felt like something noble, a worthy time and effort." A similar sentiment was echoed by others. Responding to a question about *Lolita*'s morality and overall effect on the reader, one student argued that morality is "a natural bi-product of an honest pursuit of the truth." These narratives demonstrated the intellectual and emotional labor demanded of my students while serving on *Lolita* "jury duty." More importantly, they showed the impact of the contemporary cultural and political environment on my students' everyday lives.

As we studied Nabokov's "tale of non-consent,"[4] the long overdue tsunami of #MeToo cleared the way for a national conversation about the nature of sexual coercion and the dynamics of victim silencing. As the fall semester came to an end in December 2019, President Trump's impeachment inquiry began, and the concept of truth became the subject of daily discussion and debate on every conceivable media outlet. Contributors to this volume bring our attention to the fact that teaching *Lolita* has changed because of a shift in the cultural context surrounding the novel. I agree. In my experience, students have responded to the novel with a greater sense of urgency in the #MeToo era than they ever have before. As they continue to assess *Lolita* as a groundbreaking textbook on predatory rhetoric (and its dismantling), they stand as the novel's staunchest supporters *precisely* because of its subject matter and cultural relevance.

The majority of my non–liberal arts majors arrive in class having only a vague idea about *Lolita*. However, all report a certain level of apprehension before starting the novel, aware that it is considered, as they call it, "provocative, polarizing, and unsettling." One student shared that she approached the book "with a guarded heart and head" because she was "scared to read it and did not know how it was going to affect [her]." I perceived their caution to be a necessary form of self-care, given the fact that in the fall of 2019, my students daily witnessed disturbing #MeToo-prompted revelations about crimes perpetrated and concealed for decades by men in positions of power. As the class worked through *Lolita* in the fall of 2019, billionaire Jeffery Epstein's sex trafficking scandal began to unfold. Numerous victims came forward with accounts of the abuse that they experienced as underage girls on Epstein's Virgin Islands property, known by locals as "pedophile island," and on board his "Lolita Express" jet. The Epstein crimes and their cover-up stirred up not-so-distant memories of the gut-wrenching victims' impact statements, delivered by 156 courageous young women at the 2018 trial of serial child molester and chief USA Gymnastics doctor Larry Nassar. At the same time, New York State prosecutors' 2018 lawsuit against the Weinstein Company for failing to protect its employees from Harvey Weinstein's egregious sexual harassment and abuse was moving forward. As my students' phones continued to light up with breaking news stories of crime, cover-up, victim silencing, and career derailing, they argued that Nabokov provided them with a nuanced perspective on the predator's mind, and that this somehow helped them navigate the "times of disillusionment," when their trust in the common denominator of goodness in fellow man was shaken.

As a faculty member, I wondered (and worried)—could this cultural climate of anxiety and uncertainly explain my students' genuine and continuous concern for Lolita's safety from the very opening of the novel? For the first time, my students told me that they feared Lolita "[wouldn't] make it to the last page." Most of my freshmen readers appeared to have skipped the novel's introduction and did not yet realize that the married and pregnant Mrs. Richard F. Schiller was no longer with us, having joined what I call "the silent sisterhood of Nabokov's absent, absented, and dead textual nomads."[5] Deciding not to intrude, I let the students walk themselves to the discovery of her fate. My students' eventual realization that both Lolita and her stillborn baby girl died "on Christmas Day 1952, in Gray Star, a settlement in the remotest Northwest," (4) three months after the last conversation with Humbert, came as a real sense of loss.

All students reported struggling with the novel's opening chapter given the subject matter. Some said that they gave Humbert an advantage of sorts by starting the text with an open mind about him. This advantage, however, was promptly withdrawn after reading the "intense, lyrical description" of the first page. This initial reaction was eventually overcome, as we can see from this response: "The novel came on strong from the very first chapter, and I started the text by bracing myself for his overwrought, dramatic language. However, as *Lolita* went on, Humbert Humbert's style ebbed and flowed more naturally, and I got more into the rhythm of the novel, making it easier to read in terms of language."[6] Many female students shared that they felt powerless to save Dolly from abuse and compared themselves to "helpless bystander[s], who [could] do nothing but watch from behind yellow tape as Nabokov sifts through the evidence and paints a picture of the crime scene."[7] Later in the chapter, I offer creative assignments that help alleviate the "helpless bystander effect" and give the students an opportunity to "intervene" by actively engaging with the text.

Interestingly enough, all students reported leaning on Nabokov as "an anchor to reality and sanity in a novel that takes place entirely in the mind of someone who has lost nearly all his connection to either," to borrow from my student, Elizabeth Witten. This reader-author trust is usually built in the process of studying *Invitation to a Beheading* at the beginning of the semester. An ode to the power of imagination to triumph over the abusive theatre of the absurd, *Invitation to a Beheading* gives Nabokov a certain "street cred" in terms of authorial advocacy for the most vulnerable. The novel's focus on how to write oneself out of the prison of the self helps students accept Nabokov's next invitation to explore the inner "I" of a sexual predator with unprecedented narratorial powers in *Lolita*.

In his 1964 interview with Douglas M. Davis for *National Observer*, Nabokov acknowledges that he plays with the reader, "but not as a cat with a mouse." The writer says that he avoids "teasing," adding, "I'm very honest, actually."[8] My students seem to agree. In her essay "*Lolita* as Art: The Use of Negative Space,"[9] Witten uses a design concept of "intentional absence" to explain how Nabokov's abstention from judgment helps readers open up to the idea of "being submerged deep inside the mind of a charming, educated, and worldly man with a grossly destructive wound eating him from the inside out."

> As an artist, Nabokov must always be concerned with the emotions of the reader. Nabokov's use of negative space, particularly regarding moral judgement, in his presentation of Humbert's narrative allows the reader to have space to form a more intimate connection with Humbert. While the reader's relationship with *Lolita*'s narrator may not be a fond one, that connection is made more powerful by the organic, rather than contrived, nature of its formation."

Witten, however, acknowledges a vertigo-like effect of the simultaneous freedom and constraints imposed on the reader: "There is no handholding in Nabokov's work. He is not here to mentor or preach to us, and this has the effect of disturbing the reader. Where there should be outward disdain, the reader finds a deliberate neutrality from the author. The unexpected lack of guidance is comparable to vertigo, as the readers must readjust to standing solely on their own thoughts and emotions."

The *Lolita* reading experience proves complex for students due to Nabokov's "suspended moral judgement" of his privileged narrator and each student's personal reaction to the writer's approach. As one student, Joe Armstrong, puts it: "I believe that a discerning reader, with no preconceived notions regarding morality, would initially be taken with Humbert Humbert. I think that's the point, and that's what makes the beginning of the novel difficult. It's an ascent of a despicable man to a despicable end, yet it treats neither as despicable and so feels entirely unnatural and profoundly disturbing."[10] Others, like Witten, report a numbing effect combined with fascination and desire to get to the bottom of Humbert Humbert's character, to "figure him out": "The longer that I read, the more desensitized I found myself getting. Humbert Humbert's behavior stopped coming as a shock to me, and instead became more of a resigned horror. On the other hand, the deeper inside Humbert Humbert's unravelling and convoluted mind that I delved, the greater my fascination and the desire to figure him out became."[11]

All students credit Nabokov with creating a profoundly flawed anti-hero who comes surprisingly alive on the page in his relatable angst and vulnerability. Humbert surprises the reader with his unexpected charisma. Frankie Camp writes: "Humbert Humbert, no matter how vainglorious he was, felt not only complex, but alive, and tangible, and that was a very pleasant surprise. I was able to understand his thought process, no matter how warped, and I was able to see his struggle."[12] Witten finds one of the most striking parts of the novel's construction to be "the complexity with which Humbert Humbert is developed. He is full of contradictions and incredibly human."[13] She sees the nuance of Nabokov's portrait of a predator to be the "fuel on which the novel runs" and explores the nature of the novel's unexpected reader-narrator intimacy:

> While it is the eccentricities of Humbert that draw readers in, it is his angst that keeps them hooked. Humbert is human, and by virtue of being human, he is weak. Contrary to what Humbert wishes for the readers to believe—particularly at the onset of his story—he is not undefeatable. As Nabokov presents the depths of Humbert's humanity, the readers are gifted a negative space into which they may project their own judgements in a process that brings them into an intimate and individual relationship with Humbert. It is this reader-narrator intimacy that makes *Lolita* such a gripping and versatile work of art.[14]

A CREATIVE PAUSE: INTERACT AND INTERFERE

Mid-way through the text, the class might find itself in need of a creative pause. An assignment on "*Lolita* Book Cover Redesign"[15] allows for a redirection from close reading to visual analysis, and most importantly helps alleviate the "helpless bystander" syndrome I discussed earlier. I direct the class to John Bertram and Yuri Leving's volume, *Lolita–The Story of a Cover Girl: Vladimir Nabokov's Novel in Art and Design.*[16] In "Selling Concubines: Who Is The Face of The Russian Lolita," Leving points out that "any illustration either interacts with the text or interferes with it" (202). My students want to do both. Exploring visual representation of a challenging book such as *Lolita* through personal, alternative book covers becomes the students' opportunity to interfere, intervene, and find a semblance of a solution where none are provided by the novel itself. Class time is devoted to the study of poorly thought out and market-oriented cover designs, which, to borrow from Ellen Pifer and Peter Mendelsund, "collude in the sexual exploitation of which Humbert is guilty" and "downgrade our outrage" (Pifer, 145; Mendelsund, 29). Students proceed to design their own *Lolita* book covers or select an existing re-design that appropriately reflects the spirit of the novel, and elaborate on their selection in a narrative.

Another assignment invites the class to recover Lolita's muted voice. We explore the issue of Lolita's verbal and physical absence—her wordlessness and, ironically, given the abuse every part of her body sustains, her bodylessness. In my edited volume *Nabokov's Women: The Silent Sisterhood of Textual Nomads*, I demonstrate that Nabokov's woman represents the ultimate challenge to knowability. She is what I call a "passportless wonderer without narratorial privileges."[17] By design, she is assigned a short-term tourist visa with a firm expiration date. Her departure is facilitated by death, which watermarks her into a male narrator's story, granting him an artistic release and an epiphanic sense of self-understanding. All of these characteristics apply to Lolita. As readers of the novel, we find ourselves on a narratorial diet because entry into Lolita's emotional and physical "I" is rarely granted. We are barely allowed inside pain, her loneliness, her confusion, her memories, or her dreams. Since Lolita is denied the power of the female gaze turned inward, she does not get to self-reflect, self-correct, or pursue existential quests. Students are encouraged to find cracks in the narrative that allow glimpses of Lolita's inner world or rewrite some of the scenes from her perspective. These visual and written assignments allow the class to desexualize Lolita' image, give her more agency, and even reframe the novel's trajectory.

The study of the novel can also serve as a building platform for symposia on literature, culture, and film. As part of the Rochester Institute of Technology From Russia with Love symposium, my "Dangerous Texts" class organized a student-led "Author, Narrator, Reader: Love and Morality in *Lolita*" panel that included Julian Connolly, a contributor to this volume.[18] The subsequently launched print and digital *From Russia with Love Journal* allowed my students to publish their work and join the academic conversation. A great example of such collaboration is Ashleigh Butler's provocative essay "Dolor, Dolores: The Duality of Love within *Lolita*," where she ponders the dark nature of love ("there is nothing loving about love") and argues that while "Dolores may be Humbert's captive, Humbert is her slave." Butler's essay was adopted by the University of Virginia's Department of Slavic Languages and Literatures for the study of *Lolita* in the classroom, and has since been downloaded close to three thousand times.[19]

HUMBERT'S TIGHTENING NOOSE

After "standing behind the yellow tape" and assessing Humbert Humbert's crime scene, students are very eager to dissect the ways in which Nabokov, the careful and unobtrusive stage director, sets up his narrator and the traps he lays out for him. In her 2018 award-winning essay, "Wizards and Word Games: Literary Mousetraps in Nabokov's *Lolita*," my student Abby Bratton close read both the predatory power dynamic of Humbert's narrative and Nabokov's method of punishing his narrator by "giv[ing him] enough rope to hang himself:"

> In a world of letters pressed between two covers, the one who wields the pen wields the power. . . . Like a reverse Wizard of Oz, Humbert bids the readers to pay all attention to the man behind the curtain, drawing their eyes away from whatever else might be hidden. His paragraphs paint over her pain. If Humbert is an artist, then he is the artist of Dolores' suffering.[20]

Bratton implores the readers to have the patience to "clear away the smoke and mirrors and read between the lines." She wishes them the strength of will to "ignore both the wizard and the curtain and remove the green-tinted glasses—so they can discover a traumatized Dolores behind the romanticized Lolita, a downtrodden city that is emerald in name only, a moral judgement that Humbert is unable to overturn regardless of how he sways the jury." Bratton concludes that "Nabokov's traps are set for the narrative predator rather than his prey. The author simply gives his narrator enough rope to hang himself and sits back so that the careful observer has a better view of the tightening noose."

During final discussions, students all conclude that the #MeToo era impacts the way that they evaluate *Lolita*—"a biome of the real world." They credit Nabokov for what they see as a pioneering study of "power and perspective" and recommend it as a "useful teaching tool." Here a response by Armstrong:

> In this era of awakening, it's clear to see that Nabokov was ahead of his time. His depiction of the serial predator, not as the ethereal monster under your bed, nor the outwardly threatening stranger; but simply as the man—a twisted man, for sure, but a thinking, feeling, breathing man . . . —is something that has eluded the social consciousness for decades, a deficiency that has without a doubt played a part in keeping the full scope of the epidemic of sexual violence from coming to light.[21]

Students argue that "*Lolita* has become a novel that reflects a lot of what our society has been hiding" and point out that it is an important exploration of power, obsession, and perspective. Interestingly, unprompted, students also offer their thoughts on *Lolita*'s longevity as Witten does below:

> *Lolita* has been designed in an extremely adaptable fashion, and, as the readers' environments change, the societal role that the novel plays changes as well. Like Frankenstein's monster, *Lolita* is no longer beholden to its creator. This can be seen in issues such as child abuse and sexual assault that are coming further into the forefront of social consciousness. Despite them not being a public concern at the novel's conception, *Lolita* is still able to comment on those issues in a way that is relevant to modern readers. It is precisely this changeability and a unique reader-author interaction that makes *Lolita* such an impactful work of art.[22]

CONCLUDING THOUGHTS

As my students carefully and patiently study the novel, their desire to sift through the text with a detective's lens and resurrect Lolita's voice is palpable, and toward the end of the reading process the students cheer for Mrs. Dolly Schiller. They argue that in the end she "stands up to her oppressor with a crushing and final 'no, honey, no,'" which "breaks the book and breaks Humbert" as it reveals her utter apathy and indifference in him as a romantic partner. The students are elated that "there [is] not a fraction of her he gets to keep" and lament that it is a "damn shame" that Humbert fails each time he comes close to self-reflection and empathy.[23] Some acknowledge that Humbert Humbert's search for absolution forms the heart of the novel's ending, but very few are willing to grant him the redemption he is looking for.

After becoming the unwitting witnesses of Lolita's fate, students very much want to interact and communicate with the text and the author. They want an outlet to lend their voices to the process, and innovative approaches and assignments help the students process the text, the pain, and arm themselves with the tools needed to navigate the "vertigo-like" reality of their everyday lives. After close reading this demanding novel, my students emerge informed, strengthened, empathetic, and ready to pursue the truth and the "responsibility for the last word" in the classroom and beyond. As faculty, we can help them on their journey.

In his lecture on "Good Readers and Good Writers," Nabokov pictures the harmonious fusion of the writer's vision and the reader's response as a joyous reunion and spontaneous embrace between the exhausted "master artist" and a "panting and happy" "good reader" on a windy ridge of a conquered Great Literature mountain. The meeting between the two is still on, but this time she arrives with a heavy backpack, full of questions and concerns, and very much expects the "storyteller, teacher, and enchanter" to engage with her in what might be a tough and challenging but no less fascinating conversation. I prefer the latter scenario and so do my students. And it is this conversation that will keep the two "linked forever if the book lasts forever."[24]

WORKS CITED

Bertram, John, and Leving, Yuri, eds. *Lolita–The Story of a Cover Girl: Vladimir Nabokov's Novel in Art and Design*. Blue Ash, OH: Print Books, 2013.

Boyd, Brian, and Tolstoy, Anastasia, eds. *Think, Write, Speak. Uncollected Essays, Reviews, Interviews, and Letters to the Editor*. New York: Knopf, 2019.

Bratton, Abby. "Wizards and Word Games: Literary Mousetraps in Nabokov's *Lolita*." Essay written for Elena Rakhimova-Sommers' 2018 "Dangerous Texts" class at the Rochester Institute of Technology. Winner of 2019 Kearse Writing Award.

Butler, Ashleigh. "Dolor, Dolores: The Duality of Love Within *Lolita*." Essay written for Elena Rakhimova-Sommers' 2012 "Dangerous Texts" class at the Rochester Institute of Technology and published in the *From Russia with Love Journal* Conference Proceedings: https://scholarworks.rit.edu/fromrussia/proceedings/papers/8/

From Russia with Love Journal. Conference Proceedings: https://scholarworks.rit.edu/fromrussia/proceedings/.

Iser, Wolfgang. "Interaction between Text and Reader." In *The Norton Anthology of Theory and Criticism*, ed. Vincent B. Leitch. New York, 2001, pp. 1673–82.

Leving, Yuri. "Selling Concubines: Who Is The Face of The Russian Lolita." In *Lolita–The Story of a Cover Girl: Vladimir Nabokov's Novel in Art and Design*. Blue Ash, OH: Print Books, 2013, pp. 178–208.

Mendelsund, Peter. "Fictions." In *Lolita–The Story of a Cover Girl: Vladimir Nabokov's Novel in Art and Design*. Blue Ash, OH: Print Books, 2013, p. 29.

Nabokov, Vladimir. *The Annotated Lolita*. New York: Vintage, 1991.

———. "Good Readers and Good Writers." In *Lectures on Literature*. A Harvest Book, 1980, pp. 1–9.

Pifer, Ellen. "Uncovering Lolita." In *Lolita–The Story of a Cover Girl: Vladimir Nabokov's Novel in Art and Design*. Blue Ash, OH: Print Books, 2013, pp. 144–52.

Sweeney, Susan Elizabeth. "Whether Judgements, Sentences, and Executions Satisfy the Moral Sense in Nabokov." In *Nabokov and the Question of Morality: Aesthetics, Metaphysics, and the Ethics of Fiction*. London: Palgrave Macmillan, 2016, pp. 161–83.

Rakhimova-Sommers, Eléna. "The 'Right' versus the 'Wrong' Child: Shades of Pain in *Bend Sinister* and *Pnin*." *Nabokov Studies* 6 (2000–2001): 35–51.

———. *Nabokov's Women: The Silent Sisterhood of Textual Nomads*, my Introduction, "Nabokov's Passportless Wonderer: The Study of Nabokov's Woman." Lanham: Lexington Books, 2017, pp. XV–XXXI.

Witten, Elizabeth. "*Lolita* as Art: The Use of Negative Space." Essay written for Eléna Rakhimova-Sommers' 2019 "Dangerous Texts" class at the Rochester Institute of Technology.

NOTES

1. *Think, Write, Speak. Uncollected Essays, Reviews, Interviews, and Letters to the Editor*, 300.

2. It has been a joy and a privilege to work with all of my "Dangerous Texts" classes. I want to especially acknowledge the following students who created exemplary work on *Lolita*: Abby Bratton, Elizabeth Witten, Ashleigh Butler, Joe Armstrong, Ashley Hum, Emma Woerle, Frankie Camp, Jason Carrier, Nick Laury, and Will Sugarman. This chapter includes select quotes from the work of some of these students. Abby Bratton's and Elizabeth Witten's essays are quoted at length.

3. For more on the subject, see my article, "The 'Right' versus the 'Wrong' Child: Shades of Pain in *Bend Sinister* and *Pnin*." *Nabokov Studies 6* (2000–2001): 35–51.

4. I borrow this term from Peter Mendelsund, "Fictions," in *Lolita–The Story of a Cover Girl: Vladimir Nabokov's Novel in Art and Design* (29).

5. For more on the subject, please see my edited volume *Nabokov's Women: The Silent Sisterhood of Textual Nomads*, my Introduction, "Nabokov's Passportless Wonderer: The Study of Nabokov's Woman," pp. XV–XXXI, and my chapter, "Nabokov's Mermaid: 'Spring in Fialta,'" pp. 57–75.

6. Ashley Hum, "Dangerous Texts" assignment on *Lolita*, fall 2019.

7. Elizabeth Witten, "Dangerous Texts" assignment on *Lolita*, fall 2019.

8. *Think, Write, Speak. Uncollected Essays, Reviews, Interviews, and Letters to the Editor*, p. 337.

9. "*Lolita* as Art: The Use of Negative Space," essay written for my "Dangerous Texts" course, fall 2019.

10. Joe Armstrong, "Your Initial Thoughts upon Finishing *Lolita*" assignment, "Dangerous Texts" course, fall 2019.

11. Witten, "Your Initial Thoughts upon Finishing *Lolita*" assignment, "Dangerous Texts" course, fall 2019.

12. Frankie Camp, "Your Initial Thoughts upon Finishing *Lolita*" assignment, "Dangerous Texts" course, fall 2019.

13. "Your Initial Thoughts upon Finishing *Lolita*" assignment, "Dangerous Texts" course, fall 2019.

14. Witten, "*Lolita* as Art: The Use of Negative Space," essay submitted for my "Dangerous Texts" course, fall 2019.

15. My student Ashley Hum called it "The Visual Description of an Indescribable Novel." *Lolita* re-design assignment, "Dangerous Texts" course, fall 2019.

16. Emily Temple's "60 Best and Worst *Lolita* International Book Covers" is also very helpful: https://lithub.com/the-60-best-and-worst-international-covers-of-lolita/

17. Elena Rakhimova-Sommers, "Nabokov's Passportless Wanderer: A Study of Nabokov's Woman," editor's Introduction to *Nabokov's Women: The Silent Sisterhood of Textual Nomads*, pp. XV, XVIII.

18. *From Russia With Love Symposium* information can be accessed here: https://scholarworks.rit.edu/fromrussia/

19. Ashleigh Butler's essay can be accessed here: https://scholarworks.rit.edu/fromrussia/proceedings/papers/8/.

20. Rochester Institute of Technology, College of Liberal Arts' Henry and Mary Kearse Writing Award, 2019.

21. "Your Initial Thoughts upon Finishing *Lolita*" assignment, "Dangerous Texts" course, fall 2019.

22. "*Lolita* as Art: The Use of Negative Space," essay submitted for my "Dangerous Texts" course, fall 2019.

23. Nick Laury, "*Lolita* assignment," "Dangerous Texts" course, fall 2018.

24. Nabokov, "Good Readers and Good Writers," p. 2.

Chapter Four

A *Requiem* for Dolores

Teaching Lolita *in a Russian Prison Literature Course*

José Vergara

There is, I admit, something perverse about juxtaposing *Lolita* and Anna Akhmatova's poetic cycle *Requiem*. The latter tells the story of the poet's experience during Stalin's Great Terror in a prose introduction, twelve poems, and a two-part epilogue. After her son is arrested, she must wait outside the walls of the central Leningrad prison for news. In this terrible limbo, she reflects on her youth, meets countless other women in the same circumstances, and considers what role she might play in the history of her country as a witness to such a national tragedy. The text as a whole is a form of testimony, an exploration of what it means to lose one's child to the unknown but to retain one's love and hope. Not for nothing did Akhmatova use a (mis)quotation from James Joyce's *Ulysses* in an early version of the cycle: "You cannot leave your mother an orphan." Even as Akhmatova's son was held captive by the state, she herself became a prisoner—to the government who betrayed her, to her maternal love that would not leave her.

Lolita is a much different kind of captivity tale. There is the jail, where Humbert Humbert allegedly writes his confession, but the reader never comes near it. There is suffering—all too much of it—but Humbert Humbert's prose, unlike Akhmatova's lyrics, does everything possible to render it in beautiful colors. Its author fancies himself an artist, one who transforms memories of his childhood love Annabel Leigh and of Dolores Haze into what he would wish them to be: the sad tale of a man held in the grip of tragic passion. Whereas Akhmatova's cycle foregrounds the trauma of incarceration by showing how it has wrecked the lives of many, Humbert Humbert's *Lolita* does all it can to mask Dolores's experience. Although the two works share missing children, only one of them is left orphaned by a freak accident and imprisoned by the whims of a sexual predator.

I recently had the experience of precisely this odd juxtaposition, a kind of shock to the syllabus, when teaching my course "Crime or Punishment: Russian Narratives of Incarceration and Captivity." After covering early prison texts such as Archpriest Avvakum's autobiography, Alexander Pushkin's *Prisoner of the Caucasus*, and Fyodor Dostoevsky's *Notes from a Dead House*, among many others, we moved into the twentieth century and the bloody Soviet era. *Requiem*, along with Lidia Chukovskaya's novella *Sofia Petrovna*, served as a useful primer for the tales of the Gulag and Stalin's legacy that would follow.[1] And then came *Lolita*.

I recognized from the start that it was an odd choice in several regards. In a class devoted to the Russian Prison Text, Nabokov's *Invitation to a Beheading* would be a much more logical fit. One student even proposed instead reading *The Gift*'s fourth chapter, which describes the life and incarceration of the radical nineteenth-century writer Nikolai Chernyshevsky. Anything but *Lolita*. Furthermore, these earlier novels by Nabokov were actually written in Russian. *Lolita* took us away from Russia's borders and all the way to Nabokov's mid-century America and lush English, something no other literary text in the course does. (The closest we get otherwise is the France of Peter Kropotkin's comparative study, *In Russian and French Prisons*, and of Michel Foucault's infamous *Discipline and Punish*.) Finally, as previously mentioned, it's hardly a prison text in any traditional sense. Humbert Humbert does, indeed, write his tale from the confines of a cell, but the action features no prisons as such.[2] And yet, it functions particularly well as a work about captivity, of being entirely unable to tell one's side of the story. That particular aspect of the book—the brutal narrative entrapment at its core—struck me as one important reason to feature it on my syllabus, where the majority of other texts were written by the survivors of harsh prison conditions who *can*, at least in hindsight, give meaningful shape to their experiences. Dolores, naturally, lacks this agency as she is a highly romanticized figure in someone else's narrative and has died by the novel's end. We had already read many stories from the point of view of those imprisoned within the walls of a physical prison. We had studied how various Russian and Soviet regimes had wrongfully jailed writers seeking change. But we had *not* read a text from the perspective of an unequivocally guilty criminal, one who is beyond vile and unmatched in any of the other texts save, perhaps, Victoria Lomasko's collection of "graphic reportage," *Other Russias*.[3] We had not read crime turned into art, depravity rendered as a tribute to one's victim. There was nothing so haunting as Humbert Humbert's memoir and the story of Dolores's captivity. In any event, the students seemed much more willing to sympathize with the would-be regicides of Leonid Andreev's *The Seven Who Were Hanged*.

Of course, I was also partly inspired to include *Lolita* by Nabokov's description of the ape in the Jardin des Plantes, "who, after months of coaxing by a scientist, produced the first drawing ever charcoaled by an animal: this sketch showed the bars of the poor creature's cage"—a metaphor, according to Nabokov, for Humbert Humbert's solipsistic worldview (*Annotated Lolita* 311). But the more I thought about it, the more it seemed to me that letting Humbert Humbert play the role of the ape further obscures the real captive of the story;[4] we ourselves can thus lose sight of the power Humbert Humbert does demonstrate throughout the book, both physically and narratologically. Dolores, the real captive, recedes from the picture in this Humbert Humbert-as-ape metaphor for the novice reader, as we sometimes see in the classroom.

As we began reading, there were some strong dissenters among my students, motivated, at least in part, by the events and lessons of #MeToo. The complaints were not always subtle or fully developed, but they were forceful. At least a couple of students (privately and not) raised questions about why *Lolita* should appear in this class at all. At the root of their concerns lay the question of how *Lolita* can possibly fit on a syllabus in the Russian program and in a course on prison literature. But Nabokov's allegiances have always been up for debate, haven't they? Beyond that, they charged that *Lolita* constitutes "child pornography" and that the novel encourages real abuse. Here we had an opportunity to debate the connection between art, crime, and punishment. A better combination for the class couldn't be found. For some, new to college, it was their first experience dealing with such topics as sexual abuse and rape in an academic setting; combined with the weighty course theme, this proved a lot to handle at once.

In general, my approach involved embracing the tensions of teaching *Lolita* in this context. Furthermore, I wanted to highlight how its status as an atypical work about captivity allows us to understand Dolores's plight better and lends itself to productive, #MeToo-inspired discussions on topics including guilt and power relations—perennial themes in prison literature. In other words, I ultimately sought to test the boundaries of the Russian Prison Text using what appears to be an outlier. To assuage some of these aforementioned student concerns, I opened the discussion to the topic of its relevance to our lives in 2019. The rhetorical devices Humbert deploys to hide his crimes should feel familiar, and while I am loath to use *Lolita* as a blunt moralistic tool, perhaps this is one way to bring students on board. This experience as a whole underscores *Lolita*'s flexibility; for a book whose basic plot is relatively simple and whose narrator is certainly a villain, to put it mildly, it generates rich ambiguities for readers on multiple subjects considered taboo.

What does it mean to read *Lolita*, on the one hand, as a text composed in pre-trial confinement by Humbert Humbert and, on the other, as a work that chronicles a young girl's experience of being held against her will? What does this dual perspective with its contrasting prisoners offer students? Which aspects of the book emerge in greater relief when read alongside a range of other texts that deal with crime, punishment, and captivity? These are the kinds of questions that undergirded our discussions. More to the point, students seemed eager to debate how Humbert takes over Dolores's narrative, generating a more important second-level captivity that recalls what survivors of #MeToo situations have expressed feeling. If for some readers the necessity, let alone the very appeal, of studying *Lolita* was always under serious question, then now, when we have multifarious accounts and defenses of illicit behavior filling news streams, the issue feels all the more pertinent. Students are both better equipped to read through Humbert's justifications for his actions and, in certain cases, more reluctant to appreciate the text as art(ifice).

Indeed, the course context and our #MeToo era raises yet another related, accursed question: Can a criminal-artist, fictional or real, be separated from his work? *Lolita* offers a special opportunity to deal with that tension by exploring it from various angles: criminality, guilt and justification, and public judgment. While most of the texts in "Crime or Punishment: Russian Narratives of Incarceration and Captivity" explored lasting harms and uneven power structures, they did so largely from the victims' point of view and on a national scale. Nabokov's novel complicated the question by putting the perpetrator's point of view front and center—in clear opposition to what the #MeToo movement calls for.

A brief word on logistics. Given the course's temporal range (late seventeenth century to 2014), we were only able to devote four seventy-five-minute class sessions to *Lolita*, though this was the most accorded to any work on the syllabus. I felt that this was necessary given the complexity of both the language and the content of Nabokov's book. There would be, I suspected correctly, an adjustment period brought on by the shock of the move from Stalin's Russia to Humbert Humbert's America, among the other usual sources of unease. Throughout the course, I had students hold discussions in various combinations: pair, group, and full class; they submitted a weekly, one-page response on Tuesdays where they were free to write about whatever struck them in the reading.

In the first session devoted to *Lolita*, I suggested five possible, though by no means exhaustive, ways to read Nabokov, the first three of which seem particularly relevant here: Carefully, Slowly, With Compassion, World as Art(ifice), Metatextually.[5] These approaches, I hoped, would prepare students to consider how Humbert Humbert lays out his traps for unwitting readers and how, on another level, the author ensnares his protagonist. We must, I proposed, read carefully, paying attention to the Nabokovian detail and noting how the narrator wants us to empathize with his pathologies.

Rather than only focus only on how *Lolita* should be read, I asked students to keep in mind how it should *not* be read. I wish we could have moved through it even more unhurriedly, but I emphasized the importance of slow, methodical reading to catch patterns in the narrative, as well as words that are at odds with Humbert Humbert's claims. Finally, reading with compassion and considering the various female figures in Humbert Humbert's life, we can see that the true pain of the novel has to do with the *in*ability to have Dolores's story rendered more accurately than her captor allows.[6]

These approaches in turn opened up opportunities for reflection on the real world. Perhaps the greatest #MeToo parallel provided by reading *Lolita* is the way Humbert Humbert co-opts Dolores's experience and reframes it according to his "fancy prose style" (x). Her seduction, her rape, and her captivity are all masked by Humbert's florid language, his ability to render terrible crimes through prose that is at once hilarious, touching, and delicate. While no contemporary #MeToo perpetrator, neither Kevin Spacey, nor Harvey Weinstein, has attempted to craft their own *Lolita* (yet), it struck me that there is a similarity to their statements and open letters. (I hesitate to call them "apologies," because they often are not that.) In these writings, we find the same kinds of elisions, the same familiar attempts to render past misdeeds in a more innocent light. When there *is* repentance for one's transgressions, it's often undercut by some contradictory phrasing. Humbert Humbert, of course, is a master of all these deceptions, as when he writes after the davenport scene, "Thus I had delicately constructed my ignoble, ardent, sinful dream; and still Lolita was safe, but my own creation, another, fanciful Lolita—perhaps more real than Lolita; overlapping, encasing her; floating between me and her, and having no will, no consciousness—indeed, no life of her own. [. . .] I intended, with the most fervent force and foresight, to protect the purity of that twelve-year-old child" (62–63). He speaks of his desire to protect Dolores, yet admits to constructing a "sinful dream" (62). How can it be both? He constructs this imagined avatar of the girl from whose own voice we hear little in Humbert Humbert's narrative as they begin their cross-country journey. In effect, he silences her, for what she has to say would entirely disrupt his fantasy world.

To underscore these points, I offered my students a contemporary example. Without identifying the author, I projected the statement Louis C. K. released after it was alleged that he had masturbated in front of several female comedians and while speaking on the phone with another. The accusations, circumstances, and parties involved are, of course, much different than Humbert Humbert's tale, but I wanted to focus on their use of *language* in particular. Here is C. K.'s letter in part:

> These stories are true. At the time, I said to myself that what I did was okay because I never showed a woman my dick without asking first, which is also

> true. But what I learned later in life, too late, is that when you have power over another person, asking them to look at your dick isn't a question. It's a predicament for them. The power I had over these women is that they admired me. And I wielded that power irresponsibly. [. . .]
>
> I also took advantage of the fact that I was widely admired in my and their community, which disabled them from sharing their story and brought hardship to them when they tried because people who look up to me didn't want to hear it. I didn't think that I was doing any of that because my position allowed me not to think about it. [. . .][7]

The students quickly noted that he never apologizes, constantly refers to his "dick," and draws attention to his own accomplishments. From there, they made apt connections to Humbert Humbert, who, while generally less explicitly vulgar, fails to express clear, unquestionable remorse in what is billed as his "Confessions" on the first page. Humbert Humbert, like C. K., can be quite charming. They're both wordsmiths, able to construct convincing portraits of themselves: the affable, self-deprecating comedian and the cultured, misunderstood emissary from the Old World.

After the students discussed C. K.'s statement alongside Humbert Humbert's "confession," I showed them Isobel O'Hare's erasure poem based on the former. O'Hare's poetry involves blacking out lines from statements produced by C. K. and others in order to distill an altogether different essence from them. They are as much text-based as they are graphic (here, in both senses of the word), and she renders the following from C. K.'s published statement: "My dick / is / a question / I / run from" (figure 4.1).

O'Hare's art slices through all of the comedian's posturing and language to reach the core of what he's saying—or at least one interpretation of it. *This*, students come to realize, is what we must do with Humbert Humbert's text. To avoid doing so means falling for his tricks. Failing to see what exactly he calls *his* "life" on the very first page—not even as explicit as C. K.'s—leads to ignoring the full scale of Dolores's plight.[8]

And this point, I emphasize, likewise makes *Lolita* an ideal Russian prison text. The perspective may be flipped from the prototypical one (that of the unfairly jailed), but it trains us, if we're careful enough readers, to see beyond the façade of artistry and to recognize Humbert Humbert's account for what it is: a masking of Dolores's imprisonment. It doubly underscores that her captivity is not only physical, but narratological as well. She has lost control of her story, again, much as many #MeToo survivors have reported feeling. Loss of agency takes many forms. This is but one of them. Although some have tried to recoup Dolores's side of the story, it's all for naught.[9] The trauma is long-lasting, the loss in some ways unsurmountable when your victimizer controls your narrative. Even Akhmatova could define the loss she felt after her son's arrest.

Figure 4.1. Isobel O'Hare, "a question I run from."

The broader question is an aesthetic one that my students and I wrestled with throughout the semester. As we read text after text detailing unfair incarceration, we wondered whether suffering, as Alexander Solzhenitsyn boldly maintains in his *Gulag Archipelago*, can truly offer a transformative, purifying experience. Similarly, can these stories and ideas transcend the experience of confinement without simultaneously justifying the system that produced them in the first place? Much as we might read Solzhenitsyn's or Varlam Shalamov's camp stories and question whether their composition and our subsequent reading somehow retrospectively give greater meaning or power to the terrible regimes under which they were produced, some students wondered whether their appreciation of *Lolita*'s beauty inadvertently justifies the types of crimes its plot describes.

As one of the class participants put it, *Lolita* "makes us examine what we want out of art, how we interact with art, and the relationship between art and empathy." Nabokov's novel can thus remind us of what lies beyond the boundaries of its pages. With whom do or can our sympathies lie? Can we see some humanity in Humbert Humbert's purported sufferings and pangs of guilt? Can those same abusers be admitted back into society or into the world of art? Should they? These are some of the questions that #MeToo has foisted upon the public—and rightly so. Once again, the parallels between fictionalized accounts of labor camps and a wholly fictional work such as *Lolita* are far from exact, but they are nonetheless quite instructive.[10] They speak to an anxiousness regarding addressing head on such taboo, explicit topics and their place in art.

I was particularly curious about which links between the novel and the rest of the course students would discover, regardless of whether they were the ones I had in mind myself. To begin our final day of discussing *Lolita*, I asked them to answer two related questions on an index card for a quick free-writing exercise: Why are we reading Nabokov's novel in this class, and why should we read it at all?[11] Their answers—kept anonymous even to me—ranged widely. Some considered it as an example of the "crime" in the course title ("Crime or Punishment"). Others noted that it presented a "different perspective" on captivity, though on what exactly that point of view was varied.

Curiously, some remained willing at least to entertain the possibility of Humbert Humbert as Dolores's fellow captive: "I guess in a way both [he and Dolores] are trapped." "Humbert depicts himself at times as seemingly helplessly enslaved to desires." Of course, beyond his physical incarceration by the end of the book, Humbert Humbert is at pains to depict himself as a man unable to control his urges, captive, as these students propose, to his urges for girls whom he deems nymphets: "Incarceration and/or punishment in the form of H. H.'s confinement to his role as lodger, husband to women he doesn't care for, the constant availability but unattainability of his beloved 'nymphets'? (To clarify, I absolutely think he deserves to suffer in this hell he seems to exist in—but it might be interesting to examine his view on his self-proclaimed suffering.)"

Alternatively, one student proposed, "I think it also forces the reader to hear something and witness something that they don't want to." "We can't turn a blind eye. It makes us uncomfortable and forces us to discuss our discomfort. It questions the very way we look at stigmatized topics. It brings something to the forefront that we'd rather hide." There is much to unpack in this response, which wasn't the only one of its kind. First, several students reported a sensation of being held captive before Humbert Humbert and his words. At the risk of making myself complicit in this experience(!), they suggest that the reader cannot escape from the narrator's predatory mind. There is therefore a third level to the captivity in the novel that this course's framework underscores.

This idea, in turn, linked directly to one of our other running themes: the witness. A number of our other writers, for example Anton Chekhov (*Sakhalin Island*), Lidia Ginzburg (*Journey into the Whirlwind*), and Mikhail Khodorkovsky (*My Fellow Prisoners*), clearly see themselves as witnesses who speak truth to power and expose the criminality of the state. *Lolita* places the reader in a position where s/he must observe a crime and decide how to respond.

As seen in the above cited response, students likewise viewed it as an opportunity (seemingly a welcome one) to delve into a taboo subject—again something not without its #MeToo resonance. *Lolita* challenges the reader to interrogate his/her perspectives on something that is hardly ever discussed so openly. Whether that brings on a sense of entrapment in the reader is probably just as telling. There is inherent value, some suggested in class, to considering why such issues as child abuse and incarceration are swept under the rug. If there is some link between *Lolita* and the real world, then perhaps it is in allowing the reader to "understand the mindset of criminals." Rather than dismiss an entire topic without considering its nuances, they wanted to focus on the question of perspective that *Lolita* introduces. As another student wrote, "We shouldn't stigmatize to the point that we don't talk about it." In this way, they implied, you can better understand criminality and perversions. The American justice system similarly remains an opaque subject for the public in large measure because those beyond the walls of prisons are viewed in such a negative light. Real Humbert Humberts exist, just as real Doloreses and Sally Horners do, too. By the end of our time with *Lolita*, though, many of my students seemed to feel that by studying both sides of the issue, one could come to a clearer understanding of what has happened.

Along these lines, I was particularly struck by one student's comment in a weekly reading response: "Does Lolita know that what Humbert is doing is very, very wrong? She seems to but she doesn't call the police. Is it because Humbert scared her into not doing so? Humbert makes a point of saying that it was Lolita who seduced him. Is this meant to absolve him somehow? Or just serve as more characterization of Lolita?" Reading Nabokov's novel in this context (#MeToo and Russian Prison Text) helped reify the issue of victim blaming. For the students who argued that *Lolita* does nothing but perpetuate pain and inspire abuse, I could point to this sincere comment from a student who was genuinely confused. It throws into sharp relief how victims of abuse such as Dolores often feel unable to tell their stories because of this double bind: a fear that they will somehow be viewed as the perpetrator in their trauma. It offered a way into this conversation that tied together text and life in yet another striking way and allowed students to debate the causes of and possible solutions to victim blaming. If someone as well-meaning as this young student can in this way misread *Lolita*, and thus potentially real-life accounts as well, then all the more reason to critically examine the text in this group setting as a case study in total control, to show that it *can* be a nuanced tool in revealing deeply embedded biases in society.

After our discussions, when we moved to individual analyses, several students opted to write their theoretical application paper on *Lolita* and Foucault's Panopticon. For this assignment, they had to apply one of our theoretical readings (Beccaria, Locke, Bentham, Foucault, Scarry, Forché, or Arendt) to a literary text. The goal was two-fold: how does the literary text exemplify what the theory describes, or how is the fictional (or creative nonfiction) text an example of what the philosopher or theorist describes in his/her own work? In other words, what does the theory help us understand about the selected work of art? Those who paired *Lolita* with *Discipline and Punish* saw parallels in the state Panopticon—an all-seeing, all-powerful surveillance system—and Humbert Humbert's control over Dolores. The papers evinced an attempt to understand exactly how Humbert Humbert was able to monitor all of Dolores's moves. There is, of course, his perpetual (male) gaze that dictates precisely how the reader perceives Dolores's body and mind. Even if the analogy between Humbert Humbert and the Panopticon doesn't entirely hold up, since Dolores does eventually rebel, these students recognized how he places himself at a distance, as if studying her like a guard. In Dolores's case, this means that she cannot speak out and does not expose Humbert Humbert to the policeman who pulls them over or to all the other adults in the Enchanted Hunters Hotel.

If the Panopticon is a loose metaphor for what Humbert constructs around Dolores, then Elaine Scarry's theory of the inexpressibility of pain through words also spoke to students as they read *Lolita*. In her study *The Body in Pain* (1985), Scarry examines how physical pain such as torture destroys language and how one person, even the most empathetic, cannot truly understand someone else's physical torment. She denies the claim that *psychological* pain is also inexpressible, for it "is susceptible to verbal objectification, and is so habitually depicted in art that [. . .] there is virtually no piece of literature that does not stand by ready to assist us."[12] Elena Sommers has also engaged with Scarry's writings to explain how in *Bend Sinister* and *Pnin* "Nabokov *deconstructs* the 'production' of torture in order for the reader to then *reconstruct* it in his imagination, the effect of which is a literal, physical feeling of pain."[13] Much the same might be said of what we see in *Lolita* with its child victim.

But what about sexual violence, one student in my class wondered. Using Scarry's ideas as a springboard and *Lolita* as a case study, this student suggested by way of Scarry that sexual violence features both momentary physical pain and long-lasting emotional trauma. In *Lolita*, Dolores does not literally lose the ability to speak in the way a victim of waterboarding or some other gruesome torture does, but the constant abuse warps what she can express. For evidence, the essay pointed to the davenport scene. As Humbert masturbates against her body, Dolores makes an odd noise, but says, "it's nothing at all" and later cries in the same "shrill" manner when she becomes upset while they are driving (61, 141). It is up to the reader, then, to discern the tension between her cries and what she says, between what she might be unable to express and what Humbert Humbert allows her to say in *his* narrative. Humbert Humbert furthermore ignores or silences the reality behind Dolores's school director Miss Horn's comment that Dolly "cannot verbalize her emotions" (195). He, too, chooses to focus little attention on the fact that she "sobs in the night [. . .] the moment [he] feigned sleep" (176). All of this, my student suggested, undercuts Humbert Humbert's claims that Dolores did not suffer at his hands and compels the reader to witness and engage with her pain. Dolores remains unable to express her true suffering, both because she is a child who cannot fully comprehend what is happening to her and because Humbert does not allow her the narrative voice to do so. In other works we read, we beheld similar pains, both psychological and physical. Andreev's *Seven Who Were Hanged* and Irina Ratushinskaya's *Grey Is the Color of Hope*, for instance, describe the psychological torment of knowing that you will be put to death and of hunger strikes, respectively.

In myriad ways, *Lolita* served as excellent preparation for texts about the Soviet prison system. It raised the question, as my students put it, of whether any system can ever control *all* of the human spirit. Some students maintained that no, something will inevitably slip through—an optimistic point of view that perhaps resonates with current events, as well as key works that we discussed in class. Solzhenitsyn's narrator in *The Gulag Archipelago*, for instance, proclaims, "*Bless you, prison*, for having been in my life!"[14] It would be foolish to suggest that Dolores would say something similar about her experience at Humbert Humbert's hands, and so *Lolita* provides both an instructive contrast in the despair that she undergoes and an affirmation of her will when Humbert Humbert discovers her alive and content near the novel's conclusion. With a flipped point of view, *Lolita* prepared my students to consider forms of resistance in the Gulag. The gravity and horror of the prison camp may render one artist mute, while it enriches and propels others. The students were also quite intrigued by the aesthetics of suffering. In particular, they wondered how one might read such a tale as Nabokov's in a meaningful way that does justice to it as literature and to real, not fictional, victims of abuse.

More than anything, this experience made me better appreciate the issue of context. What is the best context to read *Lolita*? (A small handful of my students had *no* idea was it was about before opening the first page.) How does context color our reading? On a literal level, a student's half-joking admission that they felt obligated to express obvious disgust while reading the novel in public spaces to make clear how they felt about doing so drew both laughter and nods of agreement. Most importantly for my purposes, *Lolita* disrupts the traditional notion of a prison text, while at the same time underscoring some of that very tradition's most significant features. Read in this particular curricular setting, it can draw readers' attention to the razor's edge of narrative control. It made us wonder about other forms of confinement and incarceration, about the limits and nuances of those phenomena. What does it take to create a prison? Is it the walls? Regulations? Guards? Terms of release? Intent? *Lolita*'s prison lacks several of these traditional elements, and still it encapsulates an ultimate loss of control. We simply have to attune our reading strategies to see its full scope, much as we must do with the prison system and with systemic sexual harassment.

In her epilogue to *Requiem*, Akhmatova ponders what kind of monument might be built in her honor as the embodiment of all the people who suffered during Stalin's reign of terror; her poems, then, also serve as a literary monument to her parental love. Humbert Humbert would have his memoirs read as a similar testament. And yet, the careful, skeptical reader can perceive its cracks, distortions, and warping. Humbert Humbert may believe he sings a tender paean to Dolores, his corrupted stepchild, but the reader only hears a requiem for her.

READING LIST

"Crime or Punishment: Russian Narratives of Incarceration and Captivity"
Cesare Beccaria: *An Essay on Crimes and Punishments* (Selections)
John Locke: *Second Treatise of Government* (Selections)
Jeremy Bentham: *Panopticon* (Selections)
Thomas Hobbes: *Leviathan* (Selections)
Jonathan Daly: *Crime and Punishment in Russia: A Comparative History from Peter the Great to Vladimir Putin*
Archpriest Avvakum: *The Life of Avvakum* (Selections)
Alexander Pushkin: *The Captive in the Caucasus*
Lev Tolstoy: "A Prisoner of the Caucasus"
Michel Foucault: *Discipline and Punish* (Selections)
Fyodor Dostoevsky: *Notes from a Dead House*
Nikolai Leskov: *Lady Macbeth of the Mtsensk District*
Elaine Scarry: *The Body in Pain* (Selections)
Lev Tolstoy: "After the Ball"
Petr Kropotkin: *In Russian and French Prisons* (Selections)
Anton Chekhov: *The Island: A Journey to Sakhalin* (Selections)
Leonid Andreev: "Seven Who Were Hanged"
Vera Figner: *Memoirs of a Revolutionist* (Selections)
Daniil Kharms: "A Man Once Walked Out of His House" and "Blue Notebook No.10"
Norman Johnston: *Forms of Constraint: A History of Prison Architecture* (Selections)
Lidiia Chukovskaya: *Sofia Petrovna*
Carolyn Forché: "Twentieth Century Poetry of Witness"

Anna Akhmatova: *Requiem*
Susan Sontag: *Regarding the Pain of Others* (Selections)
Vladimir Nabokov: *Lolita*
Hannah Arendt: *The Origins of Totalitarianism* (Selections)
Varlam Shalamov: *Kolyma Tales* (Selections)
Lidiia Ginzburg: *Journey into the Whirlwind* (Selections)
Alexander Solzhenitsyn: *Gulag Archipelago* (Selections)
Sergei Dovlatov: *The Zone* (Selections)
Irina Ratushinskaya: *Grey Is the Color of Hope* (Selections)
Nadya Tolokonnikova: *Comradely Greetings: The Prison Letters of and Slavoj Žižek* (Selections)
Angela Davis: *Are Prisons Obsolete?* (Selections)
Mikhail Khodorkovsky: *My Fellow Prisoners* (Selections)
Victoria Lomasko: *Other Russias* (Selections)
Danzig Baldaev: *Drawings from the Gulag* (Selections)

WORKS CITED

C. K., Louis. "Louis C. K.'s Full Statement." CNN, November 10, 2017. https://www.cnn.com/2017/11/10/entertainment/louis-ck-full-statement/index.html.
Dolinin, Alexander. "Nabokov's Time Doubling: From *The Gift* to *Lolita*." *Nabokov Studies* 2 (1995): 4–30.
———. "What Happened to Sally Horner: A Real-Life Source of Nabokov's *Lolita*." *Zembla*, https://www.libraries.psu.edu/nabokov/dolilol.htm.
Lomasko, Victoria. *Other Russias*. New York: n+1 Books, 2017.
Nabokov, Vladimir. *The Annotated Lolita*. New York: Vintage, 1991.
Russell, Mary Kate. *My Dark Vanessa*. New York: HarperCollins, 2020.
Scarry, Elaine. *The Body in Pain: The Making and Unmaking of the World*. New York: Oxford University Press, 1987.
Solzhenitsyn, Aleksandr I. *The Gulag Archipelago, 1918–1956: An Experiment in Literary Investigation*. Vols. 3–4. New York: Harper & Row, 1975.
Sommers, Elena. "The 'Right' versus the 'Wrong' Child: Shades of Pain in *Bend Sinister* and *Pnin*." *Nabokov Studies* 6 (2000/2001): 35–50.
Weinman, Sarah. *The Real Lolita: A Lost Girl, an Unthinkable Crime, and a Scandalous Masterpiece*. New York: Ecco, 2018.

NOTES

1. Please see full course reading list.
2. In fact, there are ways of reading the novel as entirely devoid of prisons—yet another strike against my including it on the syllabus. Alexander Dolinin, for instance, argues that textual clues in the book suggest that Dolores actually dies during her hospital stay and that Humbert Humbert makes up everything that comes afterward, including his murder of Clare Quilty. Alexander Dolinin, "Nabokov's Time Doubling: From *The Gift* to *Lolita*," *Nabokov Studies* 2 (1995): 4–30.
3. One section of Lomasko's volume documents a particularly gruesome case of slave trafficking in Moscow. See Lomasko, *Other Russias* (New York: n+1 Books, 2017), 79–105.
4. Not for nothing does Humbert Humbert refer to his "huge hairy hand" (123).
5. As I introduce each of these three topics, I draw the students' attention to particular moments in the novel:

    a. Carefully ("Caress the detail, the divine detail.")

        i. Foreword

            1. As a parody of erotic works
            2. As a parody of psychiatric works
            3. How are the characters defined in this first section?
            4. Humbert's and John Ray, Jr.'s name
    b. Slowly ("Curiously enough, one cannot read a book: one can only reread it.")
        i. Chapter 1
            1. Puns
            2. Sets of Romantic subtexts
            3. HH's solipsism
            4. Establishes HH's first line of defense
    c. Read with Compassion ("The password is pity.")
        i. Valeria
            1. 25: mislaid her virginity
            2. 27: Why does Valeria bother HH?
                a. "which was quite out of keeping with the stock character she was supposed to impersonate"
            3. 29: he drove the Humberts
        ii. Charlotte
            1. 71: Does HH actually change how he talks about Charlotte or anyone else in his narrative?
        iii. Dolores
            1. 39: First meeting in the garden and all its images
                a. What does HH focus on?
            2. 43: Our Glass Lake
            3. 57: Davenport scene
                a. What language does HH use throughout this scene?
                b. 60–62: Lolita has been "safely solipcized.
                    i. Has she?

6. Some of the questions I posed: How is this a story about captivity and imprisonment? Where do we see it in the text? How is Dolores held captive? What kind of captivity is this? Debates ensued. Indeed, while these may seem like obvious questions with equally obvious answers, responses can vary widely depending on the course context and the students involved.

7. Louis C. K., "Louis C. K.'s Full Statement," CNN, November 10, 2017, https://www.cnn.com/2017/11/10/entertainment/louis-ck-full-statement/index.html.

8. Humbert Humbert later uses this same "light of my life" metaphor to euphemistically describe his first sexual encounter with Dolores: "My life was handled by little Lo in an energetic, matter-of-fact manner as if it were an insensate gadget unconnected with me" (9, 33).

9. See Pia Pera's *Lo's Diary* (1995), which retells the plot from Dolores's perspective and takes many liberties along the way, as well as *My Dark Vanessa* (2020) by Kate Elizabeth Russell and *The Real Lolita: A Lost Girl, an Unthinkable Crime, and a Scandalous Masterpiece* (2018) by Sarah Weinman.

10. On the other hand, Nabokov did draw from the real-life case of Sally Horner's kidnapping. See Weinman and Alexander Dolinin, "What Happened to Sally Horner: A Real-Life Source of Nabokov's *Lolita*," *Zembla*, https://www.libraries.psu.edu/nabokov/dolilol.htm.

11. Why are we reading *Lolita*?

   a. Free-writing: On your notecard, please answer this question: why are we reading *Lolita*, both in general and in this particular course? You might consider the novel on its own or in relation to some of the other texts we've read (or will be reading).
   b. Again, in groups, discuss this question. Please refer to specific elements of the text.
   c. I understand that it can be jarring going from Akhmatova and Chukovskaya (to start only there) to *Lolita* and then to jump into gulag camp literature. Part of that is intentional—to see what we can read in *Lolita* given these contrasts. For instance, much of what we're reading is about state power and control, less so about individual and personal captivity. Furthermore, we see a different perspective—that of a true criminal. We could have read Dostoevsky's *Crime and Punishment*, which is another novel whose plot focuses largely on the crime rather than the punishment, but that work features a third-person narrator. *Lolita* in this way lets us examine power dynamics and the psychology of captivity in a way that trains us to look through deceptive language and the solipsism of dictators, large and small. Finally, it will resonate with Lomasko's *Other Russias* later in the course.

12. Elaine Scarry, *The Body in Pain* (New York: Oxford UNiversity Press, 1985) 11.

13. Elena Sommers, "The 'Right' versus the 'Wrong' Child: Shades of Pain in *Bend Sinister* and *Pnin*," *Nabokov Studies* 6 (2000/2001): 36.

14. Aleksandr I. Solzhenitsyn, *The Gulag Archipelago, 1918–1956: An Experiment in Literary Investigation*, vols. 3–4 (New York: Harper & Row, 1975), 617.

Chapter Five

Teaching *Lolita* in the Department of Drama

Alisa Zhulina

"Flipping the paperback over, I see a pair of skinny legs in ankle socks and saddle shoes, a pleated skirt ending above the knobby knees. In big white letters across the legs: *Lolita*. I've heard the term somewhere before—an article about Fiona Apple, I think, a description of her as 'Lolita-esque,' meaning sexy and too young." (Russell, *My Dark Vanessa* 72–73)[1]

INTRODUCTION: *LOLITA* IN A COURSE ON DRAMA?

Vladimir Nabokov's *Lolita* (1955) might seem like a surprising choice to include in a course on drama and theatre. The eruption of the #MeToo movement in the fall of 2017 has led theatre and performance studies departments to reckon with their curricula and teaching methodologies. Issues of consent, casting choices, and the choreography of intimacy have become heated topics of debate. Wouldn't *Lolita* be adding fuel to the fire? In fact, teaching *Lolita* alongside its afterlives on the stage and screen is a productive way to explore questions concerning consent, misogyny, sexual violence, as well as the process of adapting and reinterpreting problematic texts from the past.

Nabokov himself was wary of the potential adaptations of *Lolita*. Although he eventually allowed Stanley Kubrick to make a movie based on the novel in 1962, he expressed reservations: "It was perfectly all right for me to imagine a twelve-year-old Lolita. . . . She existed only in my head. But to make a real twelve-year-old play such a part would be sinful and immoral, and I would never consent to it."[2] Similarly, when describing to his American publisher what he would like to see on the book's cover, which has since seen its share of risqué images, Nabokov wrote: "There is one subject which I am emphatically opposed to: any kind of representation of a little girl."[3] Still, despite Nabokov's attempt to control the boundaries and reception of his novel, *Lolita* has inspired plays, films, a ballet, an opera, pop music, and fashion. Just as Dolly Haze eventually runs away from Humbert Humbert, so *Lolita* escapes Nabokov's authorial control. Popular culture has usurped *Lolita* against Nabokov's consent.[4] These ghosts of *Lolita*, particularly the ones that haunt the theatre and cinema, shed light on the brilliance of the novel's moral framework as well as its limitations when it comes to the representation of Dolly's body and voice.[5] No masterpiece is without flaw. Thus the cultural shift of #MeToo at once makes Nabokov's novel an urgent read and calls for a rethinking of how to contextualize it. A diverse constellation of companion texts, including those drawn from dramatic literature and featuring women's voices, will allow *Lolita* not only to weather the hurricane of #MeToo, but also to become one of the lodestars of this cultural moment.

I teach *Lolita* in an honors seminar titled "Banned: Transgression and Censorship in the Theatre." The central questions of the course are: What is the relationship between theatre-making and censorship? Which forms does censorship take and what does it look like in the digital era? How do artists evade, outsmart, or openly defy restrictions on specific content and representations and their creative freedom in general? Students, most of whom are fledgling actors, playwrights, directors, and theatre-makers, examine artistic constraints in different times and across geographical borders. Some of the central issues of the course include political and economic pressure, self-censorship, obscenity, and the relationship between art and law. Each week we focus on one specific case in theatre history, investigating why a given play or performance was banned. In addition, the course looks at stage adaptations of banned books (or books that were once banned) and asks what draws theatre-makers to transgressive content in works like Marquis de Sade's *La philosophie dans le boudoir* (1795), Pierre Choderlos de Laclos' *Les Liaisons dangereuses* (1782), and Vladimir Nabokov's *Lolita* (1955).

ADAPTING *LOLITA*

One of the first questions to arise in classroom discussions of *Lolita* is whether the novel is adaptable. After all, there has never been an aesthetically or commercially successful theatrical version of the novel, and, to this day, Stanley Kubrick's film remains the most positively received adaptation of *Lolita* into any medium. Moreover, one of the most notorious flops in musical theatre history is John Barry and Alan Jay Lerner's *Lolita, My Love* (1971). Alan Jay Lerner, the lyricist of *My Fair Lady* (1956), approached the British composer John Barry with an idea for a musical based on Nabokov's novel. Richard Burton was initially cast in the role of Humbert, but turned it down, passing the baton to Shakespearean veteran John Neville. Although critics praised Neville's performance, *Lolita, My Love* closed in Boston after just nine performances. Despite its colossal commercial failure (the production lost $900,000), many critics lauded Lerner's lyrics.[6] Song titles included "In the Broken Promise of Land of Fifteen," "March Out of My Life," "How Far Is It to the Next Town?" and "Going, Going, Gone," which became the tagline of one particularly scathing review. Graham Vickers wonders whether audiences were simply not "ready for a musical about a child molester."[7] *Lolita, My Love* would have to wait until the spring of 2019 to have its New York première, when the York Theatre Company presented a limited run of a positively reviewed workshop production as part of the Musicals in Mufti Series (on which more later).

Another infamous attempt at adapting *Lolita* for the stage was Edward Albee's *Lolita* (1981). After a tryout run in Boston, the show opened in New York and was greeted by the activist group Women Against Pornography that stood outside with placards that read "Incest Isn't Sexy" and "Rape Isn't Funny."[8] The Broadway production closed after twelve performances. America of the 1980s was a decisively different political and cultural landscape than what it had been in the 1950s, when Nabokov's novel was first published. Was it the historical situation—the height of the feminist sex wars—or was it something intrinsic to the novel itself that made Albee's adaptation problematic?

In the introduction to his ponderous screenplay of *Lolita* (which Kubrick wisely did not use), Nabokov claimed that he was "no dramatist."[9] As students are quick to point out, however, Nabokov makes numerous references to theatre, cinema, and the performing arts throughout *Lolita*. Indeed, Nabokov maintained an active interest in theatre throughout his life. During the beginning of his émigré sojourn in Prague, Berlin, and Paris, Nabokov penned plays in Russian—*The Tragedy of Mister Morn* (1923), *The Pole* (1923), *The Man from the USSR* (1926), *The Event* (1938), and *The Waltz Invention* (1938). And Nabokov's first academic appointment in the United States in 1940 was teaching drama at Stanford University. Yet, as Siggy Frank has shown, while theatre "as metaphor, structural principle, theme and context" is "an essential and pervasive element of his fiction," Nabokov, like most modernists, holds an antitheatrical prejudice.[10] To put it another way, although play and theatricality are important motifs for Nabokov, drama holds value for him as printed text and not as theatrical performance, which is associated with the loss of authorial control, deception, and even poshlost.[11] It is not by accident that Dolly's acting in the high school play *The Enchanted Hunters* is connected to her betrayal of and escape from Humbert. The play's author, Clare Quilty, is a playwright-turned-pornographer, who kicks Dolly out of his Duk Duk ranch for refusing to participate in his pornographic films. By making the "clearly guilty" character a theatre-maker and by presenting the world of theatre as a space of treachery, Nabokov exhibits an "ancient distrust of the stage" and a deep-seated hostility toward theatricality that has characterized the Western civilization since Plato.[12] Thus *Lolita*, a novel that Nabokov called "the record of [his] love affair" with the English language, is mainly invested in exploring the power of literature.[13] The moral issues at stake in the text are intricately and intimately connected to the language in which they are raised. However, despite his antitheatrical prejudice and desire for authorial control, Nabokov could not contain the contents of his novel from spilling into other media.[14] In my seminar, the students and I take the case of *Lolita*'s afterlives as an opportunity to explore Linda Hutcheon's claim that adaptation is not simply "*a formal entity or product*," but also "*a process of creation*," as "the act of adaptation always involves both (re-)interpretation and then (re-)creation."[15] Our current culture is saturated with adaptations, and it is likely that, as artists, my students too one day will be involved in the creative act of adaptation. What can the stage and screen versions of *Lolita* teach them?

The story of *Lolita*'s publication and its subsequent transmedial migrations to visual culture, the stage, the screen, and (most disturbingly) to internet pornography reads as a cautionary tale about the unsustainability of the modernist dream of medium specificity. The secondary readings that are helpful to read along with *Lolita* in order to discuss both the moral stakes of the novel and its transmedial afterlives are Clement Greenberg's "Modernist Painting," Linda Hutcheon's *A Theory of Adaptation*, and Henry Jenkins' *Convergence Culture: Where Old and New Media Collide*. In a way, *Lolita* makes a strong case for what Greenberg famously called "medium specificity," namely "the unique and proper area of competence of each art" that "coincide[s] with all that [i]s unique to the nature of its medium."[16] On the one hand, Nabokov's novel is deeply invested in the process of remediation, which Jay David Bolter and Richard Grusin define as "the representation of one medium in another."[17] There are numerous references to other art forms such as painting, photography, music, theatre, and film. On the other hand, *Lolita* continuingly emphasizes that its story should only be told within the textual universe of literature, echoing the Russian Formalist argument about the inseparability of form and content.[18] This high esteem of literature is not surprising. As Hutcheon observes, "writers and literary critics hierarchize in their own particular art's favor."[19] For all its cannibalism of American popular culture, from motels to milkshakes, at its core, *Lolita* is a difficult modernist novel whose ethical puzzle relies on the attention, empathy, and patience of a person Nabokov liked to call "a good reader."[20] The ethics of *Lolita* are bound up with the act of reading.

TIMELY OR TIME'S UP?

Although Nabokov claims in the 1956 postscript to the novel that "*Lolita* has no moral in tow,"[21] the most attentive of Nabokovian scholars have focused on how the novel offers its readers, to borrow Michael Wood's eloquent turn of phrase, "plenty of practice for the moral imagination, more than we can cope with, perhaps."[22] Indeed, *Lolita* has been taught with success in courses on ethics and literature.[23] In fact, *Lolita* has become somewhat of a usual suspect on many syllabi, so much so that the *New Yorker* book critic James Wood prefers to teach *Pnin* (1957) in his popular course "Postwar British and American Fiction" at Harvard University precisely because *Lolita* is so ubiquitous. Students interested in literature are unlikely to miss encountering *Lolita* during their undergraduate years as they are to miss *Pnin*.[24] As Sarah Herbold has noted, however, students often "worry (as they should) about whether enjoying the novel makes them complicit in it."[25] Since the explosion of the #MeToo movement, these worries have only intensified, as students are challenging the curation of texts that they see on their syllabi. *Lolita* has once again come into the spotlight, especially in debates about what to do with literature from the past that depicts the exploitation of and violence toward women.

These debates are happening both inside and outside the classroom. Anne Dwyer, for example, who has taught an undergraduate seminar on Vladimir Nabokov at Pomona since 2008, wrote an insightful piece for *Inside Higher Ed*—"Why I Teach Lolita"—based on a lecture that she delivered to her students, when they challenged her choice to teach "a book that inflicted trauma and even perpetuated rape culture."[26] Tracing the complicated relationship between aesthetics and ethics in the novel, Dwyer concludes her essay with an urgent call to her colleagues to assign "difficult books" and to the students to "read difficult books" and "come to [their] own conclusions."[27] In my experience of teaching the novel, students often arrive on the first day of class with a preconceived notion of what kind of book *Lolita* is. Their opinions are often formed by what they read online, including on social media. This is why it is crucial to address the various adaptations, riffs, and misappropriations of *Lolita* (such as a fashion line that came out with a lingerie set with the word "Lolita" stamped on it) even as we focus on what the novel does differently. Reading journalistic essays, online blogs, and even Instagram comments along with scholarly articles on *Lolita* encourages students to think of their own critical voices as contributing to a high-stakes cultural debate that is happening during their own time. This mixing of high and low culture, of course, also replicates the very aesthetic of Nabokov's novel, where allusions to French literature coexist with references to popular songs and teenage slang. Moreover, it allows students to see the differences between biased, rushed opinions and critical thinking that takes time and attention to nuance. The ability to distinguish between different types of discourses, particularly in our purported "post-truth" moment, is of paramount importance. Here are some examples of the kinds of secondary readings that the students did in the course. They were encouraged to approach all the texts with a critical eye.

In light of the #MeToo movement, several think pieces in mainstream media have asked whether *Lolita*'s framework, filtered as it is through Humbert's manipulative and seductive prose, is misogynistic, since it silences the voice of the victim. "Can *Lolita* be read as anything but a story of predation, depravity, exploitation—and specifically, rape—no matter how stunning Nabokov's prose might be?" asks E. Ce Miller in a piece titled "I Re-Read *Lolita* in the Age of #MeToo—And I'm No Longer Standing for Its Overt Misogyny." The writer concludes that *Lolita* is "a novel whose time is up."[28] In a similar vein, in her chronicle of the 1948 kidnapping case of Sally Horner (to which Nabokov alludes in *Lolita*), Sarah Weinman argues that the "abuse that Sally Horner, and other girls like her, endured should not be subsumed by dazzling prose, no matter how brilliant."[29] Those who defend Nabokov's choice of subject matter, however, point out that he is writing about the cruelty and violence that already exist in the world. When feminists in Spain criticized *Lolita* because its narrator is a pedophile, the Nobel Prize–winning Peruvian writer Mario Vargas Llosa responded: "With this criterion, literature will disappear."[30] Then there are those supporters of Nabokov who emphasize that his book remains as timely as ever precisely because of the material that it covers. "A parable about rape, misogyny, and our cultural obsession with youth is *especially* timely at the moment and aligns with movements such as #MeToo, #TimesUp, and #MuteRKelly," writes Ms. Lola for *Medium*.[31]

Significantly, Dr. John Ray Jr.'s suggestion in the fictitious foreword to *Lolita* that we be "entranced with the book while abhorring its author,"[32] that is, Humbert Humbert, anticipates one of the most polarizing questions of the #MeToo era: how to approach the art of those cultural figures who have done abominable things—Bill Cosby, R. Kelly, Picasso, Roman Polanski—the list goes on. This thorny question resulted in a rich and stimulating classroom conversation. Given how influential some of these figures have been, boycotting their art is not always possible if only because of the rampant references to and countless adaptations of their works. Yet, are we really prepared to let the art stand on its own, independent of its creator, especially in cases like that of R. Kelly, whose music (fifteen-year-old Aaliyah's "Age Ain't Nothing But A Number") closely reflects his own less than palatable predilections?

One way that *Lolita* posits the question concerning the relationship between the artist and the artwork is by teasing the reader with the deceptive doubles of Humbert Humbert and Clare Quilty. Like his name suggests,

Clare Quilty is "clearly guilty," and he gets away with abusing children because of his fame and social status. Sound familiar? Yet we do not need to worry about what to do with his "art"—it's clearly exploitative trash, tainted as it is by an association with theatre and performance. However, in the case of Humbert, a wordsmith and professor of literature, Nabokov's novel refuses to give easy answers. In the Foreword to the English edition of *Despair* (1965), Nabokov compares the unreliable narrator Hermann to *Lolita*'s Humbert, observing that they are both "neurotic scoundrels," but, while Hermann will stay in Hell forever, "there is a green lane in Paradise where Humbert is permitted to wander at dusk once a year."[33] Leland de la Durantaye suggests that this slight respite is given to Humbert for his moral awakening, however late, and for his choice, as an artist, to tell Dolly's story: "And do not pity C. Q. One had to choose between him and H. H., and one wanted H. H. to exist at least a couple of months longer, so as to have him make you live in the minds of later generations."[34] Yet what kind of image of Dolly Haze are we left with? What has Humbert accomplished as an artist? And what can Nabokov contribute to the reckonings of #MeToo?

In an essay for *The Guardian* that urges "women to rewrite the story," Sarah Churchwell calls out "Poe, Updike, Roth, Mailer," and other male writers who "have contributed to a culture in which the credibility of women is undermined." Churchwell does not, however, include Nabokov in their company, suggesting that in showing "the great tragedy" of the absence of Dolly's voice, *Lolita* reveals, in a critical and deeply empathetic manner, the ways that women have not been able to tell their stories in their own words.[35]

READ-ONLY

Defending *Lolita* in the age of #MeToo, Caitlin Flanagan writes: "*Lolita* asks us only one question: Are you a reader?"[36] One point that both the defenders and the detractors of the novel agree on is that the reader sees and hears very little of the real girl named Dolly Haze, as the book reveals only Humbert's view of her. Many good readers have taken this narrative framework, namely the loss of Dolly's voice, as a crucial piece of the novel's ethical puzzle.[37] Churchwell, for example, argues that Dolly's absence is meant to make us uncomfortable.[38] According to Sarah Herbold, the novel permits us only "a trace of the woman (or girl) who was—or could have been—present, but who can no longer truly be made present to author, narrator, or reader."[39] In a similar vein, Michael Wood argues that, although Nabokov's *Lolita* affords the reader only "a glimpse of the substantial American child," it is up to reader to find her.[40] Dolly becomes then "a product of reading, not because the reader makes her up or because she is just 'there' in the words, but because she is what a reading finds, and [. . .] needs to find, in order to see the range of what the book can do."[41] The novel's language might seduce the reader into complicity with Humbert, but it also has the potential to recover, if only partially, the victim's voice. Thus writing in Nabokov's literary universe behaves like Jacques Derrida's *pharmakon*—it's both a poison and a remedy.[42] Yet what happens when we get to see and hear the American girl on the stage or the screen?

TRANSMEDIAL TRANSGRESSIONS

In a way, Nabokov's *Lolita* resists and even prohibits adaptations and extensions of its textual world.[43] "Idiot, triple idiot! I could have filmed her! I would have had her now with me, before my eyes, in the projection room of my pain and despair!" Humbert says at one point.[44] But, within the pages of the novel, he never gets to make such a film. As Louis Menand notes, "you cannot film this story accurately and stay out of prison."[45] Dolly's age (she's twelve at the start of Nabokov's novel) has always been a problem for theatre and film directors. Sue Lyon, who played the role in Kubrick's movie, was fourteen at the start of filming. In addition to being deliberately vague about Dolly's age, Kubrick's film also expanded the storyline of Quilty, played by Peter Sollers, in order to stress Humbert's guilt from the very first scene. In the stage production of Edward Albee's 1981 ill-fated play, twenty-four-year-old Blanche Baker played the part. Dominique Swain, who starred in Adrian Lyne's 1997 screen version, was fifteen. Lyne's *Lolita* jettisoned Nabokov's dark wit, replacing it with wistful romanticism, and added obligatory Hollywood sex scenes (absent from the novel), which were simulated by Jeremy Irons and a nineteen-year-old body double. In this manner, Lyne visually extended the erotic world of the novel that Nabokov so carefully sought to restrict.[46] Nabokov composed *Lolita* on index cards with a Blackwing 602 pencil. He could not have predicted how the performing arts, cinema, digital media, and virtual reality would transform his heroine and the subsequent debate about fantasy versus reality.

In February 2019, the New York debut and workshop production of *Lolita, My Love* by the York Theatre Company took the opportunity to tell the story from a woman's perspective. Erik Haagensen revised the script from six of Lerner's drafts, including two that were composed after the musical closed in 1971. Directed by Emily Maltby, the show addressed the concerns of #MeToo head-on, reframing the musical as Humbert Humbert's confession to a female therapist, named June Ray (an utterly transformed John Ray Jr.), who offers a corrective commentary to Humbert's desires, thoughts, and actions. June Ray serves as kind of distancing device that prohibits the audience's identification with Humbert. It was Haagensen's idea to make the therapist a woman, "allowing her to serve as something of a surrogate for

Lolita, who, as in the novel, exists more in Humbert's imagination than as her own person."[47] One wonders how Nabokov would react to the presence of an analyst on stage, given his mistrust and even contempt of psychoanalysis. Although this limited run received generally positive reviews, it was impossible not to notice how lightly the image of Dolly Haze is sketched in the novel. In the unforgiving spotlight of the stage, one quickly sees how little the actor (Caitlin Cohn) has to work with. Of course, Nabokov himself predicted the challenges of transposing his story into another medium.

Seeing this production led to another thought-provoking discussion in the classroom. Even if the silencing of a victim's voice is part and parcel of the novel's moral makeup (as readers, we are supposed to condemn it), in the era of #MeToo one cannot help but ask whether such a narrative framework is enough, or whether it reenacts the silencing of women and the erasure of their stories. One student argued that Nabokov's novel was misogynistic because it doesn't take the time to explore female sexuality, echoing a critique that Eric Naiman has heard in his classroom as well, when one of his female students mentioned "the book was hostile to women because Nabokov could not bring himself to represent female sexual pleasure."[48] The cultural landscape has certainly changed. In the era of Lena Dunham's *Girls* (2012–2017) and Phoebe Waller-Bridge's *Fleabag* (2016–2019), students are more accustomed to frank depictions of sexuality and open discussions of female desire. While it is important to historicize the novel and examine how sexual mores are "historically constructed," as Anne Dwyer advises, it is equally important to put Nabokov's *Lolita* in conversation with works by women, who are addressing similar issues and telling the Lolita story (which has now unfortunately become part of our youth-obsessed culture) from the woman's perspective.

Conversely, as one student asked, was Nabokov even in the position to tell the story of a young girl? We know for a fact that Nabokov studied real case studies in psychology and rode on school buses to capture the tone and vocabulary of his teenage heroine.[49] Yet, perhaps, imagining the inner world of a teenage girl, with all of its rich and perplexing contradictions, was either something that was of no interest to Nabokov as a fiction writer or something too difficult for him to tackle. This speculation led us to a fascinating discussion about the potentials and limits of imagination. Zadie Smith's recent essay "Fascinated to Presume: In Defense of Fiction" served as our compass. Smith begins by noting that in the age of neoliberalism and identity politics the "old—and never especially helpful—adage *write what you know* has morphed into something more like a threat: *Stay in your lane*." She then asks how "our debates about fiction" would change "if our preferred verbal container for the phenomenon of writing about others was not 'cultural appropriation' but rather 'interpersonal voyeurism' or 'profound-other-fascination' or even 'cross-epidermal reanimation?'" The ever-provocative Smith doesn't offer any readymade conclusions, but suggests that part of the joy of writing about the lives of others, who are not like us, is the risk and uncertainty of the whole endeavor. At the end of the day, it is up to the reader to decide whether a book succeeds or not in telling the story.[50]

GIRLS MATTER

Perhaps then theatrical and cinematic versions of *Lolita* have not enjoyed much success precisely because the novel does not gives us the voice of a unique girl. The absence that electrifies the page doesn't translate onto the stage or screen. Since the publication of *Lolita* there have been many works, including of dramatic literature, which are inspired by Nabokov's novel, but attempt to tell the story from a woman's perspective. Reading them along with *Lolita* makes for a rich and stimulating experience, one that only heightens the pathos of the loss of Dolly in Nabokov's novel. Not all are successful, however. Pia Pera's *Lo's Diary* (1995), which relates the events from the point of view of Dolores Haze, garnered negative reviews and a lawsuit from Dmitri Nabokov.[51] Those works that feature only echoes of or allusions to Nabokov's novel, while developing their own storylines and characters, seem to have been the more successful, especially in the theatre.

To name but a few examples, plays that take on the relationship between an underage girl and an older man, who should have been her guardian, include Paula Vogel's *How I Learned to Drive* (1997), which won the Pulitzer Prize in Drama, and David Harrower's *Blackbird* (2005), which won the Laurence Olivier Award for Best New Play in 2007. Both plays echo *Lolita* in that they have charismatic male characters who know how to seduce and manipulate with words and female characters who come to terms with their childhood trauma. The key difference is that Vogel and Harrower also feature strong women who stand up to their abusers and have the opportunity to tell their stories in their own words. Vogel was actually inspired to write her play by Nabokov's *Lolita*, which she read in her twenties. She had always been unsettled by the fact that as a reader she felt sympathy for Humbert Humbert.[52] Tellingly, in the character descriptions, Vogel states that Uncle Peck is an "attractive man in his forties" and "should be played by an actor one might cast in the role of Atticus in *To Kill a Mockingbird*."[53] His name also evokes the allure of the well-respected and loved-by-the-public actor Gregory Peck. Vogel clearly wants her audience to be disturbed by the contrast between Peck's charisma and his actions. Although not an adaptation, *How I Learned to Drive* is a thought-provoking response to Nabokov's novel, from which it borrows the road motif and car imagery. The play follows the story of the erotic relationship between Li'l Bit and her aunt's husband, Uncle Peck, from her pre-adolescent years all the way through adulthood. Vogel turns the process of teaching and learning how to drive into a theatrical metaphor for the taboo affair between her two characters. In contrast to Nabokov's novel, Li'l Bit gets to sit at the wheel most of the time. The audience also gets to see a nuanced and at times troubling portrait of a young girl coming into her own, with all the messiness that ensues. For one, she experiences her own sexual awakening as both a power (that she holds over Peck) and a liability (that she doesn't quite know what to do with, so it doesn't hurt her). Further, the moral problem of the play is that the man who sexually molests Li'l Bit—Uncle Peck—is the same man who will give her one of the greatest gifts—the lifesaving skill of knowing how to drive with confidence. During one of their lessons, Peck explains the stakes:

> Men are taught to drive with confidence—with aggression. The road belongs to them. They drive defensively—always looking out for the other guy. Women tend to be polite—to hesitate. And that can be fatal.

Peck then tells Li'l Bit that he's teaching her how to drive, so that if "there's an accident, and ten cars pile up, and people get killed," she'll "be the only one to walk away."[54] As Vogel explains in an interview, Peck not only teaches Li'l Bit how to survive, but also ultimately "enables her [. . .] to reject him and destroy him."[55] The play ends on Li'l Bit checking her side mirrors, fastening her seat belt, and getting ready to hit the road. She's grown up, she's now in charge, and she's going to move on with her life. Suddenly, "the spirit of Uncle Peck" appears in the back seat of her car. What does his ghost symbolize? Is it some type of road spirit that keeps her safe? Is it her past trauma that will always haunt her? The directions also indicate that the two "are happy to be going for a long drive together."[56] So might Peck's presence in the car also stand for Li'l Bit's mixed emotions toward him—one of which, however problematic, might be called "love?"[57] His spirit is both a poison and an antidote. The contradiction remains unresolved. Even as Vogel rewrites the Lolita story from a woman's perspective, she borrows from Nabokov that same disturbing feeling that she had when she first read his novel, or what Caitlin Flanagan calls the novel's "combination of revulsion and ecstasy."[58] As Vogel notes, her play "dramatizes the gifts we receive from the people who hurt us."[59] Like *Lolita*, *How I Learned to Drive* is a nuanced and deeply empathetic work that refuses to give us an easily digestible lesson in ethics, encouraging us instead to practice our moral imagination.

Similarly, *Blackbird* stages a confrontation between Una, a woman in her late twenties, and Ray, a man in his mid-fifties, who had sex with her when she was twelve years old. Informed in part by the crimes of sex offender Toby Studebaker, Harrower's play echoes *Lolita* in more ways than the age of the female protagonist. The main male character in *Blackbird* is also a charming man who knows how to bend the narrative to make himself look better than he is. Ray manages to convince Una, along with the audience, that he has reformed and is now in a relationship with a woman of his age. When Una and Ray end up kissing, the audience might even believe that the two have a chance at a redemptive future until a girl of twelve appears on stage. She's the daughter of Ray's new partner. The audience is just as shocked as Una is. We feel that we have been duped, even betrayed. That's the point. Ray begs Una to believe him, that he "would never," but our trust in him is gone.[60] Again, while Harrower's play presents a more developed character of a young woman, it borrows from *Lolita* the act of manipulation through storytelling. Significantly, both *Blackbird* and *How I Learned to Drive* dramatize female desire and sexual pleasure without "toppling into the genre of at least soft-core pornography," as Eric Naiman rightfully worries would have happened had Nabokov chosen to depict his "heroine enjoying sexual encounters with Humbert."[61] To be sure, it is a difficult and risky endeavor, but one that many writers have taken on in recent years.

There has been a veritable explosion of plays by women, though not exclusively, who have given voice to girlhood. These works explore teenage sexuality, female desire, ambition, and coming of age in a world still dominated by misogyny and violence against women. If, as readers, we are serious about recovering the voice of the "American girl-child named Dolores Haze [who] had been deprived of her childhood by a maniac," then we would do well not only to identify the strategic lacunas in Nabokov's text, but also to imagine what her voice, thoughts, and experience might have been (while paying close attention to historical context).[62] Here are just a few examples of contemporary plays that can help the reader imagine what it is like to be a prepubescent and teenage girl in America today, a world still riven by misogyny. In Ruby Rae Spiegel's remarkable play *Dry Land* (2015), two Florida high school girls on the swim team try to do an abortion by themselves in a locker room, as they navigate the turbulent waters of their friendship. Sarah DeLappe's *The Wolves* (2016), a finalist for the 2017 Pulitzer Prize for Drama, follows a group of ferocious sixteen- and seventeen-year-old girls during their weekly soccer team practices, as they grapple with competition, adolescent love, and first sexual experiences. Clare Barron's *Dance Nation* (2019), another finalist for the Pulitzer, dramatizes the ambition and rivalry among thirteen-year-old girls who are competing for the top place in dance nationals. Many of these plays explore either taboo flirtations or relationships between older men and underage girls. Barron's *Dance Nation* features an uncomfortable scene between a female student and her older male dance teacher. The directions read as follows: "*He sort of swats her butt. It's not sexual???????? But also weird and uncomfortable for a grown-ass man to be swatting a thirteen-year-old's butt. Amina is horrified. And also, she loves it.*"[63] Nothing more ever happens between the two and the scene is left in all its disturbing ambiguity to be discussed and interpreted by the actors and their director. Julia Jarcho's *Pathetic* (2019) is a riff on Racine's *Phèdre*, in which "teen girls experiment with sex, magic and murder while mom sinks deep into lust and self-loathing."[64] (One wonders how poor Charlotte's story will be read in the #MeToo era.) During its New York première, Jarcho's production gave a nod to Nabokov by playing Lana del Ray's songs that explicitly reference *Lolita* and by having *The Stories of Vladimir Nabokov* adorn the bookcase of a high school teacher who is sleeping with one of his underage students. Yet *Pathetic* doesn't only focus on the trauma of becoming a woman or growing old in a world still full of hatred toward women. It also celebrates female desire, which in and of itself is an act of resistance. As Miriam Felton-Dansky points out in her piece about *Pathetic*, as a society, "we've persisted in understanding women's sexualities as disgusting, and female desire as maybe even a little bit reprehensible."[65] Most importantly, all of these plays move away from the pernicious trope of tracing all of a female protagonist's motivations back to an act of violence done to her. As Clare Barron eloquently notes in her "Playwright's Perspective," which accompanies the script to *Dance Nation*, she wanted "to present a different picture of teenage girls onstage. One where trauma wasn't the central narrative. One where 'being the best' was."[66] Putting texts that celebrate young girls' perseverance, not only their traumas, in dialogue with Nabokov's *Lolita* can lead to productive conversations in the classroom about what kind of stories of girlhood our culture perpetuates. This comparative exercise can also shed light on those things about Dolly in *Lolita* that Véra Nabokov wished "someone would notice"—"her heartrending courage all along, culminating in that squalid but essentially pure and healthy marriage, and her letter, and her dog."[67]

CONCLUSION

Whether or not Nabokov's novel has "contributed to a 'Lolita myth'" is up for debate.[68] Yet so many cultural symbols (like those red heart-shaped sunglasses, found nowhere in the text, and that Jeffrey Epstein Lolita Express plane) are associated with Nabokov's incendiary novel (no matter how misappropriated, misread, or corrupted) that they can no longer be ignored and should be analyzed along with the novel. My own first encounter with *Lolita* took place not by reading Nabokov's novel, which I only got to in college, but by seeing and misunderstanding Adrian Lyne's film when I was twelve. Today, thanks to the internet, children are exposed to even more inappropriate material at an even younger age. Nabokov's *Lolita*, of course, already explored this thorny question of text versus image. Studying *Lolita* together with its transmedial transgressions onto the stage, screen, and popular culture is particularly important in the #MeToo era, when social media has helped propel social movements and has also made critical reflection as urgent as ever. In particular, witnessing how Nabokov's novel does not lend itself well to a stage or screen adaptation might encourage us to turn our attention to those works that portray the trials and tribulations of girlhood. The goal is not to boycott or replace Nabokov's *Lolita*, but rather to put his novel in conversation with women-centric narratives. After all, many of these stories, like Paula Vogel's *How I Learned to Drive*, address the joy and pain of becoming a woman—a time in which reading Nabokov's *Lolita* is a formative experience.

WORKS CITED

Barish, Jonas A. *The Antitheatrical Prejudice*. Berkeley: University of California Press, 1981.
Barron, Clare. *Dance Nation*. New York: Samuel French, 2019.
Bolter, Jay David, and Richard Grusin. *Remediation: Understanding New Media*. Cambridge: MIT Press, 1999.
Boyd, Brian. *Vladimir Nabokov: The American Years*. Princeton: Princeton University Press, 1991.
Bunzel, Peter. "Yes, They Did It. *Lolita* Is a Movie," *Life*, May 25, 1962.
Churchwell, Sarah. "Pushing Back: Why It's Time for Women to Rewrite the Story." *The Guardian*, February 17, 2018. https://www.theguardian.com/books/2018/feb/17/pushing-back-why-its-time-for-women-to-rewrite-the-story.
Connolly, Julian W. "Who Was Dolly Haze?" *A Reader's Guide to Nabokov's Lolita*. Boston: Academic Studies Press, 2009. 53–66.
Couturier, Maurice. *Nabokov ou la Tyrannie de l'auteur*. Paris: Éditions du Seuil, collection Poétique, 1993.
de la Durantaye, Leland. *Style Is Matter: The Moral Art of Vladimir Nabokov*. Ithaca: Cornell University Press, 2007.
DeLappe, Sarah. *The Wolves*. New York: Samuel French, 2016.
Derrida, Jacques. *Dissemination*. Translated by Barbara Johnson. Chicago: University of Chicago Press, 1983.
Dwyer, Anne. "Why I Teach Lolita." *Inside Higher Ed*, May 14, 2018. https://www.insidehighered.com/views/2018/05/14/teaching-lolita-still-appropriate-opinion.
Edelstein, Marilyn. "Teaching *Lolita* in a Course on Ethics and Literature." In *Approaches to Teaching Nabokov's Lolita*. Edited by Zoran Kuzmanovich and Galya Diment. New York: The Modern Language Association of America, 2008. 43–8.
Felton-Dansky, Miriam. "Blood Sacrifice: Adolescence, Borderlands, and Love in Julia Jarcho's *Pathetic*." *The Brooklyn Rail*, June 2019. https://brooklynrail.org/2019/06/theater/Blood-Sacrifice-Adolescence-Borderlands-and-Love-in-Julia-Jarchos-Pathetic.
Flanagan, Caitlin. "How *Lolita* Seduces Us All." *The Atlantic*, September 2018. https://www.theatlantic.com/magazine/archive/2018/09/how-lolita-seduces-us-all/565751/.
Frank, Siggy. *Nabokov's Theatrical Imagination*. Cambridge: Cambridge University, 2012.
Gateward, Frances, and Murray Pomerance, eds. *Sugar, Spice, and Everything Nice: Cinemas of Girlhood* (Contemporary Approaches to Film and Media Series). Detroit: Wayne State University Press, 2002.
Greenberg, Clement. "Modernist Painting." In *Modern Art and Modernism: A Critical Anthology*. Edited by Francis Frascina and Charles Harrison. New York: Routledge, 1983. 5–10.
Harrower, David. *Blackbird*. London: Faber and Faber, 2005.
Herbold, Sarah. "'Dolorès Disparue': Reading Misogyny in *Lolita*." In *Approaches to Teaching Nabokov's Lolita*. Edited by Zoran Kuzmanovich and Galya Diment. New York: The Modern Language Association of America, 2008. 134–40.

Holmberg, Arthur. "Through the Eyes of Lolita." Interview with Paula Vogel. November 17, 2009. https://americanrepertorytheater.org/media/through-the-eyes-of-lolita/.
Hutcheon, Linda. *A Theory of Adaptation*. Hoboken: CRC Press, 2006.
Jarcho, Julia. *Pathetic*. Performance. The Abrons Art Center. New York, NY. June 18, 2019.
Jenkins, Henry. *Convergence Culture: Where Old and New Media Collide*. New York: New York University Press, 2006.
Karshan, Thomas. *Vladimir Nabokov and the Art of Play*. Oxford: Oxford University Press, 2011.
Kauffman, Linda S. "Framing Lolita: Is There a Woman in the Text?" In *Special Delivery: Epistolary Modes in Modern Fiction*. Chicago: University of Chicago Press, 1992. 53–80.
Kuzmanovich, Zoran, and Galya Diment, eds. *Approaches to Teaching Nabokov's Lolita*. New York: Modern Language Association of America, 2008.
Lemon, Lee T., and Marion J. Reis, eds. *Russian Formalist Criticism: Four Essays*. 2nd ed. Translated and introduction by Lee T. Lemon and Marion J. Reis. With a new introduction by Gary Saul Morson. Lincoln: University of Nebraska, 2012.
Ms. Lola. "Surviving *Lolita*: Adapting Nabokov's 'Pentapod Monsters' for the #MeToo Era." *Medium*, June 2, 2018. https://medium.com/@mslola/surviving-lolita-adapting-nabokovs-pentapod-monsters-for-the-metoo-era-9d781a8dd1d3.
Mandelbaum, Ken. *Not Since Carrie: Forty Years of Broadway Musical Flops*. New York: St. Martin's, 1992.
Menand, Louis. "Just Like a Woman." *Slate*, August 5, 1998. http://www.slate.com/articles/arts/television/1998/08/just_like_a_woman.html.
Miller, E. Ce. "I Re-Read Lolita in the Age of #MeToo—And I'm No Longer Standing for Its Overt Misogyny." *Bustle*, June 27, 2018. https://www.bustle.com/p/i-re-read-lolita-in-the-age-of-metoo-im-no-longer-standing-for-its-overt-misogyny-9567151.
Nabokov, Vladimir. *The Annotated Lolita*, rev. and updated edition, edited by Alfred Appel Jr. New York: Vintage International, 1991.
———. *Despair* [1965]. New York: Vintage International, 1989.
———. *Lectures on Literature*. Introduction by John Updike. New York: Harcourt, 1980.
———. *Novels 1955–1962*. New York: The Library of America, 1996.
———. *Selected Letters, 1940–1977*. Edited by Dmitri Nabokov and Matthew Joseph Bruccoli. New York: Harcourt, 1989.
Naiman, Eric. *Nabokov, Perversely*. Ithaca: Cornell, 2010.
Parker, Stephen Jan. *Understanding Vladimir Nabokov*. Columbia: University of South Carolina Press, 1987.
Peitzman, Louis. "An Infamous *Lolita* Musical Gets a Belated New York Debut." *The New York Times*, February 18, 2019. https://www.nytimes.com/2019/02/18/theater/lolita-my-love-york-theater-company-alan-jay-lerner.html.
Pellegrini, Ann. "Staging Sexual Injury: *How I Learned to Drive*." *Critical Theory and Performance*. Rev. and enlarged ed. Edited by Janelle G. Reinelt and Joseph R. Roach. Ann Arbor: University of Michigan Press, 2007. 413–31.
Pera, Pia. *Lo's Diary*. Translated by Ann Goldstein. Foreword by Dmitri Nabokov. New York: Foxrock, 1999.
Pifer, Ellen. *Nabokov and the Novel*. Cambridge: Harvard University, 1980.
Puchner, Martin. *Stage Fright: Modernism, Anti-Theatricality, and Drama*. Baltimore: John Hopkins Press, 2002.
Rakhimova-Sommers, Elena, ed. *Nabokov's Women: The Silent Sisterhood of Textual Nomads*. Lanham: Lexington Books, 2017.
Rampton, David. *Vladimir Nabokov*. New York: St. Martin's, 1993.
Rodgers, Michael, and Susan Elizabeth Sweeney, eds. *Nabokov and the Question of Morality: Aesthetics, Metaphysics, and the Ethics of Fiction*. New York: Palgrave Macmillan, 2016.
Rousuck, Wynn J. "Paula Vogel's Road Home: *How I Learned to Drive* Has Propelled the Maryland-Bred Playwright into Prominence and Given Her License to Take on Projects and Issues Close to Her Heart." *The Baltimore Sun*, May 3, 1998. https://www.baltimoresun.com/news/bs-xpm-1998-05-03-1998123004-story.html.
Russell, Kate Elizabeth. *My Dark Vanessa*. New York: Harper Collins, 2020.

Schiff, Stacy. *Véra (Mrs. Vladimir Nabokov)*. New York: Random House, 1999.

Skafidas, Michael. "Reading *Lolita* in the #MeToo Era." *The Washington Post*, June 27, 2018. https://www.washingtonpost.com/news/theworldpost/wp/2018/06/27/mario-vargas-llosa/.

Smith, Zadie. "Fascinated to Presume: In Defense of Fiction." *The New York Review of Books*, October 24, 2019. https://www.nybooks.com/articles/2019/10/24/zadie-smith-in-defense-of-fiction/.

Spiegel, Ruby Rae. *Dry Land*. New York: Dramatists Play Service Inc., 2015.

Sweeney, Elizabeth. "Lolita, I Presume; On a Character Entitled 'Lolita.'" *Miranda* 3 (2010): 1–12.

Vickers, Graham. *Chasing Lolita: How Popular Culture Corrupted Nabokov's Little Girl All Over Again*. Chicago: Chicago Review Press, 2008.

Vogel, Paula. *How I Learned to Drive* [1997]. *The Mammary Plays*. New York: Theatre Communications Group, 1998.

Weinman, Sarah. *The Real Lolita: The Kidnapping of Sally Horner and the Novel that Scandalized the World*. New York: Ecco Press, 2018.

Wood, James. "Pnin." Lecture at Harvard University, Cambridge, MA, April 10, 2005.

Wood, Michael. *The Magician's Doubts: Nabokov and the Risks of Fiction*. London: Chatto & Windus, 1994.

Zhulina, Alisa. "Queen Sacrifice: The Feminine Figure of Power and Nabokov's Strategy of Loss." *Nabokov's Women: The Silent Sisterhood of Textual Nomads*. Edited by Elena Rakhimova-Sommers. Lanham: Lexington Books, 2017. 19–36.

NOTES

1. Kate Elizabeth Russell, *My Dark Vanessa* (New York: Harper Collins, 2020), 72–73.

2. Peter Bunzel, "Yes, They Did It: *Lolita* Is a Movie," *Life*, May 25, 1962. PCA File for *Lolita*, Margaret Herrick Library of the Academy of Motion Picture Arts and Sciences, Beverly Hills. Quoted in Frances Gateward and Murray Pomerance, eds., *Sugar, Spice, and Everything Nice: Cinemas of Girlhood* (Contemporary Approaches to Film and Media Series) (Detroit: Wayne State University Press, 2002), 177.

3. Vladimir Nabokov, *Selected Letters, 1940–1977*, ed. Dmitri Nabokov and Matthew Joseph Bruccoli (New York: Harcourt, 1989), 250.

4. Graham Vickers, *Chasing Lolita: How Popular Culture Corrupted Nabokov's Little Girl All Over Again* (Chicago: Chicago Review Press, 2008).

5. I prefer to call the character Dolly because this is how she signs her name and not Lolita, which is the pet name used by Humbert, to distinguish between the "real" child that we don't get to see all that much and Humbert's solipsistic vision of her. See Julian W. Connolly, "Who Was Dolly Haze?" *A Reader's Guide to Nabokov's Lolita* (Boston: Academic Studies Press, 2009), 53–66, and Elizabeth Sweeney, "Lolita, I Presume; On a Character Entitled 'Lolita,'" *Miranda* 3 (2010): 1–12.

6. Vickers, *Chasing Lolita*, 132–36. See also Ken Mandelbaum, *Not Since Carrie: Forty Years of Broadway Musical Flops* (New York: St. Martin's, 1992), 189–91.

7. Vickers, *Chasing Lolita*, 135.

8. Vickers, *Chasing Lolita*, 136–41, 139.

9. Vladimir Nabokov, *Novels 1955–1962* (New York: The Library of America, 1996), 673. See also Brian Boyd, *Vladimir Nabokov: The American Years* (Princeton: Princeton University Press, 2016), 386–7.

10. Siggy Frank, *Nabokov's Theatrical Imagination* (Cambridge: Cambridge University, 2012), 1 and 47–50.

11. Frank, *Nabokov's Theatrical Imagination*, 48–49. See also Martin Puchner, *Stage Fright: Modernism, Anti-Theatricality, and Drama* (Baltimore: John Hopkins Press, 2002). For the importance of play in Nabokov, see Thomas Karshan, *Vladimir Nabokov and the Art of Play* (Oxford: Oxford University Press, 2011).

12. Jonah Barish, *The Antitheatrical Prejudice* (Berkeley: University of California Press, 1981), 1–3. Barish notes, however, that "the prejudice in question" is not "confined to the West, especially as it applies to actors," 2.

13. Nabokov, *Annotated Lolita*, 316.

14. As Maurice Couturier notes, "few authors have, as much as Nabokov, sought to orient the deciphering of their own works." Maurice Couturier, *Nabokov ou la Tyrannie de l'auteur* (Paris: Éditions du Seuil, collection Poétique, 1993), 382.

15. Linda Hutcheon, *A Theory of Adaptation* (Hoboken: CRC Press, 2006), 7–8.

16. Clement Greenberg, "Modernist Painting," in *Modern Art and Modernism: A Critical Anthology*, ed. Francis Frascina and Charles Harrison (New York: Routledge, 1983), 5–10. Originally printed in *Art and Literature* 4 (Spring 1965): 193–201.

17. Jay David Bolter and Richard Grusin, *Remediation: Understanding New Media* (Cambridge: MIT Press, 1999), 24.

18. For more on Russian Formalism, see Lee T. Lemon and Marion J. Reis, eds., *Russian Formalist Criticism: Four Essays*, 2nd ed., trans. and intro Lee T. Lemon and Marion J. Reis, with a new intro Gary Saul Morson (Lincoln: University of Nebraska, 2012).

19. Hutcheon, *A Theory of Adaptation*, 34.

20. Vladimir Nabokov, "Good Readers and Good Writers," *Lectures on Literature*, with an introduction by John Updike (New York: Harcourt, 1980), 1–6, 1.

21. Nabokov, *Annotated Lolita*, 314.

22. Michael Wood, *The Magician's Doubts: Nabokov and the Risks of Fiction* (London: Chatto & Windus, 1994), 107. For more on the relationship between ethics and literature in Nabokov and on how to read *Lolita* as a moral book, see Leland de la Durantaye, *Style Is Matter: The Moral Art of Vladimir Nabokov* (Ithaca: Cornell University, 2007); Stephen Jan Parker, *Understanding Vladimir Nabokov* (Columbia: University of South Carolina Press, 1987); Ellen Pifer, *Nabokov and the Novel* (Cambridge: Harvard University, 1980); David Rampton, *Vladimir Nabokov* (New York: St. Martin's, 1993); Michael Rodgers and Susan Elizabeth Sweeney, eds., *Nabokov and the Question of Morality: Aesthetics, Metaphysics, and the Ethics of Fiction* (New York: Palgrave Macmillan, 2016).

23. Marilyn Edelstein, "Teaching *Lolita* in a Course on Ethics and Literature," in *Approaches to Teaching Nabokov's Lolita*, ed. Zoran Kuzmanovich and Galya Diment (New York: The Modern Language Association of America, 2008), 43–48.

24. James Wood, "Pnin" (lecture, Harvard University, Cambridge, MA, April 12, 2005).

25. Sarah Herbold, "'Dolorès Disparue': Reading Misogyny in *Lolita*," in *Approaches to Teaching Nabokov's Lolita*, ed. Zoran Kuzmanovich and Galya Diment (New York: The Modern Language Association of America, 2008), 134–40, 134.

26. Anne Dwyer, "Why I Teach Lolita," *Inside Higher Ed*, May 14, 2018, https://www.insidehighered.com/views/2018/05/14/teaching-lolita-still-appropriate-opinion.

27. Dwyer, "Why I Teach Lolita."

28. E. Ce Miller, "I Re-Read *Lolita* in the Age of #MeToo—And I'm No Longer Standing for Its Overt Misogyny," *Bustle*, June 27, 2018, https://www.bustle.com/p/i-re-read-lolita-in-the-age-of-metoo-im-no-longer-standing-for-its-overt-misogyny-9567151.

29. Sarah Weinman, *The Real Lolita: The Kidnapping of Sally Horner and the Novel that Scandalized the World* (New York: Ecco Press, 2018), 32.

30. Michael Skafidas, "Reading *Lolita* in the #MeToo Era," *The Washington Post*, June 27, 2018, https://www.washingtonpost.com/news/theworldpost/wp/2018/06/27/mario-vargas-llosa/.

31. Ms. Lola, "Surviving *Lolita*: Adapting Nabokov's 'Pentapod Monsters' for the #MeToo Era," *Medium*, June 2, 2018, https://medium.com/@mslola/surviving-lolita-adapting-nabokovs-pentapod-monsters-for-the-metoo-era-9d781a8dd1d3.

32. Nabokov, *Annotated Lolita*, 5.

33. Vladimir Nabokov, *Despair* [1965] (New York: Vintage International, 1989), xiii.

34. Nabokov, *Annotated Lolita*, 309. de la Durantaye, *Style Is Matter*, 84–99.

35. Sarah Churchwell, "Pushing Back: Why It's Time for Women to Rewrite the Story," *The Guardian*, February 17, 2018, https://www.theguardian.com/books/2018/feb/17/pushing-back-why-its-time-for-women-to-rewrite-the-story.

36. Caitlin Flanagan, "How *Lolita* Seduces Us All," *The Atlantic*, September 2018, https://www.theatlantic.com/magazine/archive/2018/09/how-lolita-seduces-us-all/565751/.

37. For more on the silence of women in Nabokov, see Elena Rakhimova-Sommers, ed., *Nabokov's Women: The Silent Sisterhood of Textual Nomads* (Lanham: Lexington Books, 2017).

38. Churchwell, "Pushing Back."

39. Herbold, "'Dolorès Disparue,'" 137. See also Linda S. Kauffman, "Framing Lolita: Is There a Woman in the Text?" *Special Delivery: Epistolary Modes in Modern Fiction* (Chicago: University of Chicago Press, 1992), 53–80.

40. Wood, *The Magician's Doubts*, 115.

41. Ibid., 117.

42. Jacques Derrida, *Dissemination*, trans. Barbara Johnson (Chicago: University of Chicago Press, 1983), 71–72.

43. For more on the difference between an extension and an adaptation, see Henry Jenkins, *Convergence Culture: Where Old and New Media Collide* (New York: New York University Press, 2006), 284.

44. Nabokov, *Annotated Lolita*, 231.

45. Louis Menand, "Just Like a Woman," *Slate,* August 5, 1998, http://www.slate.com/articles/arts/television/1998/08/just_like_a_woman.html.

46. On the troubles that Lyne's *Lolita* had with distribution and the law, see Vickers, *Chasing Lolita*, 185–204.

47. Louis Peitzman, "An Infamous *Lolita* Musical Gets a Belated New York Debut," *The New York Times*, February 18, 2019, https://www.nytimes.com/2019/02/18/theater/lolita-my-love-york-theater-company-alan-jay-lerner.html.

48. Eric Naiman, *Nabokov, Perversely* (Ithaca: Cornell University, 2010), 148.

49. de la Durantaye, *Style Is Matter*, 2.

50. Zadie Smith, "Fascinated to Presume: In Defense of Fiction," *The New York Review of Books*, October 24, 2019, https://www.nybooks.com/articles/2019/10/24/zadie-smith-in-defense-of-fiction/.

51. Pia Pera, *Lo's Diary*, trans. Ann Goldstein, with a Foreword by Dmitri Nabokov (New York: Foxrock, 1999).

52. J. Wynn Rousuck, "Paula Vogel's Road Home: *How I Learned to Drive* Has Propelled The Maryland-Bred Playwright into Prominence and Given Her License to Take On Projects and Issues Close to Her Heart," *The Baltimore Sun*, May 3, 1998, https://www.baltimoresun.com/news/bs-xpm-1998-05-03-1998123004-story.html.

53. Paula Vogel, *How I Learned to Drive* [1997], *The Mammary Plays* (New York: Theatre Communications Group, 1998), 1–92, 4.

54. Vogel, *How I Learned to Drive*, 50.

55. Arthur Holmberg, "Through the Eyes of Lolita," Interview with Paula Vogel, November 17, 2009, https://americanrepertorytheater.org/media/through-the-eyes-of-lolita/

56. Holmberg, "Through the Eyes of Lolita," 92.

57. On the nuanced and complicated representation of trauma and healing in *How I Learned to Drive*, see Ann Pellegrini, "Staging Sexual Injury: *How I Learned to Drive*," *Critical Theory and Performance*, rev. and enlarged ed., ed. Janelle G. Reinelt and Joseph R. Roach (Ann Arbor: University of Michigan Press, 2007), 413–31.

58. Flanagan, "How *Lolita* Seduces Us All."

59. Holmberg, "Through the Eyes of Lolita."

60. David Harrower, *Blackbird* (London: Faber and Faber, 2005), 85.

61. Naiman, *Nabokov, Perversely*, 148.

62. For more on the risks that Nabokov took by making Dolly's voice absent from *Lolita*, see Alisa Zhulina, "Queen Sacrifice: The Feminine Figure of Power and Nabokov's Strategy of Loss," *Nabokov's Women: The Silent Sisterhood of Textual Nomads*, ed. Eléna Rakhimova-Sommers (Lanham: Lexington Books, 2017), 19–36.

63. Barron, *Dance Nation*, 51.

64. *Pathetic*, by Julia Jarcho, The Abrons Art Center, New York, NY, June 18, 2019. For more on the production, see https://minortheater.org/tag/pathetic/.

65. Miriam Felton-Dansky, "Blood Sacrifice: Adolescence, Borderlands, and Love in Julia Jarcho's *Pathetic*," *The Brooklyn Rail*, June 2019, https://brooklynrail.org/2019/06/theater/Blood-Sacrifice-Adolescence-Borderlands-and-Love-in-Julia-Jarchos-Pathetic.
66. Clare Barron, *Dance Nation* (New York: Samuel French, 2019), 7.
67. Stacy Schiff, *Véra (Mrs. Vladimir Nabokov)* (New York: Random House, 1999), 236.
68. Dwyer, "Why I Teach *Lolita*."

Chapter Six

Three *Lolita*s

The Evolution of a Cultural Icon in Fiction and Film

Julian W. Connolly

Educators and students facing the prospect of reading and discussing Nabokov's *Lolita* in a classroom will frequently face the complex set of associations sparked by the very name of the work as well as the many preconceptions that adhere to the novel's reputation. Graham Vickers has written an entire book about the many ways the image of "Lolita" has been used and abused in popular culture since the time of the novel's appearance in 1955 (see Vickers, *Chasing Lolita*). The educator will of course want to address these preconceptions at the outset, and an important component of that initial discussion might be to highlight the need for an awareness of the cultural context(s) in which the novel was written and which have shaped its afterlife in the popular imagination.

The aim of this essay is to enhance the students' understanding of Nabokov's novel through the lens of a comparative analysis, contrasting the way the original novelist sought to fashion his reader's response to his work with its subsequent cinematic treatment by two filmmakers, Stanley Kubrick, whose *Lolita* was released in 1962, and Adrian Lyne, whose *Lolita* premiered in 1997. A focused analysis of these three works will reveal how the prevailing cultural conceptions and sensitivities of the time affected both the portrayal of the work's main characters and the works' reception by audiences over the last sixty years. As Todd Bayma and Gary Alan Fine have noted, "[r]eaders bring to novels expectations and presuppositions rooted in the interpretive communities to which they belong, which may be informed by occupation, nation, race, and gender" (Bayma and Fine, "Transformation," 175). After having become familiar with these cultural contexts, students can be asked to examine or reexamine their own cultural preconceptions and evaluate how these might inform their appreciation of Nabokov's text.

Nabokov wrote the original *Lolita* in the early 1950s, an era that was very different from our own in the late 2010s. An educator may wish to begin with an introduction to Nabokov, outlining his dual status both as an established author whose early reputation was forged among the Russian émigré community in Europe in the 1920s and 1930s, and as a relative newcomer to the United States (he arrived in 1940). The writer was an acute observer of the world around him, and his cultural sensitivity led him to pick up on and incorporate into his art a variety of socio-historical and cultural forces present in American society, such as racial prejudice, anti-Semitism, anxieties about nuclear war, and so on. Students looking for a deeper appreciation of this aspect of Nabokov's art can consult several helpful articles on these topics, including Susan Mizruchi's "*Lolita* in History" and Douglas Anderson's "Nabokov's Genocidal and Nuclear Holocausts in *Lolita*." Furthermore, as Brian Boyd has pointed out in the second volume of his comprehensive biography of Nabokov (*Vladimir Nabokov: The American Years*), Nabokov sought to provide an accurate sense of time, place, and character in his *Lolita* project, and so he conducted extensive research into a diverse range of subjects, including schoolgirl slang, the design of Colt revolvers, roadside advertising, popular music, etc. (see *The American Years*, 211). Along these lines, Rachel Bowlby has chronicled the extensive role of contemporary consumer culture in the texture of Nabokov's novel ("*Lolita* and the Poetry of Advertising").

In an interesting move, Nabokov transmuted his own exquisite sensitivity about the differences between the European culture he grew up in and that of contemporary America into the unusual figure of his first-person narrator Humbert Humbert, born in Paris to Swiss and English parents, and an immigrant to America who approached his new home from a position of ostensible cultural superiority. But Nabokov's Humbert exhibits other traits more significant than this. In his earlier writing Nabokov had long been interested in cases of obsession and desire as well as the peril of overestimating the power and merit of one's subjective perception of "reality" (a word Nabokov reminds us in his afterword to *Lolita* means "nothing without quotes" ["On a Book Entitled *Lolita*," *L* 312]). The student interested in this aspect of Nabokov's work could be directed to such Nabokov works as *The Eye* (originally published in Russian in 1930) and *Despair* (originally published in Russian in 1934).

When writing *Lolita*, Nabokov coupled the themes of subjective reality and obsessive desire with another profound artistic concern: the vulnerability of children and the perverse desire of some men to possess just such a vulnerable child. The clearest reflection of this concern is Nabokov's *The Enchanter*, which was originally written in Russian in 1939 but not published during Nabokov's lifetime. However, the story of the title figure's obsession with a little girl in *Enchanter* is told in the third person, whereas *Lolita*'s tale is related by a clever, eloquent, and deceptive first-person narrator. With the figure of Humbert Humbert Nabokov sought to create a literary protagonist who was obsessed with the sexual possession of a young adolescent girl and who tried to persuade himself (and his readers) that he felt a sincere love for this child, and that this love entitled him to ignore or dismiss the constraints of conventional morality. Describing the difficulty of constructing such a complex creation, Nabokov asserted in 1953: "This great and coily thing has had no precedent in literature" (*Selected Letters*, 140), and his manuscript was initially rejected by five different US publishing houses.

One of the most crucial factors that students need to be aware of in dealing with a figure like Humbert Humbert is the inherent power of a first-person narrator in literature. Adding to the natural tendency of a reader to identify with the individual telling the tale, a narrator such as Humbert Humbert strives to control the reader's perception of events using a variety of rhetorical techniques such as direct invocations to the reader, concealing or distorting certain aspects of crucial events, and so on.[1] Indeed, as is generally the case with first-person narration, Humbert is the sole source of information on (and evaluation of) most of the events and characters in his narrative. While narrating *Lolita*, Humbert tries to exude charm, wit, cleverness, and self-deprecation, and through Humbert's narrative Nabokov demonstrates the insidious way such an eloquent figure might actually seduce his readers as well as an impressionable child. The novel thus becomes not just a blunt illustration of the evils of child abuse, but a cautionary tale about the dangers of smooth-talking snake oil salesmen in literature as in life.

And, for many readers, especially in the first few years after the novel appeared, it seems that Nabokov succeeded almost too well in making Humbert something of an appealing figure, and not a villain. Dorothy Parker called Humbert in 1958 "a man of taste and culture, who can love only little girls" ("Sex—without the Asterisks," 103). In the same year, Lionel Trilling wrote: "Humbert is perfectly willing to say that he is a monster; no doubt he is, but we find ourselves less and less eager to say so" ("The Last Lover," 14). Eight years later Martin Green would declare: "The sexually perverse enterprises of the main character are made funny, beautiful, pathetic, romantic tragic; in five or six way we are made to sympathize with him in them." He then continued: "Humbert Humbert is our protagonist [. . .] he represents a part of ourselves we are normally proud of [. . .] He is ourselves, without our inhibitions, acting out our tendencies" ("The Morality of *Lolita*," 365, 369–70). In contrast, many of the early readers and reviewers of the novel were quick to find fault with the object of Humbert's obsession, Dolores Haze. Parker described her as "a dreadful little creature, selfish, hard, vulgar, and foul-tempered" ("Sex—without the Asterisks," 103). Thomas Molnar voiced a similar view: "she is a spoiled sub-teenager with a foul mouth, a self-offered target for lechers, movie-magazine editors, and corrupt classmates" ("Matter-of-Fact Confession of a Non-Penitent," 102). Leslie Fiedler used even more extreme language in his condemnation, characterizing Dolly as "Annabel Lee as nymphomaniac, domonic rapist of the soul" (*Love and Death in the American Novel*, 327)!

How could this be? Why were these early critics so one-sided in their empathy with Humbert and their disdain for Dolly? I think we can identify two forces at work. First, of course, is Humbert's own rhetorical skill. He is a master at manipulating his reader's response to his self-presentation, deploying a broad range of rhetorical techniques. He uses wit and humor in abundance, he projects a posture of assumed equality or comradeship with his reader, and he frequently asks for the reader to sympathize with him or receive his tale with understanding. Here is one such plea: "Please, reader: no matter your exasperation with the tenderhearted, morbidly sensitive, infinitely circumspect hero of my book, do not skip these essential pages! Imagine me; I shall not exist if you do not imagine me; try to discern the doe in me, trembling in the forest of my own iniquity; let's even smile a little" (*L* 129). At one point, he even asks the reader to take part in his first attempt at stealing sexual gratification from an unsuspecting Dolly: "I want my learned readers to participate in the scene I am about to replay" (*L* 57).

Along with Humbert's own efforts at manipulating the reader, the second factor affecting his early readers' reactions to the novel is what may be called the "bad girl" stereotype that had become popular in American culture in the mid-1950s. As Todd Bayma and Gary Alan Fine have argued in their article "Fictional Figures and Imaginary Relations: The Transformation of Lolita from Victim to Vixen," several factors in the postwar years (such as "the emergence of a consumer market for teenagers, a decrease in parental authority [. . .] and greater evidence of premarital sexuality") led many adults to believe that the prevalence of sexual intercourse among teenagers was increasing, even though it had not actually increased significantly at this time ("Transformation," 169). Their article continues: "The contrast of 'good girl' and 'bad girl' became a feature of white girls' public identity and behavior, in the midst of a gender-based double standard that simultaneously encouraged and condemned the expression of sexuality" ("Transformation," 169). In Bayma's and Fine's opinion, these cultural beliefs fashioned the lens through which many contemporary critics looked at *Lolita* and its young heroine. Indeed, their research shows that contemporary reviewers, especially those who admired the novel, "depicted Dolores Haze as an unworthy, discredited person—a sexually precocious, unpleasant, and ill-willed girl, even though she is only known through her presentation by Humbert" ("Transformation," 168).[2]

However, if one approaches the text more skeptically (as succeeding generations of readers and critics have done), one sees that Humbert not only flaunts his supposed superiority and sensitivity before the reader, but he consistently downplays or minimizes the sensitivities and feelings of others, including his two wives, Valeria and Charlotte, whom he mocks mercilessly. This is especially tragic in the case of Dolly herself. One notes that Humbert consistently prefers to call the child "Lolita" rather than Dolly or Dolores, thus emphasizing his obsession with a fantasy figure that he has created for himself rather than with a real child who possesses her own identity and her own inner world.

In depicting this relationship, Nabokov skillfully shows how Humbert deploys some of the classic tactics of a child abuser both to "groom" Dolly for his predation[3] and to minimize his own responsibility for what transpires in the novel. Foremost among the latter is blaming the victim. First, near the beginning of his manuscript, he advances the theory that there is an entire class of little girls—"nymphets"—whose nature is "not human [. . .] but demoniac" (*L* 17). Such a girl stands out as a "little deadly demon among the wholesome children [. . .] unconscious herself of her fantastic power" (17). Second, he asserts that in their first sexual encounter in the Enchanted Hunters Hotel, "it was she who seduced me" (*L* 132). Characterizing this encounter further, he declares that she had been "utterly and hopelessly depraved" by "modern co-education, juvenile mores [. . .] and so on" (*L* 133). As I noted above, Humbert's point of view here proved persuasive to his early reviewers (many of whom, like Humbert, were male), and they echoed him in a chorus: from their perspective Dolly was "thoroughly corrupted already" (Nemerov, "The Morality of Art," 320), "completely corrupt" (Hollander, "The Perilous Magic of Nymphets," 558), and "singularly experienced, vulgar and depraved" (Hutchens, "Lolita," 13).

Yet the actual author of *Lolita*, Vladimir Nabokov, shapes Humbert's narrative in such a way that it becomes clear to the discriminating reader that Humbert's presentation of Dolly's corruption and her eagerness to participate in carnal relations was not quite as facile as he first intimates. As they drive away from the hotel, Dolly calls Humbert a "brute" and he himself recognizes: "This was an orphan. This was a lone child, an absolute waif, with whom a heavy-limbed, foul-smelling adult had had strenuous intercourse three times that very morning" (*L* 140). Humbert's relentless focus on Dolly's body (listing her measurements, weight, various body odors, etc.) and not on her soul, and his increasingly aggressive desire for control over that body continues in part II of the novel. Here too students will find it instructive to see how Nabokov has Humbert display the common stratagems of a child abuser: restricting access to other, using a variety of ploys to entice Dolly into giving him sexual satisfaction, and so on.[4] One particular tactic stands out: the purchase of consumer items to put Dolly in a docile mood.

Early during his stay in the Haze household, Humbert observed that "any wearable purchase worked wonders with Lo" (*L* 64) and he later called her "the ideal consumer" (*L* 148). Humbert's attitude here is perhaps modeled on a Russian novel that Nabokov translated in the mid-1950s, Mikhail Lermontov's *A Hero of Our Time*, in which the Russian protagonist, Grigory Pechorin, having arranged the abduction of young native woman named Bela, tries to win her affection by buying her clothing and fabric. His companion, Maksim Maksimich, comments cynically: "What won't a woman do for a bit of colored rag" (*Hero of Our Time*, 25). Here one notes that the theme of abduction and seduction of a young female carries with it notes of political and cultural imperialism, notes not alien to *Lolita* either.

During the second part of the novel we see another disturbing aspect of Humbert's callousness: his psychological abuse of Dolly. As he later acknowledges, it was through his "reformatory threat" (i.e., scary scenes of her being turned over to a correctional school, a reformatory, a juvenile detention home) that he "succeeded in terrorizing Lo" (*L* 151). Furthermore, he did not shy away from resorting to physical force to achieve his ends when it suited his purpose. At one point in part II when Dolly began to show signs of resistance and independence, Humbert seized her by the wrist and "in fact hurt her badly [. . .] and once or twice she jerked her arm so violently that I feared her wrist might snap" (*L* 205). In an especially significant revelation in the context of later adaptations of *Lolita*, Humbert makes it clear to the reader that Dolly never responded to his sexual demands with any reciprocal feelings of sensual arousal: "Never did she vibrate under my touch, and a strident 'what d'you think you are doing' was all I got for my pains" (*L* 266). Later in the novel, after Dolly has abandoned him, Humbert takes stock of his behavior and seems to acknowledge his consistent insensitivity to Dolly's emotional needs and wants. He writes: "Now, squirming and pleading with my own memory, I recall that on this and similar occasions, it was always my habit and method to ignore Lolita's states of mind while comforting my own base self" (*L* 287). He further recognizes that "I simply did not know a thing about my darling's mind and that quite possibly, behind the awful juvenile clichés, there was in her a garden and a twilight, and a palace gate" (*L* 284).

This was the situation that the orphan Dolly Haze had to put up with for two years. In some of the most poignant lines of the book, Humbert conveys the terrible injury he has perpetrated on his young captive. Summing up his impressions of their first road trip together, Humbert writes that as that trip came to an end, it was "no more to us than a collection of dog-eared maps, ruined tour books, old tires, and her sobs in the night—every night, every night—the moment I feigned sleep" (*L* 176). Humbert's repetition of the phrase "every night" is simply haunting. Yet the die was cast from the moment he took advantage of her during their stay at the Enchanted Hunters Hotel. At the very next hotel, they booked separate rooms, but in the middle of the night "she came sobbing into mine, and we made it up very gently." The reason? "You see, she had absolutely nowhere else to go" (*L* 142).

And yet, Dolly does eventually summon up the courage and the will to escape, even though her agent for this escape—Clare Quilty—is another pedophile like Humbert. Nonetheless, by the end of Humbert's narrative, Dolly seems to be on the way to creating a more or less "normal" life for herself. She is married, pregnant, and looking forward to moving with her husband to Alaska for new opportunities. Tragically, as the reader has learned from John Ray's introduction to Humbert's manuscript, the unfortunate young woman did not live to see this new life unfold: she died in childbirth. Although Humbert never discovers Dolly's fate (unless one accepts the reading of the tale advanced by Alexander Dolinin, who argues that Dolly died in a hospital in Elphinstone[5]), he seems to acknowledge toward the end of his narrative that he understands the damage he has done to Dolly and expresses remorse for his actions. In chapter 31 of part II, he declares that "nothing could make my Lolita forget the foul lust I had inflicted upon her" (*L* 283). And he then launches into metaphysical speculation: "Unless it can be proven to me [. . .] that in the infinite run it does not matter a jot that a North American girl-child had been deprived of her childhood by a maniac, unless this can be proven (and if it can, then life is a joke), I see nothing for the treatment of my misery but the melancholy and very local palliative of articulate art" (*L* 283, emphasis added).

On the one hand, Humbert's willingness to admit that the injuries he inflicted upon Dolly may have had the effect of validating the image of *himself* as a sensitive victim ruined by own obsessions to some of the early reviewers of the novel. Elizabeth Janeway wrote "I can only say that Humbert's fate seems to me classically tragic [. . .] Humbert is the hero with the tragic flaw. Humbert is every man who is driven by desire [. . .] Humbert is all of us" ("The Tragedy of a Man Driven by Desire," 25). And John Hutchens states: "Humbert is not the seducer but the seduced [. . .] He, rather than she [Dolly] is the victim of his obsession" ("Lolita," 13). On the other hand, Humbert's belated professions of remorse may indicate the development with Humbert of an authentic conscience and a spirit of genuine repentance. This is the view adopted by many critics of the novel in the decades following the work's initial publication. Ellen Pifer, for example, argues that Humbert "perceives the devastating effects that his solipsistic ardor has had on Lolita's life, and it is this understanding that lends such depth and poignancy to his narration" (*Nabokov and the Novel*, 165). Yet not all readers are convinced that Humbert has felt genuine repentance (or was even capable of it). Michael Wood, for one, confesses that he has a hard time accepting Humbert's profession of true love for Dolly when he sees her in the Coalmont reunion scene "pale and polluted, and big with another's child" (*L* 278): "I can't believe in Humbert's new love partly because there is nothing in his self-portrait to suggest he can rise to it, and partly because he is protesting too much, hooked on his version of *Carmen*, too anxious for us to *see* the change in him" (*The Magician's Doubts*, 139). And Brian Boyd is skeptical of the notion that Humbert has undergone some kind of moral epiphany when he discusses Humbert's desire to kill the man he assumed impregnated Dolly, even though this would mean killing the father of her unborn child: "How this planned murder of Lolita's unborn child's father would testify to Humbert's moral refinement [. . .] I cannot conceive" ("'Even Homais Nods,'" 85). This is an important debate that students can profitably engage in when discussing the book.

The indeterminacy or ambiguity that ultimately arises out of Humbert's narrative points to one of the most remarkable features of the novel. In *Lolita* Nabokov created a fiendishly double-voiced narrative. Readers who may be swept away by Humbert's manic eloquence often find themselves brought up short by a startling realization: while they may regard some aspects of Humbert's presentation to be appealing, especially at the outset, they may discover to their horror that they have been chuckling along with a very nasty individual. Ellen Pifer elucidates this reaction: "The outrage expressed by many of *Lolita*'s readers over the past fifty years may be due, at least in part, to the discomfort they feel at finding themselves taken in by the narrator's rhetoric, at realizing they have unwillingly accepted—and even identified with—Humbert's perverse desire" ("Introduction," 10–11).

What was Nabokov's own take on this? Does anything he has had to say shed light on how we should evaluate Humbert and his relationship with Dolly? Interestingly, he too seems to offer competing interpretations. In an interview conducted in 1964, Nabokov said: "I do think that Humbert in his last stage is a moral man because he realizes that he loves *Lolita* like any woman should be loved. But it is too late; he has destroyed her childhood" (Davis, "On the Banks of Lake Leman," 17). Yet just two years later, he corrected an interviewer who asserted that Humbert Humbert, "while comic, retains a touching and insistent quality—that of the spoiled artist." Nabokov retorted: "I would put it differently: Humbert Humbert is a vain and cruel wretch who manages to appear 'touching.'" And then he adds a crucial corrective: "That epithet, in its true, tear-iridized sense, can only apply to my poor little girl" (*Strong Opinions*, 94).

What is important to note here, especially in light of the #MeToo era's heightened consciousness of the victimization of women who frequently have had no voice or have had to remain passive in the face of the insults perpetrated on them, is Nabokov's redirection of the interviewer's attention to Dolly Haze: *she* is the one whose plight is authentically "touching," not that of the glib, talkative Humbert. His corrective points to one of the persistent patterns in the popular perception of who or what Dolly Haze—"Lolita"—was: a general tendency to overlook her status as victim struggling to be free from the domination of an possessive male and to overemphasize instead projected qualities of promiscuousness, precocious sexuality, etc. This creation of the "Lolita" stereotype began soon after the publication of the novel, and continued apace, much to the chagrin of Nabokov's wife Véra. Taking note of the attention showered on Humbert Humbert in the press, she wrote in her diary: "I wish, though, somebody would notice the tender description of the child's helplessness, her pathetic dependence on monstrous HH, and her heartrending courage all along [. . .] They all miss the fact that 'the horrid little brat' Lolita, is essentially very good indeed" (quoted by Stacy Schiff in *Véra*, 236).

Véra and Vladimir may have both deplored the tendency to underestimate the degree of Dolly's victimization and to overestimate her sexual precocity, but the first cinematic adaptation of the novel did not do much to dismantle those responses. In the summer of 1959, James Harris and Stanley Kubrick contacted Nabokov with an offer to write the screenplay for their proposed adaptation of *Lolita*; they had acquired the rights the previous year. Nabokov was hesitant to take on the job, however, and as he later indicated, his vision and that of the producers were not perfectly aligned. Concerned over how the censors might react, the producers wanted him to put in a scene hinting that "Humbert had been secretly married to Lolita all along" (*Lolita Screenplay*, vii). Thus he declined their offer. A few months later, however, he was again contacted by his agent with a lucrative financial offer to write the screenplay for Kubrick and Harris, and this time he acquiesced. He moved to California and began work on the screenplay, which ballooned in length to about four hundred pages.[6] Kubrick asked him to cut it down, which he did, and finally Kubrick accepted the revised screenplay. As it turned out, Kubrick would use only a small portion of Nabokov's screenplay for his movie, although he gave Nabokov full screenwriting credit. The film was released in 1962, and Nabokov was publicly very enthusiastic about it: "I thought the movie was absolutely first-rate" (*Strong Opinions*, 21). In his private diary, however, he was less laudatory, and compared the experience of watching the film to "a scenic drive as perceived by the horizontal passenger of an ambulance" (quoted in Boyd, *The American Years*, 466).

Indeed, Kubrick's film departed significantly from Nabokov's original design in several respects. For example, he gave a greatly expanded role to the character of Clare Quilty, who was played with frenetic energy by Peter Sellers. For some viewers, the film could have been called *Quilty*. Of course, of most significant for the present article is the film's treatment of Dolly, Charlotte, and other women. In his handling of the female characters and the issue of sexuality, Kubrick was very concerned about running afoul of the Motion Picture Production Code (informally known as the "Hays Code"—a neat homonym for Charlotte's and Dolly's surname), which forbade the display of various forms of "immoral" behavior—nudity, overt portrayals of sexual activity, etc.—in American films. Indeed, years later, he complained about this constraint: "because of all the pressure over the Production Code and the Catholic Legion of Decency at the time, I wasn't able to give any weight at all to the erotic aspect of Humbert's relationship with Lolita; and because his sexual obsession was only barely hinted at, it was assumed too quickly that Humbert was in love" ("Kubrick," interview by Gene Phillips, 32). He regarded this pressure as such a severe challenge that he subsequently confessed: "Had I realized how severe the [censorship] limitations were going to be, I probably wouldn't have made the film" (quoted in Boyd, *The American Years*, 466).

As a consequence of his concern, he decided in essence to *sanitize* the novel, toning down the transgressive sexual relationship between Humbert and Dolly. He eliminated all references to Humbert's pedophilia and nymphets, and he made Dolly older and more poised (Sue Lyons, the actress who played Dolly, was fifteen when the film was finished, and she looked several years older than that). This had the effect of reducing the age disparity between Humbert and Dolly, to the point where an early reviewer of the film, Bosley Crowther, wrote in the *New York Times*: "the factor of perverted desire that is in the book" is removed and Humbert's passion becomes "more normal and understandable [. . .] Older men have often pined for younger female. This is nothing new on the screen"("Lolita," 23).[7]

Further scrubbing Humbert's sexual background, Kubrick declined to depict his prior relationships with Annabel Leigh, his first wife Valeria, and the French prostitute named Monique. He also makes Humbert somewhat more inept than he might appear in the novel. Thus there is a notable slapstick scene in which Humbert haplessly (and unsuccessfully) tries to set up a cot in the bedroom of the Enchanted Hunters Hotel. Comic highlights are also added to the figure of Charlotte Haze, who, in Kubrick's treatment, becomes even more ludicrous and obnoxious than Humbert had portrayed her in the original novel. As played by Shelley Winters, Charlotte is a blowsy, sex-starved woman whose efforts to seduce Humbert are cringe-worthy. This sets the stage for many double-entendres such as a bedroom scene when Charlotte says to Humbert, "Hum, you just touch me and I go limp as a noodle." Humbert, played by James Mason with smooth aplomb, responds: "Yes, I know the feeling."

As for the title figure of the film, Dolly Haze seems much less vulnerable and childlike than the way she is presented in Nabokov's novel, and her transformation into Dick Schiller's pregnant wife gives the impression that she has made an important transition to stability and future happiness. In a stunning omission, Kubrick's film makes no mention of her premature death in childbirth, and the viewer who has not read Nabokov's *Lolita* would leave the theater with the impression that her life had turned out all right. The elision of any reference to premature death has the effect of further diminishing Dolly's condition as victim. The tag line on one of the original posters that advertised Kubrick's *Lolita* is "How did they ever make a movie of *Lolita*?" In his review of the film, Crowther gave a succinct response: "They didn't" ("Lolita," 23). As flippant as this remark may be, Crowther is essentially correct. Kubrick's *Lolita* is a different artistic work than Nabokov's. Clearly, there was a major shift from the intricate, controlling first-person narrative of Nabokov's *Lolita* to the cool command of a highly skilled cinematic auteur. And the tragedy of Nabokov's novel becomes, as the film critic Pauline Kael put it in 1962, "the first new comedy since [. . .] the 1940s [. . .] at times so far out that you gasp as you laugh" ("Lolita," 569).

As controversial or sensational as potential moviegoers believed that *Lolita* might be, the film itself proved to be much less so, and after some initial success, audience interest waned. Yet one feature of the film (or at least of the publicity for the film) retained its vital allure in the popular imagination: the poster image of the actress Sue Lyons wearing heart-shaped red sunglasses and sucking on a red lollipop. This became the iconic representation of that "Lolita" stereotype that has persisted to the present day.

When the filmmaker Adrian Lyne began efforts in 1990 to make a new film version of *Lolita*, he no longer had to worry about any adverse effects from the Production Code, which had been abandoned in the late 1960s with the institution of a rating system by the Motion Picture Association of America. Lyne had previously gained notoriety for slick movies that prominently relied on erotic and suspenseful elements—*Flashdance* (1983), *9 ½ Weeks* (1986), and *Fatal Attraction* (1987). This made some critics nervous about what he might do to *Lolita*. However, Lyne seemed to be interested not in creating a sensationalized adaptation, but something more serious, and he enlisted the help of various distinguished writers such as Harold Pinter and David Mamet before choosing a relative unknown, Stephen Schiff. The resulting film is very different from Stanley Kubrick's and it is much closer to Nabokov's original, although it contains some significant departures from that original as well.

For one thing, Schiff was insistent on recapturing the look and feel of the setting of Nabokov's original novel—the America of the 1940s, not that of a decade or so later, as in Kubrick's film. This the film does beautifully, augmented by a lush score by Ennio Morricone. Secondly, Schiff and Lyne wanted to restore to the character of Dolly the fact that she was a child, and not—as Schiff describes Sue Lyon's Lolita—"a twenty-year-old hooker" (*Lolita: The Book of the Film*, xviii). The casting of Dominique Swain as Dolly solved this problem. Although she was fifteen when filming was finished, she looks younger. But here is where the Lyne-Schiff version deviates from Nabokov's. Schiff felt that he had to "create a relationship between Lolita and Humbert, a relationship that the book's completely unreliable narrator, Humbert himself, only allows us glimpses of" (*Lolita: The Book of the Film*, xv–xvi). However, Nabokov had a specific reason for letting Humbert provide only "glimpses" of his relationship with Dolly: in essence, there *was* no relationship between Humbert and Dolly. Humbert consciously and consistently tried to ignore or block out any signs that Dolly had an independent mind or feelings of her own.

For their project, Lyne and Schiff were desperate to humanize Humbert and indicate that he and Dolly could actually have some kind of reciprocal relationship. Schiff writes about Humbert: "it seemed to me that Adrian's conception of Humbert was absolutely right: that we have to sympathize with and yes, love him even though his deeds revolt us" (*Lolita: The Book of the Film*, xvi). The resulting film character, played with great subtlety and empathy by Jeremy Irons, is a Humbert Humbert that Nabokov's Humbert would be quite pleased with. Irons portrays Humbert as a haunted being, deeply in love with Dolly and totally in thrall to her caprices and whims. Even more striking, though, is Lyne's and Schiff's conception of Dolly. Although Nabokov, through Humbert, makes it crystal clear that Dolly never responded to Humbert's sexual predations with a sensual arousal of her own ("Never did she vibrate under my touch" [*L* 266]), the Lyne film version includes a scene in which Dolly is shown having a fully erotic response to their sexual interaction. The Schiff screenplay presents the moment as follows: "She is breathing hard, and her eyes are very bright. She moans again. There seems no dividing line between her sexual pleasure and the pleasure she takes in the comics" that she is reading at the time (*Lolita: The Book of the Film*, 120).

Such a moment represents a sharp departure from Nabokov's vision of the one-sided relationship between Humbert and Dolly. It is not clear how many other such moments there may have been in the Lyne film if it were not for the intrusion of external events upon the editing process. In 1996 the US Congress passed the Child Pornography Prevention Act that criminalized not only actual child pornography but also any representation of sexual activity that make it appear as if children were involved, even if the actors are really adults. Lyne now began editing his film in the presence of a lawyer, and many scenes having to do with sex or nudity were excised. Anxiety about the new law, as well as publicity about the murder of a six-year-old beauty pageant contestant named JonBenét Ramsey in 1996, frightened potential distributors of the film, and after its premier in September 1997 at a film festival in Spain, the film saw only limited theatrical release in the United States. Viewers who watch Lyne's *Lolita* may be pleased with the look of 1940s America depicted on screen, but they will likely be disappointed with the transformation he worked in the relationship between Humbert and Dolly.

Changes wrought over time in the handling of the *Lolita* story have one element in common: they all reflect a concern with how much autonomy and sense of individual agency are given to Dolly. Humbert's narrative is the subtlest and the most challenging in this regard, for one has to read through his obfuscations and elisions to arrive at an approximate picture of the true situation. Kubrick's version is perhaps too bland, while Lyne's tips the balance too far in Humbert's favor. As this essay has attempted to show, a significant factor in the representation of Dolly and Humbert—and the way they are perceived by the reader or viewer—stems from the cultural environment in which they arose. To help enrich their understanding of this phenomenon, students living in the #MeToo era can be asked three questions: (1) What preconceptions or notions did you have about Nabokov's *Lolita* or the "Lolita" phenomenon before you read the novel? (2) Did your reading of the novel (and viewing of the films, if applicable) change after the experience of reading (or viewing) and learning about the cultural context in which the work appeared? (3) Do you think that there is anything to be gained by viewing the films after reading the novel? Does this triple perspective add depth to your understanding? When students have the opportunity to reflect on questions such as these, they may find their views changing or becoming more nuanced, and their appreciation for what Nabokov tried to do may increase as well.[8]

WORKS CITED

Anderson, Douglas. "Nabokov's Genocidal and Nuclear Holocausts in *Lolita*." *Mosaic* 29, no. 2 (1996): 73–90.

Bayma, Todd, and Gary Alan Fine, "Fictional Figures and Imaginary Relations: The Transformation of Lolita from Victim to Vixen," *Studies in Symbolic Interaction* 20 (1996): 165–78.

Bowlby, Rachel. "*Lolita* and the Poetry of Advertising." In *Shopping with Freud*. New York: Routledge, 1993. 46–71.

Boyd, Brian. "'Even Homais Nods': Nabokov's Fallibility or How to Revise *Lolita*." *Nabokov Studies* 2 (1995): 62–86.

———. *Vladimir Nabokov: The American Years*. Princeton: Princeton University Press, 1991.

Crowther, Bosley. "'Lolita,' Vladimir Nabokov's Adaptation of His Novel: Sue Lyon and Mason in Leading Roles." Review of Lolita (MGM movie). *New York Times*, June 14, 1962, 23.

Davis, Douglas M. "On the Banks of Lake Leman: Mr. Nabokov Reflects on 'Lolita' and 'Onegin.'" *National Observer*, June 29, 1964, 17.

Devlin, Rachel. *Relative Intimacy: Fathers, Adolescent Daughters, and Postwar American Culture*. Chapel Hill, NC: The University of North Carolina Press, 2005.

Dolinin, Alexander. "Nabokov's Time Doubling: From *The Gift* to *Lolita*." *Nabokov Studies* 2 (1995): 3–40.

Fiedler, Leslie A. *Love and Death in the American Novel*. New York: Criterion Books, 1960.

Green, Martin. "The Morality of *Lolita*." *Kenyon Review* 28, no. 3 (1966): 352–77.

Hollander, John. "The Perilous Magic of Nymphets." *Partisan Review* 23, no. 4 (1956): 557–60.

Hutchens, John K. "Lolita." *New York Herald Tribune*, August 18, 1958, 13.

Janeway, Elizabeth. "The Tragedy of a Man Driven by Desire." *New York Times Book Review*, August 17, 1958, 5, 25.

Kael, Pauline. "Lolita." *Partisan Review* 29, no. 4 (1962): 568–72.

Lermontov, Mikhail. *A Hero of Our Time*. Translated by Vladimir Nabokov in collaboration with Dmitri Nabokov. New York: Doubleday Anchor Books, 1958.

Mizruchi, Susan. "*Lolita* in History." *American Literature* 75, no. 3 (2003): 629–52.
Molnar, Thomas. "Matter-of-Fact Confession of a Non-Penitent." *Commonweal* 69, no. 4 (October 24, 1958): 102.
Nemerov, Howard. "The Morality of Art." *The Kenyon Review* 19, no. 2 (1957): 313–21.
Nabokov, Vladimir. "On a Book Entitled *Lolita*." In *The Annotated* Lolita. Edited by Alfred Appel, Jr. New York: Vintage Books, 1991. 311–17.
———. *Lolita: A Screenplay*. New York: Vintage International, 1997.
———. *Vladimir Nabokov. Selected Letters 1940–1977*. Edited by Dmitri Nabokov and Matthew J. Bruccoli. New York: Harcourt Brace Jovanovich / Bruccoli Clark Layman, 1989.
———. *Strong Opinions*. New York: Vintage International, 1990.
Parker, Dorothy. "Sex—without the Asterisks." *Esquire* 50 (October 1958): 102–103.
Phillips, Gene. "Kubrick." *Film Comment* 7, no. 4 (1971–1972): 30–35.
Pifer, Ellen. "Introduction." In *Vladimir Nabokov's* Lolita*: A Casebook*. Edited by Ellen Pifer. Oxford: Oxford University Press, 2003. 3–16.
———. *Nabokov and the Novel*. Cambridge, MA: Harvard University Press, 1980.
Schiff, Stacy. *Véra (Mrs. Vladimir Nabokov)*. New York: Modern Library, 2000.
Schiff, Stephen. "Introduction." *Lolita: The Book of the Film*. New York: Applause Books, 1998. x-xxviii.
Temir-Ghez, Nomi. "The Art of Persuasion in Nabokov's *Lolita*." *Poetics Today* 1, no. 1–2 (1979): 65–83.
Trilling, "The Last Lover: Vladimir Nabokov's *Lolita*." *Encounter* 11, no. 4 (October 1958): 9–19.
Vickers, Graham. *Chasing Lolita: How Popular Culture Corrupted Nabokov's Little Girl All Over Again*. Chicago: Chicago Review Press, 2008.
Williams, Lucia C. A. "Still Intrigued with *Lolita*: Nabokov's Visionary Work on Child Sexual Abuse." In *Lolita. Critical Insights*. Ed. Rachel Stauffer. Ipswich, MA: Grey House Publishing / Salem Press, 2016. 45–62.
Winters, Georgia M., and Elizabeth J. Jeglic. "Stages of Sexual Grooming: Recognizing Potentially Predatory Behaviors of Child Molesters." *Deviant Behavior* 38, no. 6 (2017): 724–33.
Wood, Michael. *The Magician's Doubts: Nabokov and the Risks of Fiction*. Princeton: Princeton University Press, 1995.

NOTES

1. For a discussion of this, see Nomi Temir-Ghez, "The Art of Persuasion in Nabokov's *Lolita*."

2. Another useful source of information about popular perceptions of teenage girls in the period after World War II and especially the relationship between girls and their fathers is Rachel Devlin's book *Relative Intimacy*. In chapter 5 she discusses *Lolita* and details how Humbert's relationship with Dolly echoes and parodies father-daughter relationships depicted in contemporary fiction and film (see pages 156–70).

3. For a concise description of the grooming process see Winters and Jeglich, "Stages of Sexual Grooming," 725–27.

4. See Lucia Williams's article, "Still Intrigued with *Lolita*: Nabokov's Visionary Work on Child Sexual Abuse" for a detailed discussion of this aspect of the novel.

5. See Dolinin, "Nabokov's Time Doubling: From *The Gift* to *Lolita*."

6. Nabokov's screenplay, in both its original draft form(s) and the version published by Nabokov in 1974, is worthy of study for its own treatment of Dolly Haze. In both versions, Dolly is given a more substantive presence than in the novel, where she is only as distinct to the reader as Humbert allows her to be. In the manuscript version, for example, she is depicted pleading with Quilty to help her escape from Humbert, and at one point, she even expresses fear that she might be pregnant.

7. A similar perspective was advanced by Herbert Gold, who interviewed Nabokov in 1966. He stated that in Hollywood and New York, "relationships are frequent between men of forty and girls very little older than Lolita. They marry—to no particular public outrage; rather,

public cooing." Nabokov's reaction to this is sharp and direct, and he offers a crucial correction: "cases of men in the forties marrying girls in the teens or early twenties have no bearing on Lolita whatever. Humbert was fond of 'little girls'—not simply 'young girls.' Nymphets are girl-children, not starlets and 'sex kittens.' Lolita was twelve, not eighteen, when Humbert met her" (*Strong Opinions*, 93).

8. This is the assignment that was given to students in an undergraduate course on Nabokov's fiction at the University of Virginia in the 2020 spring semester:

<u>Assignment on responses to *Lolita*</u>

I am interested in knowing how your reading of *Lolita* and our classes on the book may have changed any preconceptions you may have had about the book. So, *please send me by email* your response to the questions in the category that best fits your experience.

A. IF THIS WAS YOUR FIRST TIME READING *Lolita*:

Did you have preconceptions about the book? Were they changed as you read the book and participated in the class discussion? If so, how did they change?

B. IF YOU HAD READ *Lolita* BEFORE:

Did you get something out of this experience of reading the book for this course that you had not gained in your previous reading? If so, what?

FINALLY, do you have any suggestions on how first-time or re-readers of *Lolita* might get more from the experience of reading the book?

Chapter Seven

Dolores Haze

Author

Charles Byrd

Humbert Humbert's verbal pyrotechnics and sick, misogynistic humor have captivated generations of *Lolita*'s readers. In more than thirty years of teaching Vladimir Nabokov's most inflammatory novel to American undergraduates, students and I have attempted to analyze virtually every nook and cranny of Humbert's extravagant rhetoric. Yet in the fall semester of 2018, something changed. The publicity surrounding Dr. Christine Blasey Ford's testimony against Brett Kavanaugh's Supreme Court Judicial Nomination left me more than embarrassed to be teaching an at times light-hearted, trivializing fantasy of sexual victimization. Blasey Ford seemed to have a much more compelling life story to tell than her alleged abuser, and I became convinced that he same could be said of Humbert's fictional victim.

On the stand, Blasey Ford appeared the very picture of resolve, a survivor of what she recalled as a distressing incident involving Kavanaugh and one of his friends, Mark Judge, from when she was only fifteen years old. According to Blasey Ford, Kavanaugh began what she clearly perceived to be an act of attempted rape in a private bedroom for the laughter and entertainment of his classmate. I found Blasey Ford's testimony remarkable for its intrinsic duality of voicing. The voice of a traumatized teenager was distinctly audible within the rhetorical formulations of a successful professor of psychology. The anguish of the child was countered by the sophistication and courage of the adult performing what she understood to be her civic responsibility. All the details of Blasey Ford's teenage suffering were embedded in implied, larger narratives of working to overcome childhood trauma and of finding the resilience to testify before a Senate committee as divided as the nation. This was a consummate professional speaking pain to power. Blasey

Ford had suffered, but like the fictional Dolores Haze, she refused to allow herself to be defined by pain alone. In contrast, Kavanaugh's adamant denials, perhaps in part because of their brevity, struck me as flat and wooden. True, Kavanaugh's remarks were saturated with the anger and self-righteousness to be expected from a man presenting himself as falsely accused, but to put the matter strictly in terms of literary criticism, pathos trumps wrath as a system of textual creation and reception. Compare the number of sentimental, tear-jerking novels and melodramas with the scarcity of invective as an independent literary genre.

The spectacle of Blasey Ford's testimony against Kavanaugh on the Senate floor was, in essence, a competition between two strong, highly educated personalities for their audience's sympathies. Similarly, the novel *Lolita* can be interpreted as a tournament of two, for the characterizations of Humbert and Dolores are much more vivid, extensive, and consistent than those of Clare Quilty or Charlotte Haze. This is a fight between Humbert and Dolores for the reader's love and respect. The brawn and intellectualism of Humbert's discourse have long made him seem the outright winner. Fixation on the wordplay and allusiveness of Humbert's evil genius have eclipsed (in scholarship and in my teaching) the letters Dolores authors in the novel devoted to her. Blasey Ford's testimony and the #MeToo movement allowed me to see that Nabokov is careful to make of Humbert's victim a worthy opponent, for Dolores is momentarily able to usurp Humbert's narratorial privilege.

It has been convincingly argued by Eléna Rakhimova-Sommers that "readers of the Nabokovian woman find themselves on a narratorial diet because entry into her emotional and physical 'I' is rarely granted and the nuances of her pain or pleasure are rarely discussed," with Ada Veen as the "only" exception (xv). I contend that Dolores, too, is an important deviation from the general rule that Nabokov's heroine "is most often a Muse and hardly ever an artist" (xv–xvi). The present essay will show that Dolores' letters display an artistic ingenuity markedly different from Humbert's. In short, her missives can withstand extended scrutiny as aesthetically sophisticated objects detachable from Humbert's masculine voice.

Dolores is a precocious child of "very superior intelligence," to pair the wording of Lewis Terman's explication of the Stanford Revision and Extension of the Binet-Simon Intelligence Scale (78) with the IQ score of 121 that Humbert reports (107). To be sure, Dolores' number suggests no genius, but the two letters from her quoted in their entirety within the novel display emotional intelligence, including powers of empathy, more sophisticated than those of her abuser. The scientific formulation of "emotional intelligence" originated in the work of psychologists Peter Salovey and John Mayer (1990) and has been popularized by the more recent writing of Daniel Goleman (1995); but it was Nabokov's genius to have dramatized the rivalry of IQ and EQ decades before. "Emotional intelligence" includes the abilities to "persist in the face of frustrations; to control impulse and delay gratification; to regulate one's moods and keep distress from swamping one's ability to think; to empathize and to hope" (Goleman, 34).

Coincidental with Ford's Senate floor testimony was an inclination among several of my students not to refer to Nabokov's child-heroine using Humbert's favorite pet name, but to prefer instead "Dolores Haze," or more simply, "Dolores." As a long-term teacher of *Lolita*, I perceived this as newly invigorating, and I, too, began to embrace the tendency. In resisting Humbert's favorite term for his eponymous victim my students and I unwittingly affiliated with scholarly precedent. Sofia Ahlberg argues that Dolores refuses "to succumb to those other names that are given her (Dolly, Lola, Lo, Lo-lee-ta)" and that "Dolores, the feminine real," is "smuggled into the portrait of the fantasy Lolita" (16). I suggest that the abstraction of the "feminine real" is grounded in Dolores' role as an author. Another attempt to identify the "real" in the novel identifies Dolores with Sally Horner (Weinman), but we do not know Horner to have been a writer. Ellen Pifer refers to Nabokov's character as both "Dolores" and "Dolly Haze," while Julian Connolly favors "Dolly." "Dolores" is preferable for my purposes in part because it is associated with the act of signing: "She was Dolores on the dotted line" (9), which alludes to the popular expression, "Sign on the dotted line." Humbert likely has in mind his own inscription of the name on motel registry forms, but the implied motif of signature may also be taken to suggest Dolores' own handwriting. Humbert may also be imagining the legal "guardianship" papers he hopes Dolores would sign (149). "Dotted line" may further hint at the punctuation of ellipsis and the ability of Dolores to occupy the space of the unsaid.

The possessive epithet, "my Lolita," is almost everywhere in the book (32, 44 53, 66, 79, 80, 92, 111, 115, 121, 128, 134, 138, 151, 154. 166, 167, 176, 190, 198, 199, 207, 231, 241, 247, 267, 277, 278, 284, 293, 309, tabulated by Appel, 309, with my addition of 121). After being used at the climax of a single paragraph in part II, chapter 32 (284), "my Lolita" comprises the final two words of the entire novel (309). In the wake of the #MeToo movement, I wish to refrain from anything that might be misperceived as shorthand for Humbert's possessive, yet false endearment.

To call Dolores "Lolita" is already to enter a language game which Humbert adumbrates to distract his readers from the ugliness of his crimes against the child. In the novel, Charlotte Haze regularly refers to her daughter simply as "Lo," but Humbert and Clare Quilty are the only characters to call her "Lolita." Quilty's one use of "Lolita" is in the plural, "Lolitas," and does not even properly belong to him, for he is reading the poem Humbert gives him shortly before his death (300). The plural of Humbert's doggerel that Quilty quotes is probably the originary antonomasia[1] now automatic throughout the

English-speaking world. Popularly deployed to designate any seemingly seductive pubescent girl, Dolores' catchy nickname is frozen in a cliché we are called upon in teaching to struggle against. In the novel, the personality of Dolores is highly individualized, and should not be identified with the class of nymphets to which Humbert's pet name is now reflexively given. Nabokov titles the novel *Lolita*, but here the nickname refers directly to Humbert's creation as much as to the girl herself. She is not to be identified entirely with Humbert's misperceptions of her. To be sure, in Nabokov's screenplay the character is called "Lolita" and described as such in the stage directions. Many other personalities in the screenplay refer to "Lolita": Phyllis (22), an unnamed teacher (22), Mrs. Chatfield (55), Mrs. Gray (58), Miss Cormorant (143), and Charlotte (38, 40, 57, 63, 69, 71). In the scenario "Lolita" also appears in the utterance of a mysterious, unnamed voice (113) and in a song (127). "Lolita" is heard a number of times from a variety of characters in Stanley Kubrick's ensuing movie, but the present analysis of Dolores Haze as an author is confined to the depiction of her subjectivity in the first book alone, with only occasional reference to Nabokov's Russian translation of it and to his screenplay.

Pia Pera's retelling of Nabokov's novel from Dolores' point of view, *Lo's Diary*, is a much more ambitious work than mine, and shows the extent to which Nabokov's creation implies a fully realizable vision of Dolores as author. A second fictional narrative revisiting the plot of *Lolita* from Dolores' perspective, Christophe Tison's *Journal de L. (1947–1952)*, has recently been published in France (May 2019). While the present study is inspired in part by the conceit of Pera's and Tison's imaginative fictional diaries, it is surprising that Pera does not refer to Dolores' authorship of letters, and that Tison mentions Dolores's missive from Coalmont only in passing. I do not treat Pera's and Tison's books as objects of study in their own right.

> The First Letter, Part I, Chapter 19
> DEAR MUMMY AND HUMMY,
> Hope you are fine. Thank you very much for the candy. I [crossed out and re-written again] lost my new sweater in the woods. It has been cold here for the last few days. I'm having a time. Love.
> Dolly (81)

Dolores' initial short missive has been dismissed as "merely a brief note conveying little of substance about her state of mind" (Connolly, "Hearing," 149). On the contrary, this letter by the twelve-year-old girl invites interpretation. It contains the suggestive line "I [crossed out and re-written again] I lost my new sweater in the woods" (81). Given what Humbert later learns about Dolores Haze's sexual experience with Charlie Holmes while at camp, it is tempting to take "lost sweater" here as a metonym for "lost virginity."

Re-readers of the novel may remember Mona Dahl's humorous direct association of sweater and maidenhead: Dolores had "remarked that her (Lo's) sweater was of virgin wool: 'The only thing about you that is, kiddo . . .'" (ellipsis Nabokov's, 191). The three dots hint at more that might be narrated, making Dolores's sexuality occupy the space of that which is not stated directly. Not to be excluded from the realm of possibility is that Dolores originally wrote "I lost my virginity in the woods" to read aloud for the provocation and entertainment of her fellow campers, then crossed these words out for her parents' perusal.[2] Or is this merely what Humbert might want us to think? Such fanciful interpretations should not blind us to the even more basic stylistic device of the cross-out as such. This is the only passage in the novel which is explicitly stated to have been "crossed out," and thus, it clearly differentiates the voice of its humble, hesitating author from the confident, honey-tongued loquaciousness of the prose belonging to Humbert.

One may wonder, of course, if Dolores or Humbert is ultimately responsible for the cross-out. I go with the former because the presentation of this short letter from camp contrasts with the embedding of a prior letter from her mother. After Charlotte Haze's mawkish epistolary confession of love for Humbert, the rhetoric of Humbert's memory of it is extremely cautious and halting in any claim to absolute truth: "What I present here is what I remember of the letter, and what I remember of the letter I remember verbatim. . . . It was at least twice longer. . . . There is just a chance that the 'vortex of the toilet' (where the letter did go) is my own matter-of-fact contribution" (69, ellipses mine). Note the uncharacteristically clunky—for Humbert—repetition of "I remember," which calls attention to Humbert's subjectivity and potential for errors. Nabokov plants an amusing rarity in Humbert's reconstitutions of Charlotte's discourse, spelling "teeny" (68) for the more common and older "tiny." Does Humbert's infatuation with pubescent girls and his eventual desire to confine and enslave a single young teenager corrupt his orthography? On the other hand, the daughter's first letter is presented without any comparable red flags. While we know Humbert destroyed Charlotte's letter long before reconstituting it, we are inclined to assume that he has Dolores' in hand to quote because he would have treasured it as a memento. Although Humbert plays many falsifying roles throughout the novel, I see him here with Dolores' correspondence in the capacity of "very conscientious recorder" (72). Later he boasts of consulting "papers which the authorities have so kindly allowed me to use for the purpose of writing my statement" (175). Do "these papers" include Dolores' letters? The detail of the lost sweater is, furthermore, corroborated by Humbert's fragmentary reconstitution of Charlotte's subsequent epistolary response: ". . . and you had better find it because I cannot buy . . . " (99, ellipses Nabokov's) in which we infer that "it" refers to "sweater."

Everyday features of Dolores Haze's letter surrounding the image of the "lost sweater" are not devoid of interest. The cutesy salutation "Dear Mummy and Hummy" may be taken to echo Charlotte's or Humbert's own original usage, yet Nabokov's text leaves open the possibility of the reverse. Could it be that Dolores' "Mummy and Hummy" inspire Humbert's much later reconstitutions of them? When Humbert calls himself "Humbert the Hummer" (57) and "Hum" (61, 140) or reminisces that Dolores "did not condescend to have dinner with Hum and mum" (65) does he recollect his own corny coining in miniature of the pair repeated in Dolores' epistolary salutation? Or does he merely truncate the "Mummy and Hummy" which could have originated in Dolores Haze's hand in the letter or even before in her talk? Dolores is comfortable with the slight British affectation of this endearment when she asks Humbert, "When did you fall for my mummy?" (112), or subsequently complains to him: "You drive much faster than my mummy, mister" (112). Much later she asks where her "murdered mummy" is buried" (286). The spellings of Dolores' "dahrling" (199) for "darling" and "deah fahther" (220) for "dear father" imply a fascination with stylish British pronunciation. Humbert Humbert is "infinitely moved by the little one's slangy speech" (41), so we are invited to attune ourselves to her many linguistic contributions to Humbert's larger narrative. Not all of these are given directly with quotation marks. For example, when Humbert speculates that the man who leaves strange clues in motel registries is "not a common goon" one may wonder if he is quoting without acknowledgment the "vulgar vocabulary" previously listed as belonging to his stepdaughter: "'revolting,' 'super,' 'luscious,' 'goon,' 'drip'" (65). The poem Humbert claims as a "maniac's masterpiece" (257) contains a line obviously stolen from the twelve year old's speech, "Are you from Paris, mister?" (256), but not acknowledged with quotation marks.

"Hope you are fine" and "Thank you very much for the candy" seem like standard formalities, but the utter simplicity of the sentence structures opposes the complexity of Humbert's effusions and distinguishes this clearly as the voice of a child. In its concern for the well-being of others we may perceive in "Hope you are fine" an antidote to Humbert's obsessive narcissism and malfeasance. The straightforward gratitude of the second short sentence contrasts at once with Humbert's misery and with his perversely manic moments of bliss.

Dolores' "I'm having a time" is misinterpreted by Charlotte as a simple mistake with a word "left out" "before time" (81) but may also be read as an inspired instance of highly condensed ambiguity. According to the online Urban Dictionary—an admittedly asynchronous source—"having a time" has two opposite meanings: (1) "having an amazing, unforgettable time; to be so happy you never want to stop"; and (2) "having difficulty at any given time because of one's situation."[3] This is a naïve but poetic ambiguity of the seventh type catalogued by William Empson, in which "two opposite ideas are defined by the context, so that the total effect is to show a fundamental division in the writer's mind" (192). The good cheer of Dolores' opening sentences supports the first of the two contradictory meanings. Can we also divine in this usage an insouciant, elliptical reference to the joys of early sexual experience with Charlie Holmes consistent with the prior hypothesis of Dolores drafting a version of the letter to provoke and amuse her friends? In contrast, the mention of "cold" weather and lost sweater would suggest the latter, contrary sense.

Nabokov's Russian translation of the letter is interesting in regard to the temperature. Here the "cold" of the English is given a positive connotation by the use of "была свежая погода" ["the weather was cool"] (70). The adjective "свежий" has a favorable nuance, as in the commonplace "свежий воздух" [fresh air]. Moreover, Nabokov's Russian locates the "cool weather" squarely in the past, while the English progressive tense "has been" implies that the "cold" in ongoing. Because "a time" seems to be missing the adjective necessary for definitive interpretation, this usage may be called a kind of understatement. Understatement is an even more important characteristic of the next letter from Dolores included by Humbert. I follow a traditional definition of understatement as "saying less than one means" (Hüber 23). Popular conceptions of the device as typically British cohere with Dolores' playful Anglophile ostentation.

Not a single archaism ornaments Dolores's short letter, but Humbert favors antiquated usage: "poltroon" (18), "quoth" (48), "anent" (51, 161), "for the nonce" (109). Coupled with Humbert's love of Classical allusions and Latin (Larmour and Sweeney), the archaisms symbolize Humbert's plight of being mired in the past. The absence of archaisms in both of the letters Dolores authors, by contrast, suggests that she is capable of moving on. While Humbert ultimately claims to evolve away from his pedophilic obsessiveness and to grow capable of love for Dolores, Dolores is the more dynamic and compelling of the novel's two dominant personalities. Indeed, the transformation of Dolores from molested child into married mother-to-be is such that it has elicited comparison to the maturation of Tatiana in Alexander Pushkin's *Eugene Onegin*, which has been considered as a systematic source of inspiration for *Lolita* (Meyer). Indeed, what has been written elsewhere of Pushkin's heroine, "There are as many Tatiana Larins as there are readers of *Eugene Onegin*" (Hasty 3), holds no less true for Dolores and Nabokov's novel.

Another feature of Humbert's writing glaringly absent from Dolores' are his tiresome divagations into French. "Speak English" (149) and "Do you mind very much cutting out the French. It annoys everybody" (243) are Dolores' reactions to her tormentor's macaronic speech, but they can also be taken as indicating her epistolary aesthetic preference. Nabokov includes the detail of the twelve-year-old child's growing knowledge of French in her mocking apology to Charlotte, "*Pardonnez*, mother," (55) to highlight the girl's intelligence. Use of the "*vous*" form with a family member may be taken as a beginner's simple error. Or does it express Delores' desire to distance herself from the mother's excessive familiarity in telling Humbert to "slap" the child "hard" if she "interferes with" his "scholarly meditations" (55)? Dolores' strictly-in-English correspondence further contrasts with Humbert's reconstitution of a letter to her from Mona (222–23), which includes a "tongue-twister" French direct quotation of Quilty's play. Mona's letter to Dolores, at least as far as Humbert remembers it, is less compelling than Dolores' epistolary communications, for Mona's corny onomastic play—"Lollikins"—and French sound too much like Humbert's. Given an IQ score, 150, associable with genius (191), Mona displays less emotional intelligence than her addressee.

Dolores' naughty Spanish is another matter which suggests her authorial capacities for multilingual language play. According to the school headmistress Pratt, "Dolly has written a most obscene four-letter word which our Dr. Cutler tells me is low-Mexican for urinal with her lipstick on some health pamphlets . . ." (197). Dr. Cutler is mistaken, for the two four-letter Spanish obscenities that come most immediately to mind are "*puta*" (whore)[4] and "*coño*" (c—), neither of which suggest "urinal." Dolores could have meant the former as a generalized exclamation (c.f. English "f—!") or the latter as an insouciant label for an anatomical picture. But the latter is much less probable, given that "*coño*," while favored in Spain and Puerto Rico, is rare in Mexico. One may hypothesize that Dr. Cutler vaguely remembers having been summoned with the word "*puta*" by a pimp into a Mexican toilet to enjoy a prostitute's services there. Dr. Cutler could then later have confused this term with the name of the location. Such extravagant speculations adhere to Nabokov's dictum that "The reader should have imagination" ("Good Readers," 5), but should not distract us from the simple use of lipstick as a writing implement in the mischievous graffito. Dolores' bringing of the cosmetic to school testifies to her desire to appear attractive to schoolmates and hints in this way at the subjectivity Humbert attempts to minimize and restrict. Although Humbert quotes in full only a single letter from camp, he tells us clearly that there are more as he rails against Charlotte's "attitude toward my saporous darling's letters" (81). The use of the plural raises a number of questions for readers beyond the most obvious, "How many?" Does Humbert quote parts of his stepdaughter's epistolary language elsewhere in the novel without the acknowledgment he gives to the short missive fully embedded in chapter 19 of part I? Does Humbert's narrative plagiarize details from the letters he withholds?

It has been shown by Phillip Gilreath that the metaphor of "plagiarism" is especially significant with regard to the novel because it is, etymologically speaking, based on the Latin "*plagiarus*," "kidnapper." Gilreath has analyzed parallels between the literary abduction of Edgar Allen Poe's "Annabel Leigh" and the literal abduction of Dolores Haze. Michael Maar's fascinating detective work in unearthing yet another possible source, the short story "Lolita" by Heinz von Eshwege (literary pseudonym "von Lichberg"), raises the hypothesis of Nabokov's creative amnesia in fashioning the later novel. Presumably Maar never proposes that it might be Humbert along with Nabokov who remembers having read or heard of von Lichberg's tale, because we never hear of Humbert traveling to the place of its publication or of him reading obscure, early twentieth-century German stories. In any event, the possibility that Humbert reconstitutes fragments of Dolores' epistolary rhetoric while creating his own much larger text confirms prior scholarship's insistence that plagiarism is at the center of Nabokov's most famous literary enterprise.

Much of what has been argued about the opposition of Dolores' writing to Humbert's in the first letter holds for the second: this, too, is eloquent and understated in its plain American diction, a remedy to Humbert's unctuous bilingualism, rhetorical extravagance, and overstatement. Yet while the simplicity of the word choices in the first communication may be attributed to Dolores' youth, the second's plain language must be regarded as her deliberate authorial choice, since we learn from headmistress Pratt that Dolores, at fourteen, already commanded "a number of obviously European polysyllabics" in addition to "a two-hundred forty-two word area of the commonest pubescent slang" (194). Dolores crafts this later letter at seventeen.

> The Second Letter, Part II, Chapter 27
> DEAR DAD,
> How's everything? I'm married. I'm going to have a baby. I guess he's going to be a big one. I guess he'll come right for Christmas. This is a hard letter to write. I'm going nuts because we don't have enough to pay our debts and get out of here. Dick is promised a big job in Alaska in his very specialized corner of the mechanical field, that's all I know about it but it's really grand. Pardon me for withholding our home address but you may still be mad at me, and Dick must not know. This town is something. You can't see the morons for the smog. Please do send us a check, Dad. We could manage with three or four hundred or even less, anything is welcome, you might sell my old things, because once we get there the dough will just start rolling in. Write, please. I have gone through much sadness and hardship.
> Yours expecting,
Dolly (Mrs. Richard F. Schiller) (266)

When students ask me to specify a favorite line in all of Nabokov's novel I used to quote Humbert's opening words, but now I respond with Dolores' terse: "You can't see the morons for the smog." Not since Humbert's sinister generalization "You can always count on a murderer for a fancy prose style"

(9) have readers of the novel encountered use of the second-person grammatical subject outside of quoted dialogue. Dolores' friendly, chatty, down-to-earth use of "you" belies the sudden pose of superiority assumed in the insulting "morons." "Morons" is given special weight as the only two-syllable word among seven monosyllabic ones. The supercilious stance implied by this derogatory term appeals to the sense of higher intellect Humbert long attempted to force on Dolores as his pupil. Yet Dolores' posturing here is ironically playful, even self-deprecatory, since she and Dick, after all, live amid this "smog" and among these "morons." Nabokov's Russian translation of Dolores' laconic formulation alliterates: "Не видать кретинов из-за копоти" (247). Repetition of the "k" sound is cacophonous, perhaps through phonological imitation of the ancient Greek prefix "*caco-*" (bad), adding to the humorously pejorative effect.[5] The use of "for" to replace "because of" is an exemplum of condensation, the polar opposite of one of Humbert's principal stylistic foibles, wordiness. Dolores' adroitly laconic denunciation of air pollution is introduced by an understatement comparable to her prior "I'm having a time" (81): "This town is really something." The sentence is short for "This town is really something else," with "something else" understood to convey something "beyond description; unbelievable" (*New Partridge Dictionary of Slang*, vol. 2, 1815). Yet Dolores' next sentence is nothing if not a perfect, encapsulating description of her smoky city. The deceptively simple prose is thus animated by logical paradox, for Dolores' subsequent word choices capture the seemingly ineffable.

In apparent echo of the understatements of the twelve year old's letter, the contents of the later one are symmetrically framed by two especially poignant examples: the early "This is a hard letter to write" and the beautifully condensed, wise, concluding line, "I have been through much sadness and hardship" (266). The initial understatement of this second letter is highlighted by its abrupt interruption of an anaphoric pattern of prior and following sentence openings: we go from "I'm . . . ," I'm . . . ," "I guess . . . ," "I guess . . . ," to "This . . . ," then back to "I'm . . . ." The understatement is additionally emphasized by its rupture of sound sequence: the assonance of the first four long i's is broken by the sudden swerve to "This" with its contrasting short vowel. The assumption of less is more, stylistically speaking, in the first understatement prepares us to interpret the more powerful second. This longer understatement is marked with a shift from the imperative—"Write, please"—to the indicative—"I have been . . . "—grammatical mood. In its soulful deployment of a past progressive, "have been through," the latter suggests the mature ownership and working through of sexual victimization celebrated by the #MeToo movement, and prompts reflection upon Humbert's failure to own the agony of his mother's death. Dolores transcends her trauma. She is in a colloquial sense "unstuck," but Humbert is perpetually ensnared by a tangle of petrifying intellectualizations.

The understatements in both letters counter the exaggerations of Dolores' captor. Consider the following, narcissistic mess of a sentence: "Unless it can be proven to me—to me as I am now, today, with my heart and my beard, and my putrefaction—that in the infinite run it does not matter a jot that a North American girl-child named Dolores Haze had been deprived of her childhood by a maniac, unless this can be proven (and if it can, then life is a joke), I see nothing for the treatment of my misery but the melancholy and very local palliative of articulate art" (283). Overwritten, the "spectacular bathos"—to quote Nabokov on Gogol (147)—of the rhetoric belies a simple self-aggrandizing proposition, "I have deprived Dolores of her childhood." While the guilt-ridden predator imagines having robbed Dolores of her girlhood, childhood is a universal phase of human development that can only be taken away by premature death, and Humbert does not kill Dolores.

One of the most obvious devices differentiating the voice of the seventeen-year-old mother-to-be's voice from that of the manic parasite surrounding it are the nine contractions: "How's," "I'm," "he's," "he'll," "I'm," "it's," "that's," "it's," "can't." They impart to Dolores' prose a sense of urgency characteristic of the spoken word and absent from Humbert's polished, retrospective embellishments. Capitalizing all the letters of the salutation, too, conveys the dire necessity of Dolores' pressing financial need, but the capital letters also appear in the greeting at the beginning of the first missive. The capitalizations in both messages suggest the insistence of Dolores' demands for attention. I do not wish to force the point because Nabokov abandoned the use of capitalization in his Russian versions of the letters, but in metaphorical effect the English capitalizations sound loud in contradiction of Humbert's description of Dolores' epistolary voice as "small" (266). Humbert's usage is an awkward, incorrect synesthesia, since the visual and tactile sensory registers implied by "small" are mixed up with auditory perception and the voice of the letter writer is far from timid. The urgency of Dolores' financial plight is further suggested by the pun in her leave-taking: "Yours expecting" refers both to her pregnancy and to the expectation that Humbert will send a check for the inheritance she is rightfully due. Broke, financially speaking, Dolores remains unbroken in resolve. Humbert offers a dazzling array of reasons for writing his memoir, but Dolores' single purpose in crafting the second letter is clear, and does not go unfulfilled, since Humbert hands over her inheritance as a result. In a word, Dolores' prose is efficacious.

Dolores' purposeful understatements may be contrasted with Humbert's falsely trivializing ones. The succinct parenthetical explanation Humbert provides for his mother's death when he was three, "(picnic, lightning)," (10) flippantly minimizes the apparently unspeakable anguish of the boy. It may be compared to the brevity of his description of Annabel's death: "four months later she died of typhus in Corfu" (13). Both of the descriptions reflect Humbert's failure sufficiently to undertake the emotional work of mourning. Readers will remember Humbert's fears of early trauma theory: he is panicked as a boy at night by "the dreadful, mysterious, insidious words 'trauma,' 'traumatic event' and 'transom'" (70). Humbert places "trauma" and "traumatic event" in quotation marks to refer to his confrontation with them in unspecified reading material, but the usage also ironically dramatizes his failure successfully to integrate the concepts into his larger sense of self. The peculiar divagation from "trauma" to the nautical and architectural term "transom" is difficult to interpret, but one possibility is that Humbert uses the merely phonological, alliterative parallelism to escape from the troubling semantic register of "trauma" and "traumatic event." Only near the end of the novel does Humbert offer a fuller, speculative description of his mother's death to counter the early pretense of "cheerful motherlessness" (11):

> When my mother, in a livid wet dress, under the tumbling mist (so I vividly imagined her), had run panting ecstatically up that ridge above Moulinet to be felled there by a thunderbolt, I was but an infant, and in retrospect no yearnings of the accepted kind could I ever graft upon any moment of my youth, no matter how savagely psychotherapists heckled me in my later periods of depression. But I admit that a man of my power of imagination cannot plead personal ignorance of universal emotions. (287)

"Livid" here means primarily "dark blue gray," but the automatic associations of the adjective with bruising and with wrath provoke a retort: it is Humbert, much more than the dress, who must be angry, to put the matter in terms of the "universal emotions" Humbert appears to denigrate. On one level Humbert implies that he cannot be subject to the Freudian Oedipus complex, since he lost his mother early, but the intricacy of the rhetoric hides a simple truth of his ongoing emotional illiteracy: Humbert has failed to acknowledge and work through the anger he must feel over the untimely loss of a parent. Humbert is so "drunk on the impossible past" (282) that his capacities for empathy, a crucial component of emotional intelligence, are forever stunted.

In contrast, Dolores's second letter shows her concern not only for the protection of her husband, but also for the feelings of her former abuser. Dolores justifies the decision to avoid giving a home address, opting instead, we presume, for a P.O. box number, because "you may still be mad at me, and Dick must not know." Fearing for the life of her husband and mindful both of Humbert's wrath and of his proclivity to impetuous violence, Dolores has compelling reasons to be cautious. Yet in addition to concern for Dick's life, the passage expresses a desire to spare him the shock of learning about Dolores' prior anguish. In the management of emotions, some secrets are best left unshared. Now master of her sorrow, Dolores regulates her moods sufficiently to shelter Dick from awareness of her troubled past. She is also solicitous of Humbert's sentiments: "How's everything," "Pardon me . . . ," "Please . . . ," ". . . please" (ellipses mine). Because these politeness formulae can characterize discourse with strangers, they suggest Dolores' achievement of psychological distance from her abuser. In short, she has transcended Humbert's illusions of intimacy at the same time as she remains polite and emotionally regulated toward him. In the final analysis, publicity surrounding Blasey Ford's Senate testimony and the larger #MeToo movement prompted this reevaluation of Dolores' role as an author of letters in *Lolita*. Plucky yet desperate for cash, mischievous but dignified, emotionally intelligent, wise and efficacious, the multilayered voice of Dolores as letter-writer contrasts vividly with Humbert's, but the understated elegance of Dolores' prose is such that her authorial role cannot be defined exclusively in terms of its opposition to her captor. Humbert's admission that there are more letters from Dolores than he quotes directly raises questions about Humbert's possible plagiarism of them. Does Humbert not steal and ventriloquize, in his construction of the novel, language originally belonging to Dolores? A full listing of moments in *Lolita* when readers can detect the implied voice of Dolores as co-author has not been given here, but would constitute an intriguing future project for scholars and students alike. The present study has suggested possible echoes of Dolores' letters in Humbert's writing, but Dolores's speech is such a wellspring of wisecracks that it, too, deserves comprehensive analysis as an influence on Humbert's stylistics. One may object that Dolores' untimely death at seventeen outweighs the celebration of her as an emotionally intelligent, fellow survivor of sex crimes suggested by the #MeToo movement, but Dolores outlives her abuser. More importantly, Nabokov's killing of the heroine at a young age underscores a fundamental irony of the book: at seventeen, Dolores dies an emotionally intelligent, young adult, while the neurotic Humbert is perpetually trapped in his boyhood, and expires as less than a man.

WORKS CITED

Ahlberg, Sofia. "Via Dolores: The Passage of the Feminine as Contraband in Nabokov's Fiction." In *Nabokov's Women: The Silent Sisterhood of Textual Nomads*, edited by Eléna Rakhimova-Sommers, Lanham: Lexington Books, 2017, pp. 3-18.

Appel, Alfred. Notes. In *The Annotated* Lolita by Vladimir Nabokov, ed. Appel. New York: Vintage, 1991, pp. 311–457.

Burke, David. *Street Spanish Slang Dictionary and Thesaurus*. New York: John Wiley and Sons, 1999.

The Cassell Dictionary of Slang. Ed. Jonathan Green. London: Cassel, 1998.

Connolly, Julian W. "Fetching Yet Faithless: Problematic Mistresses in Nabokov's Fiction." In *Women in Nabokov's Life and Art*, edited by Nailya Garipova and Juan Jose Torres Nuñez. New York: Peter Lang, 2016.

———. "Hearing the Female Voice in Vladimir Nabokov's Fiction." In *Nabokov's Women: The Silent Sisterhood of Textual Nomads*, edited by Eléna-Rakhimova-Sommers, New York: Lexington Books, 2017, pp. 143–54.

Curtius, Ernst Robert. *European Literature and the Latin Middle Ages*. Trans. William R. Trask. New York: Pantheon, 1953.
Empson, William. *Seven Types of Ambiguity*. London: Chatto and Windus, 1947.
Fontanier, Pierre. *Les figurs du discours*. Paris: Flammarion, 1977.
Gilreath, Philip. "Kidnapping Annabel, Plagiarizing Dolores Haze: Literary and Literal Appropriation in Vladimir Nabokov's *Lolita*." M.A. Thesis, The Graduate School of the University of Charleston, South Carolina, 2016.
Goleman, Daniel. *Emotional Intelligence: Why It Can Matter More than IQ*. New York: Bantam, 1995.
Hasty, Olga Peters. *Pushkin's Tatiana*. Madison: University of Wisconsin Press, 1999.
Herbold, Sara. "'Dolores Disparu': Reading Misogyny in *Lolita*." In *Approaches to Teaching Nabokov's* Lolita, edited by Zoran Kuzmanovich and Galya Diment. New York: The Modern Language Association of America, 2008, pp. 134–41.
Hüber, Axel. *Understatements and Hedges in English*. Philadelphia: John Benjamins, 1983.
Larmour, David. "Nabokov Philomelus: The Classical Allusions in *Lolita*." *Classical and Modern Literature: A Quarterly* 10, no. 2 (1990): pp. 143–51.
Maar, Michael. *The Two Lolitas*, trans. Perry Anderson. New York: Verso, 2005.
Meyer, Priscilla. *Find What the Sailor Has Hidden: Vladimir Nabokov's Pale Fire*. Middletown, CT: Wesleyan University Press, 1988.
Nabokov, Vladimir. *The Annotated Lolita*, ed. Alfred Appel. New York: Vintage, 1991.
———. "Good Readers and Good Writers." In *Lectures on Literature*, edited by Fredson Bowers. New York: Harcourt Brace Jovanovich, 1982, pp. 1–6.
———. *Nikolai Gogol*. New York: New Directions, 1961.
———. *Lolita: A Screenplay*. New York: Vintage, 1997.
———. *Лолита: Роман*, trans. Nabokov. New York: Phaedra, 1967.
The New Partridge Dictionary of Slang and Unconventional English, 2 vols. Edited Tom Dalzell and Terry Victor. New York: Routledge, 2006.
Pera, Pia. *Lo's Diary*, trans. Ann Goldstein. New York: Foxrock, 1995.
Pifer, Ellen. "Art as Pedagogy in Lolita." In *Approaches to Teaching Nabokov's* Lolita, edited by Zoran Kuzmanovich and Galya Diment. New York: The Modern Language Association of America, 2008, pp. 83–88.
———. "Nabokov's Novel Offspring: Lolita and Her Kin." In *Vladimir Nabokov's* Lolita*: A Casebook*, edited by Ellen Pifer. New York: Oxford University Press, 2003, pp. 85–109.
Rakhimova-Sommers, Eléna. "Introduction—Nabokov's Passportless Wanderer: A Study of Nabokov's Woman." In *Nabokov's Women: The Silent Sisterhood of Textual Nomads*, edited by Eléna Rakhimova-Sommers. New York: Lexington Books, 2017, pp. xv–xxxi.
Rancour-Laferriere, Daniel. *Out from under Gogol's Overcoat: A Psychoanalytic Study*. Ann Arbor: Ardis, 1982.
Salovey, P., and Mayer, J. D. "Emotional Intelligence." *Imagination, Cognition, and Personality* 9 (1990): pp. 185–211.
Shute, Jenefer P. "'So Nakedly Dressed': The Text of the Female Body in Nabokov's Novels." In *Vladimir Nabokov's* Lolita*: A Casebook*, edited by Ellen Pifer. New York: Oxford University Press, 2003, pp. 111–20.
Sweeney, S.E. "Io's Metamorphosis: A Classical Subtext for *Lolita*." *Classical and Modern Literature: A Quarterly* 6, no. 2 (1986): pp. 79–88.
Terman, Lewis M. *The Measurement of Intelligence: An Explanation of and a Complete Guide for the Use of Stanford Revision and Extension of the Binet-Simon Intelligence Scale*. Boston: Houghton Mifflin, 1916.
Tison, Christophe. *Journal de L (1947–1952)*. Paris: Éditions Gouttes d'Or, 2019.
Urban Dictionary. "Having a Time." www.urbandictionary.com/define.php?term=having+a+time.
Weinman, Sarah. *The Real Lolita: The Kidnaping of Sally Horner and the Novel That Scandalized the World*. New York: HarperCollins, 2018.

NOTES

1. Figurative use of a proper name to designate a whole class of persons. Fontanier defines antonomasia as "synechdoche of the individual" (97, trans. mine). Curtius cites the examples of calling a rich man a "Croesus" or a patron of the arts a "Maecenas" (416).

2. In proposing that Dolores jokes about virginity, I follow Sara Herbold's invitation to ponder Dolores' "layered" nature, not only as a victim, but also as "a powerful agent, in whom erotic desire and creativity are as closely intertwined as they are for Humbert (and Nabokov)" (137–38).

3. None of the book-format dictionaries of American and English slang I have consulted include listings for "having a time."

4. All the dictionaries of Spanish slang I have checked concur that "*puta*" is potentially much more offensive than the usual English literal translation of "whore" would suggest.

5. It has also been argued that "repetition of the occluded velar [k] inevitably reminds the listener of fecal matter, of the universal ka-ka word" (Rancour-Laferriere, 95).

Chapter Eight

Nabokov and #MeToo

Consent, Close Reading, and the Sexualized Workplace

Eric Naiman

> "Or, and this is the worst thing a reader can do, he identifies himself with a character in the book." (Nabokov, *Lectures on Literature* 4)

#METOO

Right away the #MeToo movement runs up against a basic incompatibility when it comes to Nabokov's understanding of fiction. While there are many ways to define the movement—or movements, because its adherents and spokespersons have had different though overlapping goals and practices—it burst onto the national scene and continues to function as a social media phenomenon through a dynamic of nearly instantaneous identification. Reading an account of sexual victimization occurring in a situation where one person has significantly more power than another, or where one person takes advantage of an environment rife with sexual inequality to hurt another, the reader responds by identifying with a character in that story and by affirming that identification through a hashtag and often by the addition of her own narrative of abuse and survival. Of course, to refer to the account that evokes that reaction as a *story* with *characters* is already to imply that it might be fiction. With a MeToo hashtag, the reader is declaring an implicit belief that the account isn't just a story but should be accepted as the truth, and that its subject is not a character but a person.

This insight ought to hint not at an incompatibility between #MeToo and Nabokov but at a deeper compatibility. The dynamics of the #MeToo movement are predicated on the call to identify with narratives accepted as true:

#MeToo narratives are not read as fiction. Nabokov does not envision reading as an identificatory practice, but that is partly because when reading or writing fiction he does not prioritize truth. For Nabokov, fiction is about deceit. He views the story of "The Boy Who Cried Wolf" as a parable about the birth of art (*Lectures on Literature,* 5). Lying is basic to art, and one of the worst things a person can do is to confound art with life.

This procedural lesson about the sin of identificatory reading has its moral correlative in Nabokov's fiction, where the line between art and life is breached when characters—most often, narrators—seek to objectify other characters as the material for art. Turning a person into an object of art is wrong because it deprives that person of the ability to change and imprisons her within literary form.[1] In this respect, the creation of a character is always a form of character assassination. (Nabokov's *Invitation to a Beheading* captures this paradox, when it introduces its hero and pronounces his death sentence in the novel's first words: "In accordance with the law the death sentence was announced" [11]). Nabokov makes his readers aware that it is difficult for novelists to avoid assassinating their characters; character assassination is a regrettable necessity in the creation of fiction, but people shouldn't treat their fellow human beings in this way.

The dynamic of character assassination is also central to the #MeToo movement, although as a negative principle against which the movement defines itself. The abusive behavior of people in positions of power that led both to the #MeToo movement and to the discourse resisting that conduct relies—and triply so—on various sorts of character assassination. First the abuser objectifies his target, depriving her of volition and subjectivity, then he either destroys her career or protects himself through a non-disclosure agreement. (And if he fails and the abuse is publicized, *he* often claims his own character is being destroyed.) Survivors seek to reclaim for themselves the agency and—regaining control over their lives—contingent future which no literary character can possess. So the #MeToo movement and Nabokov's fiction ought to be able to exist without contradiction; the divergence in their stances on reading as an identificatory practice is predicated on a shared distinction between the real world and fiction. A contradiction between the goals of the #MeToo movement and Nabokov's program for reading and writing fiction need never trouble the student or reader who supports the first and appreciates the second, secure in the knowledge that literature and life are conceptually and morally distinct.

Nabokov, however, complicates the matter in several ways. First, the principle that the absence of identification between reader and character serves as the best guarantee for the independence of art from life often operates in his work less as a rigid rule than as part of an ongoing game of temptation played with the reader. Indeed, this game may be the real subject of all Nabokov's fiction. Of Nabokov's injunction not to identify, Anne

Dwyer, a contributor to this volume, writes: "To my mind, that is one of those (slightly bullying) Nabokovian instructions that has to be taken with a grain of salt. Identification is deeply wired in the human psyche. This is how we engage with narrative." Nabokov tells us not to identify with characters, while at the same time writing stories that urge the reader to bond with them. The opening lecture in his "Masters of European Fiction" class at Cornell, where he insists on the evil of reader-character identification, includes a vignette about an ideal reader with whom the actual reader *is* urged to identify: "Up a trackless slope climbs the master artist, and at the top, on a windy ridge, whom do you think he meets? The panting and happy reader, and there they spontaneously embrace and are linked forever if the book lasts forever" (*Lectures on Literature,* 2). Nabokov intends this image as the culmination of a story about how to read fiction, and he clearly expects the good readers in the class to call out something like Me Too (without the hashtag!).

Second, Nabokov writes metafiction, in which the creation of fiction within the diegesis is frequently portrayed as a sin that paradoxically produces wonderful literature. Humbert objectifies Dolores as a nymphet and produces *Lolita*. The narrator of the immensely entertaining *Pnin* tries to transform an émigré intellectual into a pathetic, clueless object of fun. Nevertheless, Nabokov wants the reader to understand that metafiction is fiction, too. If the reader remains cognizant of the difference between a true story and an invented one, she should be able to treat literature and life as separate realms with separate rules. She can believe survivors, practicing empathy and building solidarity, while disbelieving—along *with* Nabokov—in the truth of his created world; moreover, this disbelief can play an important role in the celebration both of Nabokov's playful deviousness and of the pleasure that comes from his language and his version of author-reader complicity.

Third, and perhaps most obviously, good writers do not make everything up out of whole cloth. Nabokov insists on the creative power of authors: they recombine the world "in its very atoms": "The material of this world may be real enough (as far as reality goes) but does not exist at all as an accepted entirety; it is chaos, and to this chaos the author says 'go!' allowing the world to flicker and to fuse" (*Lectures on* Literature, 3). This is an exercise in creative laundering—good writers take fragments of their actual world to create the world of their fiction without, Nabokov asserts, incorporating the social forces that have shaped those objects and that still reside in them.[2] Good readers are supposed to shake themselves free of these forces, but that, like the injunction not to identify, is an impossible task.

So the harmonious compatibility of Nabokov's good readers and the #MeToo Movement, both ostensibly committed to the importance of a rigid line between fiction and fact, is probably a literature professor's fantasy, but it may be a productive, heuristic illusion because it offers the potential for exploring in the classroom ways in which literature is not like life and for analyzing how principles of interpretation and concepts of predation central to the #MeToo movement function but function differently in a work of art. Conceptually, the #MeToo movement ought not to extend to Nabokov's fiction, but when it does, it defamiliarizes the process of reading and reveals ways in which Nabokov can prove an unexpectedly kindred, as well as an expectedly antithetical, interlocutor.

In the pages that follow, I'll explore three concepts pertinent to the reading and teaching of Nabokov in the era of the #MeToo movement. These concepts are interlocking and overlapping, and their separation is artificial, so at the end I'll bring them together with some concrete suggestions about teaching.

CONSENT

Let's begin with "A Nursery Tale," a story first written in Russian in 1925, about a man who makes a deal with the Devil. The hero, Erwin, likes to move through his pretty German town seeking additions to an imaginary harem. He has had very little sexual experience: "Only once in his life, taunted by rascally comrades, he had accosted a woman, and she had said quietly: 'You ought to be ashamed of yourself. Leave me alone'" (*Stories*, 161). Every morning and evening he sits safely in the streetcar, looking through its windows as he selects his imaginary prey. The Devil, sidling up to him in middle-aged, female form, offers him all the women he chooses in the course of the next day, provided that by midnight he has collected an odd number. Erwin begins by selecting a young woman playing with her dog. She is the choice whose person and environment are described in the greatest detail, but Erwin, caught up in accumulating and counting desirable women, soon recalls her as "the most artless of the lot" (168). Nearing the end of the day, Erwin has made eleven selections, but with time growing short he glimpses "a little girl, . . . a child of fourteen or so," and adds her to his collection, which now has an even number that threatens to turn his harem into a jury (170). Needing one more to keep his total odd, Erwin pursues a young woman who moves through a narrated cityscape that in various ways should recall the first girl's surroundings to him. (Erwin cannot read the text he is in and is in too great a hurry, and nearly all first-time readers, rushing on to the story's conclusion, miss the signs, too.) When he discovers that the thirteenth girl is the same as the first, it is too late. The clock has struck midnight and he is left empty-handed.

When we discuss this story at the second meeting of my semester-long course on Nabokov, nearly all the students understand that its form suggests a fable, and that "A Nursery Tale" must have a moral. They find it difficult to formulate that lesson, however. "Don't have sex with more than eleven women at once" cannot be right; "don't be greedy" is far too general. I've taught the story at least ten times over two decades; not once has any student said "you shouldn't have sex with people without their consent."

That isn't the moral of the story, either, though it might seem odd that among fifty university students who have been through online and in-person sessions on sexual consent the issue of consent doesn't suggest itself. This is all the more striking because the climax of the story is an explicit denial of consent. The woman Erwin attempts to claim turns her face toward him:

> and by the light a streetlamp cast through emerald leaves, he recognized the girl who had been playing that morning with a woolly black pup on a graveled path, and immediately remembered, immediately understood all her charm, tender warmth, priceless radiance. [. . .]
> "You ought to be ashamed of yourself," she said quietly. "Leave me alone." (171)

Her denial of consent, coming after the preceding, evocative paragraph, establishes a link with the beginning of the story and puts the seal on the story as a work of art.[3]

It would be comforting to say that the story enshrines the denial of consent as an aesthetic marker in and of itself. Or at least that it aestheticizes the importance of an object of desire's subjective sexual volition. That, however, is not the moral of the story, either, for this woman presumably would not have had the opportunity to speak or resist had Erwin not muffed his count. Erwin could have claimed his harem had he only studied his victims longer. Most of his choices come with a touch of kinkiness—one looks like a boy, two others are probably twins—but Erwin's appreciation doesn't go beyond these superficial details. He doesn't spend enough time ogling the women nor noticing their individual traits; if he had, he would have recognized the first one sooner, appreciated her beauty, and then not wasted precious time going after her again. So one moral of the story is that getting what you want depends on noticing things and looking them over carefully.

Gazing through the window of the bus at the world outside, Erwin is essentially a stand-in for the reader. Real readers understand that Erwin is a contemptible figure, but their position as readers works to establish a structural affinity with him. And real readers rarely worry about seeking the consent of characters, as they follow the author in a study of the characters that would probably be regarded as invasive if the characters could perceive it. Readers become aware of their potential status as stalkers only when the author troubles the line between real people and characters that most readers, however they might identify with characters, rarely perceive as a moral question in their reading of fiction.

The issue of consent is often treated cavalierly in works of literature by male writers. In Marcel Proust's *Swann's Way*, a novel Nabokov taught and acclaimed one of the four greatest literary masterpieces of the twentieth century (*Strong Opinions*, 57), the initial sexual encounter between Swann and Odette unfolds in such complete accordance with all the strictures of affirmative consent that it could be used as an example for an online module on the topic. At each new moment of intimacy, as he moves aside her flowers or touches her in a new way, Swann asks Odette if she minds. This securing of consent, however, is portrayed not only as erotic but also ludicrous, in part, because none of the many men who have "possessed" Odette in the past have ever asked so explicitly for permission (240–42). Proust's narrator asks for consent of all sorts at many points in the novel—it would be hard not to, French is a polite language, after all—but shockingly, he later abuses a young girl in the first four sentences of a very long paragraph, an act not censured and almost immediately forgotten by the novel itself (*The Prisoner and the Fugitive*, 399).[4]

This act of physical transgression is less interesting to Proust than the penetration of another's mind. His narrator returns repeatedly to his fantasy of possessing the thoughts, desire, and past of another. He wants to make a lasting impression on the peasant girl he meets in a village: "I wished that the idea of me, in entering her, in becoming part of her, might attract not only her attention, but her admiration, her desire, and might force it to keep a memory of me against the day when I might be able to benefit from it" (*In the Shadow*, 296). Indeed, the reader suspects that any future physical benefit to be gained would be less crucial than this initial mental impression.

Lolita and *Pnin*, written almost simultaneously, take up this paradox and explore its tension. In the first novel, the heroine's body becomes the narrator's plaything, but he almost never gains access to the thoughts and emotions of Dolores Haze. In the second, the hero's body is a source of mirth, but the narrator's chief concern is the predatory exposure of his hero's mind, a tampering that the hero views as unwelcome. Read together, the two books offer a meta-fictive twist on #MeToo, for in both cases the abuser's narrative is the same as the narrator's abuse.

Humbert Humbert objectifies Dolores's body. He takes her measurements, clothes and unclothes her, and insists on using various parts of her anatomy as the focus for his lust. He is interested in Dolly's language, but more as though her words were material extensions of her body than because they offer a clue to what is going on in her mind. He suspects that she is concealing something from him, but in one particularly brutal scene he seeks the evidence of her designs in her body rather than her mind:

> I said nothing. I pushed her softness back into the room and went in after her. I ripped her shirt off. I unzipped the rest of her. I tore off her sandals. Wildly, I pursued the shadow of her infidelity; but the scent I traveled upon was so slight as to be practically undistinguishable from a madman's fancy. (215)

If Humbert were to listen more closely to Dolores, she might not be able to hide from him her plans to escape with Quilty. At only a few points does the opacity of Dolly's mental processes even occur to Humbert as a fact, let alone a problem. When he overhears Dolores saying to a friend, "you know, what's so dreadful about dying is that you are completely on your own," it suddenly strikes him that "I simply did not know a thing about my darling's mind and that quite possibly, behind the awful juvenile clichés, there was in her a garden and a twilight, and a palace gate—dim and adorable regions which happened to be lucidly and absolutely forbidden to me" (284). Commenting on this passage, Dana Dragunoiu observes that Dolores "possesses that kernel of inviolable personhood that remains inaccessible even to the worst kinds of violence inflicted upon her" (*Vladimir Nabokov and the Poetics of Liberalism,* 117).

As a noun or a verb, the word "consent" never appears in *Lolita*. Legally, the notion of consent is irrelevant to the sexual relations between Humbert and the twelve-year-old daughter of his late wife; in the eyes of the law Dolores Haze is too young to give her consent to a sexual relationship, try as Humbert might to relativize the concept by referring to bygone epochs and earlier nympholepts who also wielded a pen. Humbert does use an adjectival form of the word "consent" once, at the moment of greatest erotic tension in the novel, when Humbert masturbates on a sofa by manipulating himself against Dolly's legs and bemoans having to work "more hastily than was consensual with deliberately modulated enjoyment" (59). The word "consensual" seems to be appearing here in the guise of its secondary, physiological meaning: "designating involuntary action or movement accompanying, or correlative with, voluntary action or movement" (*Webster's New International,* 567), except that that meaning doesn't fit so well here, either, and readers probably interpret "consensual with" to mean "conducive to." If they dwell on it, however, they will see that the word flaunts its inappropriateness, as though Humbert means to raise the specter of consent before dismissing its relevance, transforming an illegal, non-consensual sexual rapport into a purely sensual one focused on the reaction of only his own body.

Pnin offers a completely different case of a character's non-consensual penetration. Where Humbert penetrates Dolores's body, the narrator of *Pnin* penetrates Pnin's mind. At first, his facility at reading Pnin's thoughts seems to occur within the context of an omniscient narrator's use of free indirect discourse, or what Dorrit Cohn calls "narrated monologue" (99–140). The first time reader of *Pnin* initially sees nothing wrong with this practice, until we come to an odd digression mid-way through the first chapter:

> I do not know if it has ever been noted before that one of the main characteristics of life is discreteness. . . . Man exists only insofar as he is separated from his surroundings. . . . Death is divestment, death is communion. It may be

> wonderful to mix with the landscape, but to do so is the end of the tender ego. The sensation poor Pnin experienced was something very like that divestment, that communion. He felt porous and pregnable. (20)

The novel here captures what it might feel like to have one's thoughts narrated by someone else. For the first six chapters of the novel, the narrator gains access to Pnin's mind and even his mouth virtually at will, a process that becomes increasingly disturbing as the reader begins to realize that the narrator, too, is a character in the story.[5] Eventually, the narrator's ability to see into Pnin's mind no longer satisfies him, and in the seventh and final chapter of the book, he has himself appointed to the faculty of the college where Pnin has been teaching, effectively kicking Pnin out of his job. At this point, however, Pnin gains a life-affirming opacity and an ability to contest the veracity of the narration; in the final pages, he ignores the narrator's interpellation and drives his own car right out of the book to an unknown destination "where there was simply no saying what miracle might happen" (191).

The narrator's emergence as a character in *Pnin* essentially bares the device of a type of narration that goes on in fiction all the time. Characters are never asked to consent to the penetration of their minds, nor do readers feel uneasy or complicit about sharing such insight with the author or narrator. *Pnin* suggests that this dynamic might be seen as an abuse of power, that it is narratologically unethical. Juxtaposition of *Pnin* with *Lolita* shows that at the same time, Nabokov was writing two books about the misuse of authority and the disregard of consent: in one case parental authority and sexual consent, in the other narrative authority and mental consent. From the anachronistic perspective of #MeToo, Nabokov cements this parallel with the narrator's treatment of Liza Bogolepov, Pnin's future wife. In the seventh chapter, when the narrator makes his descent down from the heavens to meddle, like a god, in the lives of his characters, he admits to having been attracted at one time by this "striking looking young girl in a black silk sweater." Although he initially expresses his opinion that her poems are terrible, he leaves room for revision when he spies her in another café, "sitting at a long table, abloom and ablaze among a dozen young Russian poets": "We talked. I suggested she let me see those poems again in some quieter place" (181). A few sentences later, we learn that "in the result of emotions and in the course of events, the narration of which would be of no public interest whatsoever, Liza swallowed a handful of sleeping pills" (182). This episode draws together the twin novels' forms of abuse. Just as a priest should not take advantage of his parishioners or a teacher have sex with his students, so an omniscient narrator has no business sleeping with his characters. The text punishes him by refusing to restore his license: he ends the novel imprisoned in the book like any other character and retrospectively, the reliability of his entire narrative is opened to question.

Both *Lolita* and *Pnin* deal with the non-consensual penetration of an eponymous hero by the narrator. That penetration provides the backbone for both novels, and each luxuriates at length in the narrator's pleasure and the hero's pain that are derived from the violation of the latter's physical and mental integrity. (The brilliance of both books is that the reader is induced to partake in both those sensations: the pleasures of narrative power and the pain of being a fictional character). Crucial to each of these texts, however, is the way they end with the newly empowered hero's denial of consent. Before saying good-bye, Dolores's final words to Humbert are "No . . . no" when denying his invitation to come away with him. (Indeed, this denial of consent is emphasized through repetition: "No, honey, no"; "No, it is quite out of the question, I would sooner go back to Cue"; " 'No,' she said smilingly, 'No'" [279–80]). Pnin refuses to speak to the narrator directly, but he declares to the outgoing head of his department: "I will never work under him" (170). These are characters who at the end transform themselves from victims into survivors. In *Lolita*'s penultimate paragraph, Humbert predicts that "Dolly Schiller will probably survive me by many years" (308). He is wrong about the length of time, but the reader should not slight the first six words of that sentence, which—like the scene in Coalmont that portrays her as a resilient, if, in Humbert's eyes, diminished, adult—establish her as a survivor.[6] This is not quite the notion of survival envisioned by the #MeToo movement—not only will Dolores soon die in childbirth, but neither she nor Pnin will ever take firm control of their narratives. Though there are isolated, touching moments, such as the letter Dolores writes to Humbert—"I have gone through much sadness and hardship" (266) or the note Pnin writes to Hagen at a roughly equivalent point after the miraculous salvation of his bowl (173)[7]—their denials of consent can be seen as precipitating the end of their abuser's narrative, but not as initiating the production of their own.

The sexual abuse in *Lolita* is immediately more troubling because Dolores's lack of mental transparency makes her more like a person in the real world, and a traumatized person at that. Paradoxically, the mental transparency that might serve to make a character in a novel seem more like us can also work to make us more conscious throughout that we are dealing with a work of fiction. (If we can read a person's thoughts, she can't be real). Can we imagine a narrator who asks, in the manner of Swann's series of questions to Odette, "do you mind if I uncover this thought, or this one," cognizant that only yes means yes and that consent may be withdrawn at any minute? The penetration of Pnin's mind makes us aware of how disturbing being (or reading about) a character can be.[8] The fear of some readers of *Lolita* in the #MeToo era might be that that novel normalizes pedophilia; looking at *Lolita* alongside *Pnin* reveals how the disregard of consent is normalized in literature in general.[9]

This normalization of non-consent is an underappreciated aspect of what Mikhail Bakhtin described as an author's creative love for his characters. Such love is envisioned by Bakhtin as a generous act in which the author directs his full attention to all aspects of his hero, pierces his secrets, understands him completely, *and* thus deprives him of the freedom to act in surprising, unanticipated ways: "The aesthetic embodiment of the inner man anticipates from the very outset the hero's hopelessness with respect to meaning [on his own terms]" (131). In its limitation of the hero's freedom and curtailment of his future, this gift of creation is also akin to a death sentence: "Throughout the entire course of an embodied hero's life, one can hear the tones of a requiem" (131). There have been attempts to portray Nabokov as sharing Bakhtin's positive portrait of authorial love, but an essential difference between Nabokov and Bakhtin is that Nabokov views the process of aesthetic consummation not only from the point of view of the author, as does Bakhtin, but also from that of the character, who can perceive authorial love as a fundamental breach of personal dignity, as a physical or mental molestation. Humbert Humbert and the narrator of *Pnin* can be considered bad or corrupt artists, but they lay bare the aggressive, non-consensual principle at the heart of much fiction. Nabokov's novels, by implicitly encouraging the identification that the author explicitly censures, brings the pain of this non-consensual process to the fore.

Stephen Blackwell convincingly makes the case that Nabokov's treatment of Pushkin entails the loving conversion of the poetic forerunner into a character (427–31), an act which might be treated as a powerful repudiation of the anxiety of influence. Blackwell notes that Bakhtin's depiction of an author "linger[ing] intently over an object, to hold and sculpt every detail and particular in it" is "precisely" what Humbert "fails to do in his aesthetic portrayal of Dolly Haze (because he lingers only over his solipsized image of her)" (429). Humbert, though, *does* linger, even if his lingering is tainted by sexual desire. It is worth noting that Bakhtin admitted that he took his metaphor of aesthetic consummation from sexuality to begin with: "It should be evident, of course, that we are abstracting here from the sexual features, which cloud the aesthetic purity of these irreversible actions" (42). Nabokov, who never read Bakhtin's work on artistic creation, which remained unpublished until shortly before Nabokov's death, seems to have anticipated Bakhtin's approach, and a reading of the former suggests that the latter's view of disinterested authorial love may be impossibly pure. Even should such unalloyed authorial affection be possible, Nabokov often finds abusive authorial love, like Tolstoy's unhappy families, to provide richer and more interesting material for meta-fictive storytelling.

The comparison of penetration in *Lolita* and *Pnin* has at least one more facet. *Pnin* is a novel that registers the importance of privacy—and the cruel necessity of invading it in the service of the novel. Pnin insists: "special privacy is now to me absolutely necessary" (34). The novel relentlessly attacks all sorts of group activities. "It is nothing but a kind of microcosmos of Communism—all that psychiatry," wails Pnin: "Why not leave their private sorrows to people? Is sorrow not, one asks, the only thing in the world people really possess?" (52). *Lolita* concerns itself with a different sort of privacy, the space for sexual abuse society would condemn or punish if it were committed flagrantly in the open. Within this protected space, the privacy of Dolores's body is assaulted. The novel repeatedly activates the link between privacy and sexual organs still retained in expressions like "private parts"; the word private frequently refers to sex and often to sexual abuse: "Let me be her private tutor for a year," Humbert considers saying to Dolly's mother (83). "The majority of sex offenders," he claims, "merely ask the community to allow them to pursue their practically harmless, so-called aberrant behavior, their little hot wet private acts of sexual deviation without the police and society cracking down upon them" (88). In a passage resonant with genital references, Humbert speaks of his "private aesthetics": "for I simply love that tinge of Botticellian pink, that raw rose about the lips, those wet, matted eyelashes" (64). Humbert quotes from a parenting book with advice on dealing with a recalcitrant daughter: "Let her take the brunt of your displeasure in private" (185). Here is a different meaning of privacy, "secrecy, concealment, discretion; protection from public knowledge or availability," as opposed to the "freedom from interference or intrusion" (*Oxford English Dictionary*) or the "discreteness" so important to Pnin. The ease with which these meanings of privacy can collapse into one another speaks to the subtle way in which a concept that has been used to support liberal freedoms and independence, as well as, in the law, bodily and reproductive freedom, has also served as a tool for sexual oppression.[10] Pnin the hero is opposed to disclosure, *Pnin* the novel regrets its aesthetic necessity; Humbert Humbert fears disclosure, as does Dolores, but *Lolita* loudly and eloquently embraces it. Which position is closest to or farthest from the politics of #MeToo?

CLOSE READING

Let's return to "A Nursery Tale," and to a consideration of what I have already hinted is the perverse moral of that story. The sin for which Erwin and, by conflation, the reader, is punished is not greed, nor is it the sexual objectification of others or failure to secure consent. It is rather a failure to read closely. Had Erwin selected and objectified with a sharper eye for detail, he would not have mistaken the first woman for the last. Had the reader spent more time on the text, and on the moments describing the choice of Erwin's women, she would have grasped before Erwin who this final woman was. By the logic of the narrative, Erwin is punished largely for being a poor reader, and not primarily for having excessive desires. The reader, however, should catch a subtler, ancillary message. The story has established at least an oblique rapport between disregarding sexual consent and close reading; close reading can facilitate successful sexual predation or at the very least it can serve as a complement to—and, perhaps, as a metaphor for—sexual molestation.

This link between close reading and sexual predation should not come as a surprise to those who have reflected on the #MeToo movement. As a social media phenomenon, the movement has flourished through a dynamic of quick response and an absence of hermeneutic suspicion paradoxical because in the realm of personal reflection it can be accompanied by heightened awareness about what may have been undetected abuse in the past. #MeToo encourages taking a new, retrospective look at experience and advocates powerfully for the necessity of close rereading, of wondering about the possibility of claims of abuse not made, which may contrast with a lack of suspicion about claims made in the present. It is not that the movement enshrines gullibility concerning current claims or is necessarily blind to the tenuous nature of truth. Indeed, Sarah K. Burgess situates the movement within "post-truth logics," where truth may be less important than what a claim of truth can accomplish: social change, resistance to an oppressive, patriarchal power structure, and the building of an empowered community, empathetic to survivors, and buoyed by political momentum. These goals may override the importance of whether a #MeToo claim is true in every specific instance, or whether the specific truth of a particular claim warrants the sanctions in which the claim results:

> The movement employs affective claims as truth claims. . . . The hashtag is a password of sorts meant to permit entry into the scene of address in which a subject's speech is presumed to be true, believable, and actionable without question. . . . In this context, it makes sense then that one of the demands consistently made by the movement is that people who question or critique the movement should apologize, even though the apology, when offered, does not reconcile the apologizer with those in the movement or the scene they occupy. (360–61)

In other words, while the #MeToo movement is founded on a discourse of belief in the truth of survivors' claims, it also relies on an understanding that at some point a necessary fiction may become—due to its political and moral efficacy—the truth.

Close reading can take several forms and can profit from at least two affective modes. On one hand, it can be aggressive and suspicious, looking for symptoms that expose contradictions. In this sense it has much in common with cross-examination, which seeks to destroy the coherence of a narrative and can pose an obstacle to the litigation or prosecution of #MeToo claims. On the other hand, close reading can be reverential, focused on the way in which a text succeeds aesthetically as it achieves its ends. The feminist literary scholar Jane Gallop once attempted to draw a bright line between the two modes, which she saw respectively as the properties of deconstruction and the new criticism it had dethroned. Calling the latter "close reading" and the former "symptomatic reading," she took pains to emphasize the differences: "Where new critical close reading embraces the text in order to more fully and deeply understand its excellences, 'symptomatic reading' squeezes the text tighter to reveal its perversities. New criticism is appreciative, even worshipful. Symptomatic reading tends to be demystifying, even aggressive" (*Around 1981*, 7). Within a few years, however, as deconstruction began to be challenged by new historicism, Gallop saw more affinity than difference between these two forms of close attention to a text ("Historicization," 182–83). As she argued for their commonality, she was implicitly deconstructing the opposition between worship and aggression. As in an abusive relationship, devout admiration and savage disparagement can go hand in hand.

Nabokov's approach to close reading contains both readerly postures identified by Gallop. On one hand, Nabokov was a savage reviewer, with a penchant for finding the soft spots in another writer's (or critic's) work and ripping it apart.[11] His review of W. W. Rowe's analysis of sexual symbols in Nabokov's work serves up a fireworks display of style and one-upmanship, endeavoring to show that Rowe has a clear understanding of neither Nabokov's prose nor—not coincidentally—the female body (*Strong Opinions*, 305).

Close reading of a more reverential kind—"kindness to authors"—is described by Nabokov in sensual terms: "In reading, one should notice and fondle details." In Nabokov's description of its ideal practice, close reading can sound a lot like groping. (It isn't surprising that Rowe's inept close reading should be characterized through a lack of familiarity with the female anatomy.) The work by Nabokov that most celebrates close reading, "The Vane Sisters," begins with what looks, retrospectively, like a #MeToo narrative. Sybil Vane, one of the narrator's students, is involved in an affair with one of his colleagues, "D." The narrator helps to put an end to the attachment, but he himself is clearly jealous and obsessed with Sybil. At his class's final exam, he looks at her very closely indeed. His gaze repeatedly reverts to her ("so childishly slight in close-fitting gray") for two and a half hours as he studies her make-up and searches for "visible openings into her beauty" (621).

Afterward his desire for Sybil is betrayed by the eagerness with which he picks her exam out of the pile: "I [. . .] came prematurely to Valevsky and Vane" (621). Finding a suicide note at the end of the exam, the narrator rushes to Sybil's house, but it is too late—what is left is "the tumbled bed from which a tender, inessential body, D. must have known down to its last velvet detail, had been removed" (622). The narrator spends the rest of the story haunted by Sybil and her recently deceased sister Cynthia, trying to find hints of their ghostly presence in his life. In a frenzy he close reads a variety of texts in ludicrous ways, but he misses the acrostic in the final lines that serve as the sisters' signature of the entire story. (One might say that the narrator is punished for his leering at flesh by an inability to discern the signs of spirit.) Despite the narrator's limitations, here, as in "A Nursery Tale," unwanted attention to women is linked to close observation of texts. As Nabokov might have said, only one rung on the alphabetic ladder separates a sexual from a textual predator.[12] And even though Sybil Vane secures a vengeance of sorts, veiling herself from the narrator and then co-authoring his story without his knowledge, the moral is muddled. Students are supposed to fondle the details of a text, a formulation that seems to confer interpretive and sexual agency on them. Yet since, as in "The Vane Sisters," Nabokov's work is always read under the specter of one single correct solution, the text knows what it wants. Learning how to caress a work by Nabokov as he thinks the text should be caressed opens up only a limited latitude for interpretive agency. The student who has learned to fondle the text may begin to discover that the text is groping her back.

THE SEXUALIZED WORKPLACE

Texts can't object to being fondled. Characters can object or consent to the erotic advances of other characters, but, as we have seen, the issue of whether they can agree to be penetrated by the reader has to be wrenched into the reader's consciousness. Nabokov often inscribes his reader into his texts: the moment of identification that is not supposed to occur, but on some level nearly almost does, can be extremely disquieting. "A Nursery Tale" was first published in English in *Playboy*, where the reader, following the continuations of the story throughout the issue, had to turn past dozens of photos of naked women, thus becoming another Erwin. The taboo identification may have been further reinforced by readers of *Playboy* recognizing their own anxiety in the first and last woman's retort to Erwin: "You ought to be ashamed of yourself." After all, Nabokov's presence in the magazine was designed to ensure its intellectual gravity, but here his story calls that respectability into question.

And the reader, in the world in which Nabokov established his American reputation, was often a student. The erotic pedagogic inscription already on evidence in "The Vane Sisters" emerges with even greater salience in that opening lecture Nabokov gave to his class at Cornell:

for my plan is to deal lovingly in loving and lingering detail with several European masterpieces. A hundred years ago, Flaubert in a letter to his mistress made the following remark: *Comme l'on serait savant si l'on connaissait bien seulement cinq à six livres*: What a scholar one might be if one knew well only some half a dozen books. (*Lectures on Literature,* 1)

There was no need to mention the addressee of Flaubert's letter, nor to quote it in French, other than for the purpose of equating sexual knowledge with the knowledge of books. Later the identification would be reinforced in the disparagement of "buxom best sellers that are hawked around by book clubs under the heading of historical novels" *(Lectures on Literature,* 1). The link in Nabokov's pedagogy between the study of books and the sexualization of women is made even clearer when we listen closely and hear the name of Humbert's object of desire, so tenderly evoked at the opening of his confession, in Professor Nabokov's opening rhapsody about "*lo*ving and *li*ngering de*ta*il."

If we discount a summer at Stanford, Nabokov began his American teaching career at Wellesley, a woman's college to which he referred by the shorthand of "Looks and Books" (*Think, Write, Speak,* 211). Young women there, he told an anonymous young interviewer, have "been educated to listen closely," so that "the lecturer can feel in contact with his audience" (*Think, Write, Speak,* 211). To judge from his frequent appearances in the campus newspapers, Nabokov cut a flirtatious and fascinating figure on the Wellesley campus. Whether anything he did there would have provoked #MeToo posts today is less important than the firm impression that his pedagogy at Wellesley had what in *Pnin* will be called an "erotic undercurrent" (181).[13]

To what extent does this eroticization carry over into the classroom today when Nabokov's books and lectures are taught and discussed? How do we deal with the possibility that close reading of Nabokov's fiction might become something of a hostile workplace for women?[14] At issue here is not only the topic of pedophilia but also the punning sexual wordplay that suffuses much of Nabokov's American prose. Pnin's classroom is chaste, but the narrator's animus toward Pnin is reflected in a penchant for surrounding him with bawdy double entendres that take as their model Gertrude's treatment of Ophelia. Mermaids with their "amusing parts," "vulgar old cats," pussies, a Russified Frenchman named *Kon*stantin *Chat*eau, tributes to Pushkin's and Shakespeare's most ribald moments, douches, French beavers and Prussian sham shower baths all lead back to the narrator's world, in which he contemplates everything as he does the "Paphia Fritillary," a butterfly he enjoys spreading—"underside up"—in "concentrated ecstasy" (177).[15] The squirrel, an image in the novel for predatory, artistic invention and structure, at one point metamorphizes into a "beastly grey tangle," formed by "a communal supply of athletic supporters" in a prep school locker room (95). What is the best way to approach, in class, this philological locker room in which male authors and critics bandy about the bodies of young women? Students should be made aware of this stratum of the novel, but they should also be encouraged to think about the potential stakes—the gendered costs and benefits—of these authorial winks.

One could adopt an absolutist free speech position and argue that where literature is concerned, sensibilities in the college classroom should not be taken into account. A ringing defense of the virtues of art under attack from puritanical forces was recently undertaken by the premier Nabokov scholar in France, Maurice Couturier, in a letter he wrote after *Le Monde* had failed to list *Lolita* among the 100 novels that had most provoked the enthusiasm of the paper's reviewers. Noting that *Le Monde* had long displayed an admirable "openness of spirit" on subjects touching on sexual morality, and pointing out that the paper had praised Nabokov in the past, Couturier complained: "Up until the end of the 1990s, you did not stop showering Nabokov with praise, but now you consign him to oblivion, preferring a crowd of authors who don't come up to his ankles. Has political moral correctness struck again? Have you fallen victim to the 'MeToo' syndrome?" (*The Nabokovian*). Such a position is disappointing for two reasons. First, it suggests that "open-mindedness" in regard to sexual morality and admiration for *Lolita* are both fundamentally under threat from a movement that draws attention to sexual harassment and sexual assault. To call from a position of grievance the #MeToo movement a "syndrome" or to refer to those who are influenced by it as *the movement's* "victims" is itself problematic, reflecting at best a militant indifference to the experiences from which #MeToo has sprung. Deploying such terms as part of a defense of *Lolita* may serve to confirm the unfortunate suspicion that aesthetic pleasure in general—not to mention admiration for Nabokov in particular—tends to be incompatible with compassion for real-world suffering. Second, where *Lolita* is concerned, this position, paradoxically, works against appreciation of the book's merit, part of which is the complex, entangled position of the reader who is thrilled by Nabokov's (and Humbert's) language and appalled by the use in the story to which it is being put. Rather than deploring the #MeToo movement as a hostile force, a teacher or critic can engage its concerns to enrich our appreciation of the novel.

We can admit, first of all, that the narrative and philological space in which *Lolita* or *Pnin* unfolds is essentially misogynistic. In the wake of the resignation from the United States Senate of Al Franken, Lauren Berlant wrote an insightful essay about moments where "the jokester" and "the predator" function in similar ways: "Power shows its ugliest tentacles most clearly in these [two] figures" even though they may seem miles apart:

It is hard for people to get their minds around this. It can seem like a false equivalence between the predator and the jokester. Like all analogies, it's partial. But now it's powerful to link them, because both are clearly protected by privilege over time and space and the framing of consequences in domains of capital, labor, institutional belonging and speech situations where the structurally vulnerable are forced to "choose their battles" or just act like a good sport.

Defenses of *Lolita* often insist implicitly on the line separating these two figures. Humbert is the predator, Nabokov is the jokester. Nabokov himself, however, challenges this division, intermittently calling attention to the predatory nature of his humor. Perhaps the most striking such moment in *Lolita* comes when Humbert adopts his most repentant tone:

> Unless it can be proven to me—to me as I am now, today, with my heart and by beard, and my putrefaction—that in the infinite run it does not matter a jot that a North American girl-child named Dolores Haze had been deprived of her childhood by a maniac, unless this can be proven (and if it can, then life is a joke), I see nothing for the treatment of my misery but the melancholy and very local palliative of articulate art. (283)

As a defense of art, this is a weak one, but what should not be missed is the parenthetical qualification, for in much of the novel the word "life" *has* been a joke, a genital reference stemming from an old French erotic poetic device that plays on the homonymic overlap between the words for penis (*vît*) and life (*vie*): "Light of my life, fire of my loins"; "less than six inches from my burning life"; "My life was handled by little Lo in an energetic, matter-of-fact manner as if it were an insensate gadget unconnected with me" (9, 130, 134).[16] The insertion of the parenthetical qualification—"and if it can, then life is a joke"—reveals at least a conditional awareness of the costs of such joking, undercutting the ribald frame of reference in a merger of the jokester and the predator that questions the entire game of lexical hide and seek. Yet even as he exposes the violence of his joke, Nabokov keeps telling it. The passage quoted above speaks less to the harm done to Dolores than to Humbert's continuing obsession with himself. (With what might strike a contemporary reader as prescience, at the start of that passage Humbert even rebuffs the solidarity of the #MeToo movement by solipsistically inverting its call: "to me, to me"!)

Long before #MeToo, Sarah Herbold explored the predicament of the female reader of the novel, arguing that reading *Lolita* can be empowering for women, if they see Dolly's sexual pleasure as an important element in the plot and take comfort in, or even enjoy, her manipulation of Humbert.[17] This insight does not excuse Humbert's violent behavior, and Herbold does not neglect the scenes that focus on Dolores's pain, but Herbold's suggestion does allow the female reader, through *metafictive* identification, to see the possibility for interpretive agency and aesthetic pleasure. Taking as her focus one of the most erotic scenes in the novel, where Humbert furtively uses Dolores's body to bring himself to orgasm while seated on a sofa, Herbold suggests:

> The "magic friction" between Humbert's penis and Lolita's thinly clad buttocks [. . .] is also occurring between reader and author. That is, the reader is pleasurably and painfully rubbing himself or herself up against (and or being rubbed by) the shifting layers of the story. If Lolita is a full participant, or even in control, then both men and women readers occupy different positions, both sexually and in terms of narrative irony, than if she is merely a naïve catalyst for Humbert's onanism. As long as Humbert seems to be in control and to tell a simple story, ordinary relations of dominance and submission prevail: men are aggressors and women are passive, adults know more than children, and narrators tell the truth and readers meekly absorb it. But if Humbert, Nabokov, and Lolita are all playing games (and they are) none of these assumptions holds. (83)[18]

To be sure, Herbold's is a resolutely redemptive enterprise which foregrounds the category of gender at the expense of that of age; her Lolita is a figure for the female reader, not for the child the female reader once was. Herbold begins with the conviction that women reading *Lolita* need to be given a position from which to enjoy the novel that is not primarily masochistic. Herbold goes on to show how both men and women are forced by Nabokov to play a compromising game, in which they are alternatively excited (at least aesthetically) and then shamed (morally) by the text. She argues that the appreciation of that dynamic is ultimately liberational, and that the reverse position, rejection of the novel on account of its sexism or hostility toward women, is predicated on reaffirmation of established stereotypes. Nabokov, she writes, "does not permit women and men to have entirely separate experiences of the story, but neither does he construct their experiences as simply equivalent":

> Each is induced to see through the divide that separates pornography from art, sadism from masochism, sincerity from fraud, and privacy from publicity. Imaginatively and even viscerally, the reader is forced to occupy only one side and also both sides of such divisions, all of which are buttressed by the idea that women are—or should be—chaste readers as well as citizens. (92)

Herbold emphasizes that the actual audience for whom Nabokov was writing in the 1950s was male, and her article is an attempt to break down the boundaries of Nabokov's audience, allowing a reader who remembers her gender to appreciate the novel nonetheless. The notion of play is crucial to her reading. The reader needs to play with the text, with and against Humbert, Nabokov, even Dolores. A censorious perspective deprives the female reader of this opportunity, which may be the most exhilarating part of reading Nabokov.

Herbold anticipates in this respect the vision of sexual justice recently articulated by Joseph Fischel, who attempts to move beyond a preoccupation with consent in an effort to decide more consistently what conduct to penalize in the realm of sexual harassment. Taking his cue from the journalist and culture critic Rebecca Traister, he observes that #MeToo "is not only or even primarily about sexual assault but also about sex, sexual innuendo, sexual advances, and sexual trespasses that constitute but one component of a larger discriminatory culture impeding women's equality and advancement" (179). Effective teaching of *Lolita* should make students aware of the ways in which the novel both sustains and critiques that culture, and how various readings support one or the other of those dynamics. Fischel writes that an important commonality in #MeToo incidents is their place in what he calls "a scaffold of undemocratic hedonism and sexual one-sidedness that structures the more violent, nonconsensual, harassing, and discriminatory behaviors of men in power" (181). The behavior that has come under the critique of the #MeToo movement relies on structures that compromise women's sexual autonomy:

> The #MeToo men insure against risks of rejection; they maintain positions of gendered dominance by extracting sex and pleasure from exploited subordinates. But what the #MeToo men also deny is women's (and sometimes other men's) risk, their "dignity of risk"; that is, risking sex on any terms other than the terms men set through power. How do we facilitate access for people less privileged by power to risk more and then to "demand better"? How might we democratize sexual culture? (182)

Whether *Lolita* works for or against the democratization of sexual culture depends on how it is taught and read.[19] Can we teach our students how to approach Nabokov's texts in a way that emphasizes both the pleasure and play of reading him while demonstrating a compassionate awareness of the repressive structures that have limited the ability of women to enjoy and play as equals? (This balance may be difficult to maintain. In 1925 Nabokov lauded the importance of play, elevating it to a kind of life force. In that essay, however, he showed a dangerous blind spot to play's limits: "the Germans have lately realized that the goose step won't take you far, and that boxing, football and hockey are more valuable than military or any other drills" [*Think, Write, Speak*, 33]). Can we encourage an approach that directs the attention of textual interpretation both to the text's richness and to the processes and gendered complexity of interpretation itself? Rather than ignore the world of #MeToo or agree to an obliteration of the lines between the real world and fiction that would impoverish both the curriculum and our understanding of individual texts, the classroom study of Nabokov should reaffirm these lines but point out the risks and pleasures that pushing against them makes possible.

THEORY INTO PRACTICE

Paying close attention to the concerns and practices of the #MeToo movement can contribute to the self-conscious study of literature in general and to appreciation of Nabokov's complexity in particular. The inclusion of consideration of the #MeToo movement in class discussion of the novel should not make the teaching of *Lolita* apologetic, but, rather, more interesting. We should keep in mind, moreover, that the rapport of #MeToo is far from the only way to contextualize the book. The novel's place in the history of American, Russian, or European fiction is obviously relevant, as is its status as a work of metafiction or of, as Alfred Appell calls it, "involution" (*The Annotated Lolita,* xxiii–iv). The novel's critique of and contribution to American culture also offer a rich theme. Teaching strategies, moreover, will obviously depend on the course in which the reading occurs. (Students in a semester-long class on Nabokov are unlikely to return their tickets.) If the book is being taught at a lower-division level or in a reading and composition class, it should not be forgotten how surprisingly difficult the language may be for some readers. Occasionally, one may have to ask in a very basic way "what just happened?" This is true no less on the level of the sentence than for that of a scene or chapter.

The issues I've raised above can be incorporated into the classroom in many ways: for senior and graduate seminars an entire session (or more!) can be set aside for the topic of "literature and consent" or "sex and close reading." For less sophisticated settings, here are some strategies that engage and highlight these and related issues:

1. Try to shift the axis of identification from student/character to student/reader. In 1950 Walker Gibson, a contemporary of Nabokov in the pages of the *New Yorker,* wrote an accessible, thought-provoking essay entitled "Authors, Speakers, Readers, and Mock Readers." The mock reader is not the person holding the book but the "fictitious reader whose mask and costume the individual takes on in order to experience the language" and, we might add, even the ideology of a book (2). The mock reader is "a projection, a fictitious modification" of the actual reader. Students do not have to read Gibson, but they can pay attention to the sort of person a book asks them temporarily to pretend to be. "A bad book," Gibson says, "is a person in whose mock reader we discover a person we refuse to become, a role we will not

play" (5). In the course of reading *Lolita* the instructor might at various points ask the students to write a page on "who is this book for" and to consider whether they fit (or can make themselves fit) into that category. This exercise allows reluctant students who are reading the book out of a feeling of curricular compulsion to engage productively with an aspect of consent that is not limited to what happens within the text but between reader and text.

2. Nabokov's own vision of his mock reader may be the one he describes in his lecture: the reader has climbed a mountain and, "panting and happy," meets the master-artist at the top and slips with him "simultaneously" into an embrace. Potentially, a #MeToo scenario if there ever was one, with an unwanted and prolonged hug a reward for intellectual and aesthetic discernment! Nabokov emphasizes the one-on-one relationship of author and reader. The reading of a book can be seen as the development of a close and often submissive relationship with a strong author who establishes the rules and expects the reader to follow his instructions in a manner that combines cleverness with compliance.[20] The pleasures of such a rapport are not to be dismissed; regardless of gender, for some readers such pleasure can be fundamental to the excitement of reading Nabokov. This sort of pleasure, a blend of insight and submission, which acquires marked sexual connotations in Nabokov's work, can be brought into connection with some of the recent fiction by women writers that explores paradoxes of female desire especially fraught in the #MeToo era (Rooney, Popkey). A reader of Nabokov, moreover, can alternate between following the rules and questioning them. Collective reading of Nabokov is a particularly conducive approach to the latter mode. Not surprisingly, Humbert's ideal model of pedagogy is private tutoring; discussion groups, such as the female one at the Planned Parenthood clinic in *Pnin*, inspire disgust and contempt. Nabokov's lecturing called attention to himself as an authoritative figure, and that focus must also have worked against the establishment of a sense of intellectual collectivity among his students. (One imagines that students addressed one another in Nabokov's Cornell classrooms infrequently, if at all). It is a platitude that encouraging student participation is a good idea, but when discussing Nabokov, allowing students to direct discussion should be a particular imperative. The instructor should call attention to the way Nabokov cultivates the parallel between the author and reader, on one hand, and the teacher and student on the other; for some readers the classroom can be a forum for undoing and even reversing this form of transference, especially where it might be reinforced by the instructor's gender.[21] While this is easier to accomplish in a seminar—a form of learning antithetical to Nabokov's celebrated lec-

tures—even in a larger class an instructor should try to encourage students to address one another and to cede at least temporarily the podium to brief student presentations (of individual sections of the novel, or of critical approaches to the text). It is useful to make the students aware that play with different forms of teaching can facilitate play with different modes of reading. Finally, discussion of the relevance of #MeToo to a reading of *Lolita* can raise productive questions about the advantages and drawbacks to collective and individual readings of literature in general.

3. On the occasion of the novel's fiftieth "birthday," *The New Republic* invited ten women—writers and critics—each to take a short section of the book as the basis for a short essay. All are clearly engaged with the book, nearly all of them also push against it. A wide range of identificatory responses are employed, from Alexandra Schwartz's telling a story of her own objectification on a disturbing date all the way to Hannah Gold's comment on the novel's road trip: "hilarious, brief, totally unrelatable" ("*Lolita* Turns Sixty"). This short publication models individual and collective gendered reading. It also shows how individual readers change their assessments over time. The wonderful thing about these contributions is the way their authors interpret without passing judgment. (Humbert asks for judgment, why honor *his* request?) It is as though these ten authors were given the remit "You don't have to *decide* anything now." It is worthwhile asking students to do something similar with five to ten pages of text.

4. Close reading is essential, and instructors should not shy away from scenes such as the one on the davenport analyzed by Herbold. In all cases, give the students the opportunity to consider *how* they react—not only to the subject matter and not only to the language, but to the experience of close reading itself. Consider putting together close reading anthologies—all the students submit five short comments about a given section, which the instructor then turns into a single document, with the entries shuffled and anonymized. Combining individual and collective reading, this exercise makes the rich playfulness of the novel readily apparent. The advantage of having students write multiple comments is that it frees them initially from the burden of formulating a single interpretive position as they would in an analytical essay. (They can even experiment with donning the identity of different mock readers.) Short, multiple responses open up room for play with the text and encourage students to make imaginative suggestions that they might otherwise be reluctant to propose. (After further reflection and discussion, some of these comments can later germinate into conceptual essays.) At some point during my semester class on Nabokov, I ask the students to reflect on whether close reading makes

them into better people and how it carries over, if at all, into everyday life. (Is close reading a value or a skill, and how does it relate to other values and skills?) Some negative answers are to be expected, even from students who later become graduate students and professors in the humanities.

WORKS CITED

Bakhtin, M. M. *Art and Answerability.* Trans. Vadim Liapunov. Austin: University of Texas Press, 1990.

Berlant, Lauren. "The Predator and the Jokester." *The New Inquiry,* December 13, 2017. https://thenewinquiry.com/the-predator-and-the-jokester/.

Blackwell, Stephen H. "Calendar Anomalies, Pushkin and Aesthetic Love in Nabokov." *Slavic and East European Review* 96, no. 3 (2018): 401–31.

Burgess, Sarah. K. "Between the Desire for Law and the Law of Desire: #MeToo and the Cost of Telling the Truth Today." *Philosophy & Rhetoric* 51, no. 4 (2018): 342–67.

Clandfield, Peter, and Conley, Tim. "'You Talk Like a Book, *Dad,*' Pedagogical Anxiety and *Lolita.*" *Soundings* 88, no. 1–2 (Spring–Summer 2005): 15–41.

Cohn, Dorrit. *Transparent Minds: Narrative Modes for Presenting Consciousness in Fiction.* Princeton: Princeton University Press, 1978.

Couturier, Maurice. "Letter to *Le Monde.*" *The Nabokovian,* September 29, 2019. https://thenabokovian.org/node/35813.

De la Durantaye, Leland. *Style Is Matter: The Moral Art of Vladimir Nabokov.* Ithaca, NY: Cornell University Press, 2007.

Dolinin, Alexander. "Nabokov's Time Doubling: From *The Gift* to *Lolita.*" *Nabokov Studies* 2 (1995): 3–40.

Dragunoiu, Dana. "The Afterlives of Odette and Albertine in *Lolita*'s Final Chapters." *Comparative Literature* 72, no. 3 (September 2020): 340–60.

———. "*Lolita*: Nabokov's Rewriting of Dostoevski's *The Brothers Karamazov.*" *Nabokov Studies* 13 (2014/2015): 31–52.

———. *Vladimir Nabokov and the Poetics of Liberalism.* Evanston: Northwestern University Press, 2011.

Dwyer, Anne. "Why I Teach *Lolita,*" *Inside Higher Ed,* May 14, 2018. https://www.insidehighered.com/views/2018/05/14/teaching-lolita-still-appropriate-opinion.

Dyne, Thomas. "'That's the Horrible Part: I Understand Everything!' The Narrative Ethics of Misreading the Other in Dostoevsky's *Poor Folk* and 'The Meek One.'" Forthcoming in *Slavic and East European Journal.*

Fischel, Joseph J. *Screw Consent: A Better Politics of Sexual Justice.* Oakland: University of California Press, 2019.

Gallop, Jane. *Around 1981: Academic Feminist Literary Theory.* New York: Routledge, 1992.

———. "The Historicization of Literary Studies and the Fate of Close Reading." *Profession* 2007: 181–86.

Gibson, Walker. "Authors, Speakers, Readers, and Mock Readers." In *Reader, Response Criticism from Formalism to Post-Structuralism,* ed. Jane P. Tompkins. Baltimore: Johns Hopkins University Press, 1980, 1–6.

Herbold, Sarah. "'(I have Camouflaged everything, my love)': *Lolita* and the Woman Reader." *Nabokov Studies* 5 (1998/1999): 81–94.

Kokinova, Kate. "Lolita Reading *Lolita*: Rhetoric of Reader Participation." *Nabokov Studies* 14 (2016): 59–77.

"*Lolita* Turns Sixty." *The New Republic,* December 15, 2015. https://newrepublic.com/article/125536/lolita-turns-60.

Meek, Michelle. "Lolita Speaks: Disrupting Nabokov's 'Aesthetic Bliss.'" *Girlhood Studies* 10, no. 3 (Winter 2017): 152–67.

Milano, Alyssa. Tweet of October 15, 2017. https://twitter.com/Alyssa_Milano/status/919659438700670976.
Nabokov, Vladimir. "A Nursery Tale." *Playboy,* January 1974: 99, 100, 116, 268–69.
———. *The Annotated Lolita.* Ed. Alfred Appel, Jr. New York: Vintage, 1991.
———. *Invitation to a Beheading.* Trans. Dmitri Nabokov in collaboration with the author. New York: Vintage, 1989.
———. *Lectures on Literature.* New York: Harvest, 1980.
———. *Nikolai Gogol.* New York: New Directions, 1961.
———. *Pnin.* New York: Vintage, 1989.
———. *The Stories of Vladimir Nabokov.* New York: Vintage, 1995.
———. *Strong Opinions.* New York: Vintage, 1990.
———. *Think, Write, Speak: Uncollected Essays, Reviews, Interviews and Letters to the Editor.* Ed. Brian Boyd and Anastasia Tolstoy. New York: Penguin, 2019.
Naiman, Eric. *Nabokov, Perversely.* Ithaca, NY: Cornell University Press, 2010.
The Oxford English Dictionary. Online edition.
Patnoe, Elizabeth. "Discourse, Ideology and Hegemony: The Double Dramas in and around *Lolita.*" In *Discourse and Ideology in Nabokov's Prose*, ed. David H. J. Larmour. London: Routledge, 2002, 111–36.
Popkey, Miranda. *Topics of Conversation.* New York: Knopf, 2020.
Proust, Marcel. *In the Shadow of Young Girls in Flower.* Trans. James Grieve. New York: Penguin, 2002.
———. *The Prisoner and the Fugitive.* Trans. Carol Clark and Peter Collier. New York: Penguin, 2002.
———. *Swann's Way.* Trans. Lydia Davis. New York: Penguin, 2002.
Rooney, Sally. *Conversations with Friends.* New York: Hogarth, 2017.
Schiff, Stacy. *Véra (Mrs. Vladimir Nabokov).* New York: Random House, 1999.
Stockton, Kathryn Bond. *The Queer Child: On Growing Sideways in the Twentieth Century.* Durham: Duke University Press, 2009.
Vogler, Candace. "The Moral of the Story." *Critical Inquiry* 34, no. 1 (Autumn 2007): 5–35.
Webster's New International Dictionary. 2nd. ed. Ed. William Allan Neilson. Springfield, MA: G. and C. Merriam, 1952.
Youtube. "Lolita 1997—Deleted Scene—The Sofa." https://www.youtube.com/watch?v=7sq5FoG1QSQ&list=PL7Cp79okrwtj_UClV3KVQqWnw7VgrzkfO&index=3.

NOTES

I am grateful for the perceptive and extremely helpful responses of Dana Dragunoiu, Elizabeth Geballe, and Eléna Rakhimova-Sommers to earlier versions of this chapter.

1. This point has been made by various astute readers of Nabokov, including Dolinin, Dragunoiu ("*Lolita*: Nabokov's Rewriting"), and de la Durantaye, who sees Hermann, in *Despair*, as exemplary of several "criminal artists" in Nabokov's work who are "guilty of applying the 'methods' destined for *art* to *life*" (51, emphasis in the original).

2. Bad readers of fiction "concentrate on the social-economic angle" or hope to learn about the past (*Lectures on Literature*, 3).

3. In the original Russian version of the story, Erwin's first selection is referred to as a girl (*devushka*) when he initially sees her, but a woman (*zhenshchina*) in her second appearance. Her rapid maturation seems to have endowed her with a subjectivity that allows her to say "No." In the English version of the story, she reverts to a "girl" at the moment of Erwin's recognition. In any case, with the exception of the fourteen year old, there is no suggestion that—unlike Dolores Haze—any of Erwin's selections are below the age of consent.

4. The narrator's interaction with Albertine, his principal object of desire, is more complicated. During her first visit to his room, he ignores her denial of consent and she rings for help.

On her second visit, she consents to a kiss, whereupon the narrator decides to save up her consent for use on a future occasion.

5. The narrator is able to dial up the intensity of Pnin's accent at will, and his mocking "possession" of Pnin's language is epitomized by the feeling Pnin has after having obtained dentures: "when the plates were thrust in, it was like a poor fossil skull being fitted with the grinning jaws of a perfect stranger" (38).

6. For a different approach to the question of *Lolita*'s survival, one which takes into account the calendrical discrepancies of the novel, see Dana Dragunoiu, "The Afterlives of Odette and Albertine in *Lolita*'s Final Chapters," 349–54.

7. If we use word count as a measure of length, Dolores's letter reaches Humbert after 86 percent of the novel has been read, while Pnin pens his note at the 90 percent mark.

8. In the novel's final pages the narrator is characterized by Pnin as a "dreadful inventor" (185), an aspersion that is part of the narrator's descent from omniscience to the role of a character. It is conceivable that the narrator has invented all of Pnin's thoughts, but this possibility is not raised before the concluding chapter of the novel, and throughout most of the text the reader feels with Pnin the pain of being penetrated, parasitized, and read.

9. My thinking here has been influenced by the forthcoming work of Thomas Dyne, an important and transformative extension to Russian realism of critical work on the ethics of narration, such as Constance Vogler's analysis of the function of mental opacity as a dividing line between art and life.

10. Dana Dragunoiu sees in *Lolita* "an ambivalence toward liberal values" which is "generated by a communitarian sensitivity to the ways in which a commitment to personal freedoms undermines the state's capacity to protect not only itself but also its most vulnerable members." "The liberal state," she adds, "turns a blind eye to the exploitation and violence that America's commitment to personal privacy can occlude" (*Vladimir Nabokov and the Poetics of Liberalism*, 130).

11. His recently published analysis of Thomas Mann's "A Railway Accident" offers a fine case in point (*Write, Think, Speak*, 229–32).

12. See Nabokov's comment in his book on Gogol: "the difference between the comic side of things, and their cosmic side, depends upon one sibilant" (142).

13. On Nabokov at Wellesley, see Schiff, 138–42.

14. Elizabeth Patnoe, who has raised this issue in the context of a graduate seminar, tells the story of how a discussion of *Lolita* with other students in a café led to one student who had been sexually molested precipitously leaving the table (116–17). A striking aspect of this scene is that the student who left was triggered not by reading *Lolita* herself nor by a classroom discussion of the novel but by Patnoe's expression of outrage about the book.

15. In Nabokov's dictionary the figurative meaning of that word, *paphian*, is given as "pertaining to love, esp. illicit love, or wantonness" (*Websters*, 1768).

16. See Patnoe's discussion of Nabokov's use of this word (125–26).

17. As Kathryn Bond Stockton has noted, what has made filming *Lolita* so problematic has not been showing rape or even statutory rape, but the problem of how to represent "a sexual child" (33). Neither released film version of *Lolita* contains the scene on the sofa, although Adrian Lyne did film it before cutting it out. Youtube, "*Lolita* 1997."

18. For a reading of the novel that raises questions about the complexity of adolescent desire and its place in both criticism and rewritings of *Lolita*, see Meek. A strikingly different reading of the reader's role in this scene is provided by Clandfield and Conley, 27.

19. See Clandfield and Conley's remark that "the case of *Lolita* would seem to bear out . . . that teaching and learning require some degree of risk, and some level of involvement with intractable kinds of impulses and desires" (35).

20. On Nabokov as an author whose poetics are predicated on instruction, see Kokinova.

21. Clandfield and Conley once again provide eloquent advice: "we need to encourage students to speak as themselves—or, if that phrasing suggests too tall or presumptuous an order, at least to encourage them to subsume *without subduing* the voices of the text with a critical discussion. We must quote and analyze key passages in order to make the text an engaging presence in the classroom; we must also persuade students to tell us, and each other, of their responses to the book" (19).

Chapter Nine

Resisting Humbert's Rhetorical Appeals

A Reevaluation of Lolita*'s Ethics*

Lisa Ryoko Wakamiya

In the 2008 volume *Approaches to Teaching Nabokov's* Lolita, I published "Humbert's 'Gendered' Appeals to the Jury Not of his Peers," in which I reflected on my experiences teaching Nabokov's novel.[1] At the time I had asked my students to examine Humbert Humbert's calculated addresses to the presumed "gentlemen" and "gentlewomen" who judge his actions. The students considered the sort of man Humbert imagined as his peer, and the assumptions that accompanied his creation of the "frigid gentlewomen" whom he regards with disdain even as he begs their forgiveness. Ultimately, Humbert's credibility as a narrator and his alternating appeals to male fantasy and traditional values proved so unstable that the students quickly shifted their focus from his rhetorical practices to evaluating how they should approach them as readers.

Since writing that piece, my approach to teaching the novel has changed. I have changed, as have my students and the climate in which they encounter the novel. We have grown wary of public apologias—the non-apologetic statements that public figures issue to explain actions that they regret only if they inadvertently happened to have caused anyone harm. While such statements primarily reside in the realm of public relations, they inevitably color my students' responses to *Lolita*. Already in 2007 James Phelan observed that readers "determined not to be taken in by Humbert" and who resist "all of his rhetorical appeals, including those that arise from his self-condemnations at the end of his narrative," are more common now than they were in 1961, when Wayne C. Booth focused his attention on readers "taken in by

Humbert's artful narration."[2] Based on how my students responded to *Lolita* in 2008 and 2018, few, if any, allowed themselves to be seduced by Humbert's "Confession of a White Widowed Male." But if my students twelve years ago wondered how they should read *Lolita*, with some eventually ascribing agency to the briefly glimpsed, married and pregnant Mrs. Dolly Schiller, my students in 2018 struggled to read as they evoked the apologias of Harvey Weinstein, Kevin Spacey, and others that emerged in the wake of #MeToo. Their responses revealed their distrust of a form they associated with high-profile sexual predators who sought to defend their public reputations, and the challenges presented by rhetorical situations in which neither accusers nor the accused can be confident that others are open to the message they hope to communicate.

The present study addresses my students' difficulty engaging with *Lolita*, a consequence of the continuing shift in reception that Phelan discerned and of substantive changes in the genre of the apologia over time. This chapter considers the repercussions of these changes, as *Lolita* becomes at once thoroughly relevant to the present and detached from evolving discourses around inclusiveness as they relate to reading practices and pedagogy. Finally, this study will examine its own attention to generic criticism and rhetoric, as well as recent apologias for teaching *Lolita* and "bad-faith millennial bashing" over "cancel culture" and the perceived sanctimony of #MeToo,[3] all of which suggest that anxiety over the changing reception of *Lolita* bespeaks the unsettled relations between the novel and the ethical situations encountered in our daily lives.

In his study of bonding and estranging unreliability in *Lolita*, Phelan argues that the potential for misreading *Lolita* is built into the very structure of the novel. While Humbert remains an unreliable narrator throughout, the "complex coding of Humbert's narration in Part One" has the "paradoxical result of reducing the interpretive, affective, or ethical distance between the narrator and the authorial audience."[4] According to Phelan, readers of part I who narrow the distance between Humbert and themselves are mistaken, but so too are those readers who so thoroughly reject the equivocations of part I that they dismiss part II, in which Humbert admits that "Had I come before myself, I would have given Humbert thirty-five years for rape."[5] While some would argue that the latter is not a misreading, but a possible and even ethical reading that can be sustained by Humbert's narration itself, for Phelan both are "unintended negative consequences of Nabokov's brilliant experiment with estranging and bonding unreliability."[6] Phelan concludes that Nabokov must bear some responsibility for those readers who fall into the traps he set for them, as must readers for not recognizing and overcoming those traps.

Turning to the appreciable increase in readers who feel estranged from Humbert's narrative, according to Phelan this phenomenon should be attributed in part to greater reader fallibility. The consequences of "misreading" part II of *Lolita* are that Nabokov will not "make us feel moved" by "Humbert's change from the beginning of his narration," and the ensuing absence of empathy in the reader will dangerously mirror that of Humbert, whose neglect of others adds to his catalog of cruelty. These consequences are only a problem, however, if one assumes the primacy of authorial intention over reader autonomy and if the reader is bothered by lack of empathy for a self-admitted pedophile and rapist. But what Phelan's study implies, and what cultural critics and scholars make explicit, is that the "misreading" offers a position of ethical certainty that is denied when the reader remains torn between Humbert's charm and abuse. Lionel Trilling argued that "Literature is the human activity that takes the fullest and most precise account of variousness, possibility, complexity, and difficulty,"[7] yet fewer readers now find Humbert's condition complex. Humbert's *narration* remains complex and difficult to be sure, and while some might argue that an unwillingness to engage with complexity is what alienates today's readers from *Lolita* and perhaps from "serious literature" altogether, setting ethical certainty and reader autonomy against ethical ambiguity and authorial intention only gets us so far. Approaching literature from a position of ethical certainty is not easily evaluated in terms of its correctness or incorrectness, but this approach is symptomatic of a larger change in the condition of reading in which Nabokov's "traps" no longer function as they once did.

For the reader to "feel moved," or at least to be willing to work through Humbert's narration, she must recognize that the novel allows her to access something—whether knowledge, experience, understanding, or something else that the reader herself may not even be able to articulate—that makes the novel worth reading. The imaginary relations that the reader constructs as she reads the novel acknowledge that she is undertaking a quest for knowledge that can be fulfilled through the act of reading. Reading reviews and studies of *Lolita* provides insight into this dynamic and what readers were seeking (or if they did not know what they were seeking, what they found) when they read it. Take, for instance, Erica Jong's 1988 review of *Lolita*, written thirty years after the novel's publication, which establishes upfront her identification with the author: "As one whose literary debut was also steeped in scandal, I know intimately the ambivalent feelings of an author who gains wide fame and commercial acceptance through a misunderstanding of motives. Much as one wants the acceptance conferred by best-sellerdom, it is bittersweet to win this by being thought a pervert."[8] While ostensibly demonstrating her identification with the *author*, Jong's slip in characterizing *Lolita* as a "literary debut" brings her identification with *Humbert* into focus. Immediately following the description of her intimate understanding of Nabokov's circumstances, she acknowledges that "Nabokov knew that he had been toiling in the vineyards of the muse since adolescence. The public did not [. . .] With eleven extraordinary novels, a study of Gogol, an autobiography, numerous short stories, poems and translations behind him, the author of 'Lolita' was hardly a literary novice."⁹ On the one hand, this elaboration allows Jong to differentiate herself from the Anglophone public that was likely unfamiliar with Nabokov's long literary career before *Lolita*. On the other, it makes her initial characterization of *Lolita* as a "literary debut" all the more curious, as this more accurately describes Humbert's "Lolita, Confession of a White Widowed Male" than it does Nabokov's novel.

When Jong turns to her discussion of what can be gained from reading *Lolita*, her identifications with Humbert's narrative become more closely foregrounded. "The book works, above all," she writes, "because it is so clearly the story of a man maddened by an impossible love, the impossible love for an impossible object: a banal little girl who calls him 'kiddo.' Are not all impossible, obsessional loves inexplicable to other people? Do our friends ever understand what we see in them? Isn't that inexplicability the wonder and the terror of obsessional loves?"[10] Jong's questions call on the reader to identify with her reading of *Lolita*, in which Humbert's "impossible" love gradually transitions into one's own "obsessional loves," which are simultaneously transgressive and an object of wonder, always awash in a field of alterity. Behind or beyond her identification with the *image* of an other, Jong has identified what is mysteriously, desirously, Other in herself. Jong's characterization of Nabokov's novel as a "masterpiece" grounds it firmly in the realm of the symbolic (i.e., that of hierarchy, order, and the Law), as a supposed subject of knowledge, and when she begins to discuss "impossible" or "obsessional loves" against this symbolic locus, one easily recognizes a transferential relationship in which the reader's "demand for recognition of his or her own unconscious story" is answered by "the other who refuses to behave like an other, [but] is really the Other in the patient's being," the other in whose discourse the reader finds an echo of her own discourse, and subsequently finds knowledge.[11] Calling on her reader to acknowledge the inexplicability of desire, she finds Humbert's condition to be universal ("Humbert is every man who is driven by desire.").

My students were unmoved by Humbert's narration and found little, if any, grounds for identification with it. Given the option to write their final projects on a subject of their choosing, only two students chose to write about *Lolita*. One of those students, hereafter identified as "D," wrote the paper that I will now discuss. Her paper is remarkable in that despite an unreceptive attitude toward Humbert's narrative the student looked for something in it that made the novel worth reading, and like Jong and other readers, saw Humbert's narration as an entry point to the knowledge she sought.

The premise of "D"'s paper was to demonstrate "how Humbert fits into particular categories of sexual offender" identified in criminological discourse, how "the effects of sexual assault" are exhibited in young women, and "how Dolores Haze displays those symptoms."[12] In her analysis, "D" recognizes the value of the novel and of Nabokov's achievement in that they corroborate empirically derived data found in criminological studies of sex offenders, particularly in cases of child sexual victimization. As a post-#MeToo reading of *Lolita*, "D"'s study displays a structure identical to that found in Jong's reading, but the points of identification and transference have been replaced with new coordinates. Where Jong identified *Lolita* as a "masterpiece," placing it firmly within a canon of literary works that "seem always to have existed, unopposed"[13]—a synecdochic *figure* of regulating law—"D" found a compatible domain, identifying it with *the* law, regulating social behaviors and actions. Jong recognizes (and is recognized by) Nabokov as a canonical author, a subject of knowledge and locus of transference, whose creation Humbert Humbert opens the way to knowledge of the self; "D" recognizes Nabokov as an (imaginary) fellow expert on the behavior of criminals. Humbert's unreliable narration still remains the object of analysis, only here the reader's "unconscious story" is not that of messy desire, but— speaking purely structurally—that of an obsessional need for order. In the imaginary guise of an expert criminologist much like "Nabokov," "D" allows for the story of sexual assault of a minor to find its recognition in the law. Where Jong identifies with transgression, "D" identifies with regulation.[14]

Students' responses to Lolita are an integral part of its pedagogy, and as I read "D"'s paper I realized that I could not have asked for a better argument for incorporating not only the context that gave rise to *Lolita* into my teaching, but the context in which it is read. This includes the #MeToo movement, in which women spoke publicly about their experiences of sexual harassment and violence, foregrounding subjective acts of enunciation to enact social justice and engage in a wider debate about sexual coercion. It includes multiple news stories in which acts of sexual violence committed by public figures were recounted in detail, and in which the accused denied the allegations and issued a "fauxpology."[15] All of this might be said to be part of a larger condition in which "literary art, as Trilling defined it, has been largely displaced by life—or, at least, by the pictures of life ceaselessly produced by the all-powerful media—as the realm in which we lose ourselves in a moral problem."[16] In reference to Dylan Farrow's wrenching account of how her adoptive father, the director Woody Allen, sexually molested her when she was seven years old, Lee Siegel writes, "The alleged abuse is heinous— there's nothing 'artistic' about it—yet the arguments of each party are suffused with the kind of rich, if indeterminate, emotional, psychological, and intellectual twists and turns that literature seeks to delineate."[17]

Against this backdrop, a reevaluation of mid-century literary classics is underway. John Updike was the subject of reevaluation in 2019 following the Library of America's reissue of his first four novels. One review, printed in the *Times Literary Supplement,* was titled "Giving Him His Due," with its online publication subtitled "Claire Lowdon on Why We Should Still Read

John Updike."[18] Another, written by Patricia Lockwood for the *London Review of Books*, makes its intent clear from its opening sentences: "I was hired as an assassin. You don't bring in a thirty-seven-year-old woman to review John Updike in the year of our Lord 2019 unless you're hoping to see blood on the ceiling."[19] Despite coming at Updike from seemingly opposite directions, both Lowdon and Lockwood acknowledge that the passage of time has changed how we read. Lowdon cites Updike's first rule for reviewing ("Try to understand what the author wished to do, and do not blame him for not achieving what he did not attempt"), then adds, "But 2019 wants to know why we should play by Updike's rules. Increasingly, fiction is judged on content over style. Updike chooses to write about an asshole with a penis: if you don't want to read a book about assholes with penises, then Updike has written a bad book."[20] The inconsistent relation between content and style shapes Lockwood's reading: "Updike's reliably beautiful descriptions, always his strength far above dialogue, plot and characterisation, now betrayed my faith on every other page: how can a man who lights on the phrase 'tulip sheen' to describe the skin of a woman's breast use a racial slur to describe another woman's labia in the same book?"[21] In these reappraisals of Updike's work, Lowdon and Lockwood recognize that the elevation of content over style and the value in reading Updike's work, that is, gaining a better understanding of the past, stand out as significant changes in reception. The sublime quality of Updike's prose that led earlier generations to appreciate his writing—Nabokov, in conversation with Alfred Appel, "talked admiringly and often wittily of the work of Borges, Updike, Salinger, Genet, Andrei Sinyavsky ('Abram Tertz'), Burgess, and Graham Greene"[22]—is not intrinsic and everlasting. Where style once occupied an exalted place in the fantasy space correlative with the symbolic system of literature (as the symbolic hierarchy itself is reordered), it now falls into a less-exalted place, with something else now in the eminent position.[23]

These reviews, "D"'s paper, and Siegel's proposal that the news is replacing literature as the field in which we explore ethical questions, take as an underlying premise that one generation's sublime object, elevated and worthy of admiration and analysis, has been replaced with another. In the case of my student "D," style—correlative with literature qua Great Art (what Lacan calls its *objet petit a* or in lay terms its "je ne sais quoi")—has been replaced by the "arguments" correlative with the law. Lowdon uses "2019" as a collective noun, implying that a widely shared system of values now elevates content above style. Referring back to Phelan's observations about the shift in interpretations of part II of *Lolita*, ethical certainty is favored over uncertainty. The new sublime object, in each of these cases, is something that is not typically associated with art, yet now occupies the position that style once did. These acts of sublimation do "not involve directing the drive to a different object"—after all, both Jong and "D" read the same novel and the supposition that reading it led to knowledge remained constant—"but rather changing the nature of the object to which the drive was already directed."[24] In the example of "D"'s turn to the law, there is the supposition that the law provides justice. Even if the belief that justice can be found in law is a "necessary structural illusion,"[25] it is the illusion on which social order rests. For "D," people are subject to the law and must uphold it. The potential for justice lies in this contract, as does the possibility for truth to be derived from the empirical data gathered in criminological studies, leading her to sublimate legal "argument" and to reorder literature into the form of the law.

These searches for certainty at a time of reevaluation have been accompanied by unforgiving media characterizations of the post-#MeToo generation, and giving students an opportunity to respond to these characterizations would be a welcome addition to pedagogy. In her article "Would Any Publisher Dare to Publish *Lolita* Now?" Rachel Johnson asks, "Would any publisher have the balls to publish a book by an old white man about an old white man rogering an underage girl, given that the list of too-hot-to-handle topics (as described by [Lionel] Shriver) include 'anything to do with gender, sex, race, immigration, disability, social class, obesity and Islam?'"[26] The question assumes that "the novel of the 20th century that stood the test of time," "listed as one of the 100 best novels ever written by *Le Monde*, *Time*, and newspapers passim,"[27] would never be published in a climate in which artists and publishers have been browbeaten into submission by #MeToo. Johnson voices her misgivings about the post-#MeToo search for ethical certainty and social justice by juxtaposing her anxiety about the of-the-moment influence of the #MeToo movement against *Lolita*'s timelessness. This leads her not to articulate *Lolita*'s artistic merits, but to ring false alarms about the potential future classics that aren't being published due to a new censoriousness in the publication industry, and speculate about the retroactive disappearance of classics that have been in print for over sixty years. The recently retired publisher Dan Franklin, then at the Vintage imprint Jonathan Cape, responded to Johnson's question with an unambiguous, "No. I wouldn't publish *Lolita*. What's different today is #MeToo and social media—you can organize outrage at the drop of a hat. If *Lolita* was offered to me today, I'd never be able to get it past the acquisition team—a committee of 30-year-olds, who'd say, 'If you publish this book we will all resign.'"[28]

Laura Waddell, a self-described millennial in the publishing industry, responds to such speculation with vehemence: "Alongside trigger warnings and safe spaces, the imaginary millennial war on *Lolita* has become an oddly specific cultural trope. As a stick to beat us with, it's rotten. Nobody making this statement seems to have consulted any millennials for their thoughts."[29] Waddell's statement creates an opening for discussion in its recognition that manufactured outrage over a hypothetical situation in which *Lolita* cannot be published stands in for the fact that *Lolita* is being read and discussed in the classroom. It also opens the door to acknowledging that many students are active participants in discussions around #MeToo, and may have performed a range of rhetorical stances in these conversations, from "calling out" perpetrators for their actions, to debating the complexities of #MeToo as a movement, and acknowledging that a hashtag does not require victims of trauma to publicly share their stories.[30] Students may also have recognized the discursive frames that shape these online debates, which "maintain an ideal female victim (repentant), male savior, and the grotesque and rare male rapist," and often include counter claims that are made to "to discipline the situation."[31] The disciplining of post-#MeToo voices is a counterpart to the excessive and ubiquitous nature of many of today's public apologias.

Public statements issued in the wake of #MeToo present rhetorical situations and genres such as the apologia, in which the initial accusation is accompanied by discursive framing that presents counter claims intended to question the credibility of the accuser, as well as the accused's refusal to claim responsibility for his actions. These discursive frames sound very much like those that organize Humbert's narration, and as long as readers see that connection, they are bound to evaluate Humbert's apologia in much the same way that they respond to those they encounter in their public lives. Nabokov could hardly have anticipated a scenario in which readers of his novel would be inundated by the public apologias of sexual offenders seeking exoneration, and examining the reasons and contexts behind the apologias released by public figures and how they contribute to their meaning provides a useful framework for acknowledging the role of allusion in Nabokov's novel, which revealingly draws the title of Humbert's narration from case histories of psychiatric works while parodying the "titillating confessional novel" and "the expectations of the reader who hopes Lolita will provide the pleasures of pornography."[32]

As a genre, the apologia is less identifiable as a form than as "a catalog of options available to rhetors."[33] Of critical importance is the function of the apologia: "Stemming from the interplay between a rhetor's purpose and an audience's expectations within a certain context," the function of the apologia "constitutes its meaning, or the way it is used in any given time to satisfy collective needs."[34] Tracing the function of the apologia from the Classical period to the present, Sharon D. Downey observes that contemporary apologias differ substantively from those of previous periods. After noting that previous apologia required an accusation, setting, audience, and resolution, and typically produced "some kind of demonstrable effect," she states that those of the contemporary period have lost these situational markers. The contemporary apologia:

reflects contradictory, self-serving motives, "masks moral responsibility," exploits audience ignorance and emotions while championing the same values breached by the apologist, undermines facts and accuracy and shuns confrontation of issues. The net effect was a staged event, a decisive rhetoric of manipulation. That this subversive form persisted implies the existence of some pragmatic purpose. In the absence of rules for the conduct of apologia, contemporary apologia may well have functioned as delay or postponement tactics—a view intimating that time heals, distorts, forgives, and forgets.

These subversive features are recognizable in the apologias published after #MeToo,[35] even in their more unconventional forms. These include John Hockenberry's essay "Exile: And a Year of Trying to Find a Road Back from Personal and Public Shame," in which Hockenberry embeds a rereading of *Lolita* within an autobiographical essay about being dismissed from Public Radio International after allegations of his sexual misconduct became public,[36] and the video "Let Me Be Frank," in which Kevin Spacey delivers a monologue in character as Frank Underwood, the villain he played on the series *House of Cards* until sexual assault charges were filed against the actor.[37] In the former, Hockenberry finds himself "identifying with Lolita, her innocence lost along with any identity other than sexual." He also compares American women to the religious police in Iran.[38] In the latter, Spacey double-speaks for both himself and Underwood, with lines such as: "You wouldn't rush to judgment without facts, would you?" "I showed you exactly what people are capable of. I shocked you with my honesty, but mostly I challenged you and made you think." "We're not done, no matter what anyone says. And besides, I know what you want. You want me back."

In these interventions, the accused defends himself against media annihilation. The sublime object (intellectual work, style) no longer serves the subject, and now is being performed for the enjoyment of the other. As "staged events," to use Downey's term, they obscure the search for ethical certainty. Searches for "Kevin Spacey's bizarre video" draw our attention away from the thirty individuals who have come forward with allegations of sexual misconduct. In her essay "Quit Using Lolita to Absolve Your Guilt, John Hockenberry," Sarah Weinman, author of *The Real Lolita: The Kidnapping of Sally Horner and the Novel That Scandalized the World*, redirects our focus: "as more #MeTooed men step forward to reclaim what they felt they were always entitled to, let's keep the focus on those they harmed, who always mattered more—and always will."[39]

An unconventional apologia that must be considered as students read *Lolita* is Nabokov's own "On a Book Entitled *Lolita*." This afterword, which Nabokov wrote to accompany the first American publication of excerpts from *Lolita* in *The Anchor Review* for 1957, has been included in most subsequent editions. It begins with the suggestion that after impersonating John Ray Jr. in the foreword, Nabokov may be offering "an impersonation of

Vladimir Nabokov talking about his own book."[40] Marilyn Edelstein points out that *Lolita* is unique in Nabokov's oeuvre for being bookended by the fictional editor's foreword by John Ray Jr. and the afterword by Nabokov, and as a consequence, many scholars have focused on the relationship between the two paratexts.[41] Yet as an apologia that immediately follows Humbert's apologia, the afterword identifies its audience, explains the author's rationale for writing, and defends against accusers. Like Humbert's apologia, and some of its readers, the afterword proposes that *Lolita* can be read well (correctly) and poorly (incorrectly). Nabokov's apologia calls attention to its incorporation of the genre's features, the processes by which artistic style is sublimated, and outlines its own challenge in acknowledging the fall of the sublime object through an attempt at its recuperation through explication.

It is evident from reading "On a Book Entitled *Lolita*" that Nabokov was troubled by how the book had been read. The publishing houses to which he sent the manuscript placed content above form: "Their refusal to buy the book was based not on my treatment of the theme but on the theme itself."[42] Nabokov laments the "gentle souls who would pronounce *Lolita* meaningless because it does not teach them anything." Some pronounced the book "anti-American." Others read "in a spirit of 'Why did he have to write it?' or 'Why should I read about maniacs?'" In response, Nabokov goes on to explain exactly why he had to write it, detailing the novel's origins in "The first little throb of *Lolita*" that "went through me late in 1939 or early in 1940." Around 1949, "the throbbing, which had never quite ceased, began to plague me again." Echoing Humbert's climactic "throb of the longest ecstasy," Nabokov "energetically resume[s]" his work to completion after nearly destroying it twice. The manuscript lives on the brink of destruction at his own hands, and despite this, and despite its completion, does it not become a shared object of the sublime for all readers? Acknowledging that not everyone shares his estimation of the work or reads it "correctly," Nabokov proceeds to explain that some of the allusions ("certain techniques in the beginning of *Lolita*") did not have their intended effect; he points out that pornographic writing, like detective stories, must be devoid of artistic originality so that "style, structure, imagery" do not distract the reader. He distinguishes art from "topical trash."

Readers have cited Nabokov's assertion in the afterword that "a work of art exists only in so far as it affords me what I shall bluntly call aesthetic bliss," and extrapolated it to wider discussions of Nabokov's artistic method. To a degree this indicates that the afterword succeeded in creating a shared system of values where Humbert's narration did not. The success of the afterword-apologia is especially evident when Nabokov laments his "private tragedy" of abandoning Russian for a "second-rate brand of English," a tragedy "which cannot, and indeed should not, be anybody's concern." Alfred Appel responds that it "*is* our concern," "it involves us all," for "only words can bridge the gulf" of "the distance between people."[43] "It is a necessary act of love to try," Appel opines, "and perhaps Nabokov succeeds with the reader where H.H. failed with Lolita."[44]

Yet the shared enjoyment of *Lolita* as Great Art, aided by the afterword, still did not extend to all readers, particularly those of later generations. Eric Naiman notes that the anxiety provoked by Nabokov's anti-didacticism led some readers to seek real-world redemptive value in reading *Lolita*. Readings aimed at providing "support to readers of political, sexual, or hermeneutic coercion," according to Naiman, are "indicative of the pressures Nabokov places on his readers."[45] They are also indicative of the pressures readers place on themselves to find meaning in the act of reading when the text has lost its fascination, when it becomes topical,[46] when legal "argument" is elevated to the place of the sublime. "Maybe poetry is all just artifice," Dean Young declares at the outset of his poem "Non-Apologia."[47] "Words never stop escaping back/into meaning," yet at the same time, "Don't we love words too for themselves"? In his explication of the poem ("The Poet on the Poem"), Young describes his love of occasioned poetry, of which "Non-Apologia" may be considered an example. "It sets up an energy field between the poles of improvisation and law, abandonment and purposefulness [. . .] It's always one thing *and* the other," he emphasizes, paraphrasing a line in the poem.[48] Although it predates the #MeToo movement by nearly ten years, the poem is a reminder that at a time of social and rhetorical instability, when justice is not guaranteed, when post-#MeToo voices get disciplined and our attention deflected away from suffering, the cost of abandonment stimulates a turn toward purposefulness that is resented by some, defended by others, and remains undefined even as it guides our conversations about literature, *Lolita*, and everyday ethics.

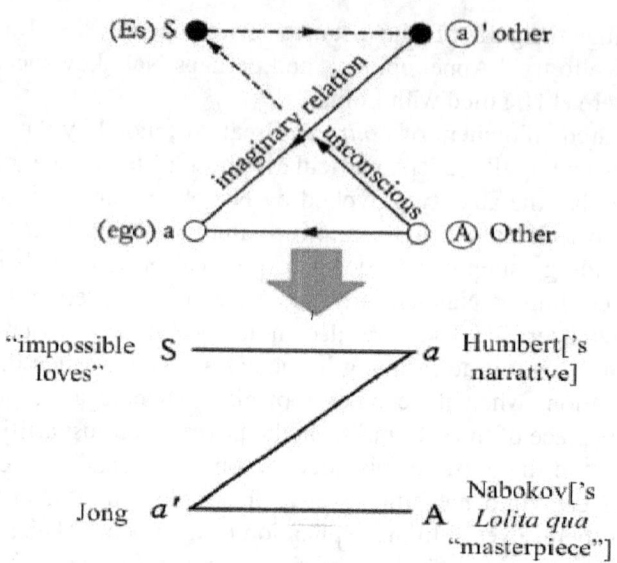

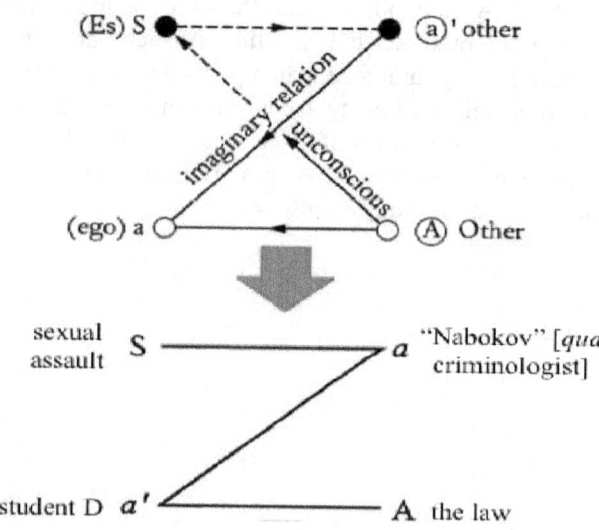

Figure 9.1.

WORKS CITED

Appel, Alfred. *The Annotated Lolita.* New York: Vintage, 1991.
Downey, Sharon D. "The Evolution of the Rhetorical Genre of Apologia." *Western Journal of Communication* 57, no. 1 (1993): 42–64.
Edelstein, Marilyn. "Before the Beginning: Nabokov and the Rhetoric of the Preface." In *Narrative Beginnings: Theories and Practices*, ed. Brian Richardson. London and Lincoln: University of Nebraska Press, 2009: 29–43.
Evans, Dylan. *An Introductory Dictionary of Lacanian Psychoanalysis.* London: Routledge, 1996.
Hewitson, Owen. "The Dora Parallax." August 4, 2014. https://www.lacanonline.com/2014/08/the-dora-parallax/.
Hockenberry, John. "Exile: And a Year of Trying to Find a Road Back from Personal and Public Shame." *Harpers*, October 2018. https://harpers.org/archive/2018/10/exile-4.
Johnson, Rachel. "Would Any Publisher Dare to Print *Lolita* Now?" *The Spectator*, March 9, 2019. https://www.spectator.co.uk/2019/03/would-any-publisher-dare-to-print-lolita-now/.
Jong, Erica. "Time Has Been Kind to the Nymphet: 'Lolita' 30 Years Later." *The New York Times*, June 5, 1988; Section 7, pg. 3.
Lanius, Candice. "Torment Porn or Feminist Witch Hunt: Apprehensions About the #MeToo Movement on /r/AskReddit." *Journal of Communication Inquiry* 43, no. 4 (2019): 415–36.
Lockwood, Patricia. "Malfunctioning Sex Robot." *The London Review of Books* 41, no. 19 (October 10, 2019): 19–24.
Lowdon, Claire. "Giving Him His Due." *The Times Literary Supplement*, no. 6066 (July 5, 2019): 3–5.
Naiman, Eric. *Nabokov, Perversely.* Ithaca and London: Cornell University Press, 2010.
Phelan, James. "Estranging Unreliability, Bonding Unreliability, and the Ethics of *Lolita*." *NARRATIVE* 15, no. 2 (May 2007): 222–38.
Ragland, Ellie. "Who Is Transferring What to Whom?" Academy for the Psychoanalytic Arts. http://www.academyanalyticarts.org/ragland-transferring.
Shepherd, Tory. "It's Scary that the Pseudo-Sorry Has Started to Echo through the #MeToo Campaign." *The Advertiser* (Adelaide, Australia), Sec. OpEd, October 10, 2018, p. 18.
Siegel, Lee. "Is the News Replacing Literature?" *The New Yorker*, February 12, 2014. https://www.newyorker.com/books/page-turner/is-the-news-replacing-literature.
Spacey, Kevin. "Let Me Be Frank." https://www.youtube.com/watch?v=JZveA-NAIDI.
Trilling, Lionel. *The Liberal Imagination.* New York: NYRB Classics, 2008. xxi.
Waddell, Laura. "Nabokov's Lolita: The Latest Thing Millennials Have Apparently Ruined." *The Guardian*, March 8, 2019. https://www.theguardian.com/books/2019/mar/08/nabokovs-lolita-the-latest-thing-millennials-have-apparently-ruined.
Wakamiya, Lisa Ryoko. "Humbert's 'Gendered' Appeals to the Jury Not of His Peers." In *Approaches to Teaching Vladimir Nabokov's Lolita*, eds. Galya Diment and Zoran Kuzmanovich. New York: Modern Languages Association, 2008. 141–46.
Weinman, Sarah. "Quit Using Lolita to Absolve Your Guilt, John Hockenberry." *The Cut*, September 14, 2018. https://www.thecut.com/2018/09/quit-using-lolita-to-absolve-your-guilt-john-hockenberry.html.
Wood, L. A., and Rennie, H. "Formulating Rape: The Discursive Construction of Victims and Villains." *Discourse & Society* 5, no. 1 (1994): 125–48.
Young, Dean. "Non-Apologia." *American Poetry Review.* (May–June 2008): 27.
Young, Dean. "The Poet on the Poem." *American Poetry Review.* (May–June 2008): 27.
Žižek, Slavoj. *Looking Awry.* Cambridge, MA; London: MIT Press, 1992.
———. *The Sublime Object of Ideology.* London, New York: Verso, 1989.

NOTES

1. The author wishes to thank Terry Coonan, Jennifer Adams, and Robert Romanchuk for their support. Lisa Ryoko Wakamiya, "Humbert's 'Gendered' Appeals to the Jury Not of his Peers." In *Approaches to Teaching Nabokov's Lolita*, eds. Zoran Kuzmanovich and Galya Diment. New York: Modern Languages Association, 2008: 141–46.
2. James Phelan, "Estranging Unreliability, Bonding Unreliability, and the Ethics of *Lolita*." *NARRATIVE*, 15, no. 2 (May 2007): 223.
3. Laura Waddell, "Nabokov's Lolita: The Latest Thing Millennials Have Apparently Ruined." *The Guardian*, March 8, 2019. https://www.theguardian.com/books/2019/mar/08/nabokovs-lolita-the-latest-thing-millennials-have-apparently-ruined (Accessed December 4, 2019).
4. Phelan, 225.
5. Phelan, 308.
6. Phelan, 236.
7. Lionel Trilling, "The Liberal Imagination." New York: *New York Review of Books*, 2008 (1950), xxi.
8. Erica Jong, "Time Has Been Kind to the Nymphet: 'Lolita' 30 Years Later." *The New York Times*, June 5, 1988; Section 7, pg. 3.
9. Jong, 3.
10. Jong, 3.
11. Ellie Ragland, "Who Is Transferring What to Whom?" Academy for the Psychoanalytic Arts. http://www.academyanalyticarts.org/ragland-transferring
12. D, "Final Paper." 2018.
13. Jong, 3.
14. Mapped onto the "L schema" from Lacan's Seminar IV, Jong's "impossible loves" and her Canonical Author "Nabokov" are placed in the symbolic positions of Ragland's "unconscious story" and "Other in the patient's being," respectively; "Humbert's narrative" and Jong herself are in the imaginary/identificatory positions. Likewise mapped onto the "L schema," Student "D"'s "sexual assault" and "the law" are placed in the symbolic positions of "story" and "Other"; the criminologist "Nabokov" and Student "D" are in the imaginary/identificatory positions. (Adapted from Owen Hewitson, "The Dora Parallax." August 4, 2014. https://www.lacanonline.com/2014/08/the-dora-parallax/.) See figure 9.1.
15. Tory Shepherd. "It's Scary that the Pseudo-Sorry Has Started to Echo through the #MeToo Campaign." *The Advertiser* (Adelaide, Australia), Sec. OpEd, October 10, 2018, p. 18.
16. Lee Siegel, "Is the News Replacing Literature?" *The New Yorker*, February 12, 2014. https://www.newyorker.com/books/page-turner/is-the-news-replacing-literature (last accessed December 4, 2019).
17. Siegel, 2019.
18. Claire Lowdon, "Giving Him His Due." *The Times Literary Supplement*, no. 6066 (July 5, 2019): 3–5.
19. Patricia Lockwood, "Malfunctioning Sex Robot." *The London Review of Books*. 41, no. 19 (October 10, 2019): 19–24.
20. Lowdon, 3.
21. Lockwood, 21.
22. Vladimir Nabokov in Alfred Appel, *The Annotated Lolita*. New York: Vintage, 1991. xli.
23. "The sublime quality of an object is not intrinsic, but rather an effect of its position in the fantasy space." Slavoj Žižek, *Looking Awry*. Cambridge, MA; London: MIT Press, 1992: 84.
24. Dylan Evans. *An Introductory Dictionary of Lacanian Psychoanalysis*. London: Routledge, 1996: 198.
25. Slavoj Žižek, *The Sublime Object of Ideology*. London, New York: Verso, 1989: 38.
26. Rachel Johnson, "Would Any Publisher Dare to Print *Lolita* Now?" *The Spectator*, March 9, 2019. https://www.spectator.co.uk/2019/03/would-any-publisher-dare-to-print-lolita-now/.

27. Johnson, 2019.
28. Johnson, 2019.
29. Waddell, 2019.
30. For a range of sample responses gathered from online discussions, see Candice Lanius, "Torment Porn or Feminist Witch Hunt: Apprehensions About the #MeToo Movement on /r/AskReddit." *Journal of Communication Inquiry* 43, no. 4 (2019): 423–26.
31. L. A. Wood and H. Rennie, "Formulating Rape: The Discursive Construction of Victims and Villains." *Discourse & Society* 5, no. 1 (1994): 125–48, cited in Lanius: 433.
32. Appel, 319.
33. Sharon D. Downey, "The Evolution of the Rhetorical Genre of Apologia," *Western Journal of Communication* 57, no. 1 (1993): 43.
34. Downey, 43.
35. The blog SorryWatch catalogues and dissects "apologies of all sorts": "We praise the good ones (and discuss what makes them good) and fling metaphorical monkey poop at the bad ones (using savage words and holding them up to ridicule)." http://www.sorrywatch.com/.
36. John Hockenberry, "Exile: And a Year of Trying to Find a Road Back from Personal and Public Shame." *Harpers*, October 2018. https://harpers.org/archive/2018/10/exile-4.
37. Kevin Spacey, "Let Me Be Frank." https://www.youtube.com/watch?v=JZveA-NAIDI.
38. Hockenberry, 2018. One also gathers from Hockenberry's post-#MeToo reading of *Lolita*, beyond his explanations of events and calls for compassion, is a resentment that extends to Nabokov for not having suffered any apparent professional consequences for having had an extramarital affair and writing a book that offends public decency to such a degree that Hockenberry got off the subway for fear that "even being seen with the book in public would confirm my offenses."
39. Weinman makes this pronouncement amid her observation of the phenomenon that "more people, particularly men, are clinging to *Lolita* to absolve their own terrible behavior." https://www.thecut.com/2018/09/quit-using-lolita-to-absolve-your-guilt-john-hockenberry.html.
40. Nabokov, in Appel, 453.
41. Marilyn Edelstein, "Before the Beginning: Nabokov and the Rhetoric of the Preface." In *Narrative Beginnings: Theories and Practices*, eds. Brian Richardson. London and Lincoln: University of Nebraska Press, 2008: 34–39.
42. Nabokov, cited in Appel, 314.
43. Appel, 456.
44. Appel, 456.
45. Eric Naiman, *Nabokov, Perversely*. Ithaca and London: Cornell University Press, 2010: 136–37.
46. In Naiman's words: "The price of literature's relevance may be the diminution of its literary value" (2010: 147).
47. Dean Young, "Non-Apologia." *American Poetry Review*. (May–June 2008): 27.
48. Dean Young, "The Poet on the Poem." *American Poetry Review*. (May–June 2008): 27.

Chapter Ten

Reading *Lolita* as a Teenage Girl

Francesca McDonnell Capossela

INTRODUCTION

Late one night, crossing a bridge over the Tiber, I asked a friend why he would no longer listen to Michael Jackson, but would read a book by J. D. Salinger (who was predatory toward young girls), or William Golding (who tried to rape a fifteen year old). This was 2019 and "Leaving Neverland," a film that documents the child sexual abuse allegations against Michael Jackson, had just been released. My friend had a good answer, the best answer I've heard to the question: music affects you differently than other art forms. When you listen to "Billie Jean," he said, you become the beat; you become Michael. When you read *Catcher in the Rye,* you judge the text, you analyze. The latter is less personal, less blinding, and less binding. You are not so intimately entwined with the text.

But if any book captures the seductive rhythm of a Michael Jackson song, it is *Lolita*. If books typically exist at a distance from the reader, able to be judged and analyzed, *Lolita* sidles up as close as it can; it breathes on your neck. We can still analyze it—we must—but it is hard to see the thing clearly, and even more difficult to understand through what lens we should be examining it.

The questions *Lolita* raises are timely, as well as timeless. In the age of identity politics and the #MeToo movement, how do we approach a text in which the narrator—and seemingly the novel itself—is oppressive? And doesn't any novel, simply by having a narrator, introduce some hierarchy of power, some kind of oppression?

I have always been reticent to dismiss any novel as immoral. I have no interest in mapping gender studies theories onto literature; I study literature because I am interested in texts themselves. But when I read *Lolita* in college, my second time reading the novel, I began to wonder if the novel itself, and not just the content it was depicting, was oppressive. And if a novel could actively oppress, rather than simply represent oppression, could it be considered art?

Lolita's aesthetic merit, to me, came down to whether the novel, like Humbert himself, silenced Lolita. As Nabokov says in an essay on Dickens in his *Lectures on Literature*: "a great writer's world is . . . a magic democracy where even some very minor character . . . has the right to live and breed" (*Lectures on Literature*, 124). A novel, to me, is democratic; it does not silence, or insist on one meaning. To know whether the book was truly artistic, I needed to determine whether Lolita had a voice within the text.

PERSONAL READING EXPERIENCES

When I was fifteen, I picked up a paperback copy of Nabokov's *Lolita* at JFK airport and read it on a flight across the country. My mother sat next to me as I fell dizzyingly in love with the novel. I don't know if she thought twice about buying me the book. I don't even know why exactly I picked it out (do all Hudson News stores sell Nabokov?), but my best guess is that I had heard the title enough times to know that it was a classic, and at that point in my life I was obsessed with reading every book in the Western literary canon.[1]

When I read *Lolita*, I was primed to empathize with Humbert Humbert. In his thought-provoking examination of *Lolita*, Leland de la Durantaye records Alfred Appel Jr. saying that "Humbert enlists us, against our will, on Humbert's side . . . Humbert has figuratively made the reader his accomplice in both statutory rape and murder" (*Style Is Matter*, 224). In my experience, most readers struggle against this enlistment, finding themselves appalled by Humbert's actions, even as they are drawn further in. But I do not remember being appalled at fifteen. I remember being convinced that morality had no place in art. I remember thinking the book's disturbing aspects were a mark of genius. I got a lot out of *Lolita*, even then. The language of the book was unlike anything I had ever encountered. It was—and is—the sweetest, richest book I have ever read. But I did not consider that I was a teenage girl reading about the rape and subjugation of a teenage girl.

A lot changed between my sophomore year of high school and my sophomore year of college, when I next encountered the novel. Identity politics surged to the forefront of national conversations. When I was a freshman in high school, I knew one other queer person. By the time I graduated, middle schoolers were coming out. Likewise, in junior year in high school, my Latin teacher asked who identified as a feminist and he and I were the only ones who raised our hands. One year later, half the school was participating in a feminist meeting group. Weeks before we graduated, two women came to speak to my grade about the sexual assault crisis. We went around the room counting up to four. Every fourth person stood up, to represent how many of the women in our class would be assaulted by the end of college. I was a four; I stood.

My long-lived love of *Lolita* was one of the reasons I took a "Novels of Vladimir Nabokov" course my sophomore year at Pomona College, taught by Professor Anne Dwyer, a fellow contributor to this book. We read the novel over spring break. I was in the Southern California desert with my dad, visiting Joshua Tree and Las Vegas. We stayed in a motel in Palm Springs and played tennis every other day. As I read about the motels of *Lolita*, and Lolita's forehand, about the driving and the Americana, I found myself continually having to put the book down. The novel felt too present; it invaded my week. It shaped my view of the tennis court. I was angry at *Lolita*; I remembered being fifteen and loving the book, and I felt like I had been duped into supporting a rapist. Like Alfred Appel Jr., I felt that in reading the novel, I was assisting Humbert Humbert. I was allowing violence.

This was 2016, before the #TimesUp or #MeToo movements had become mainstream, before Donald Trump's Access Hollywood tape had been released, but well into a growing consciousness around sexual assault. Nevertheless, I hesitate to present the question of "oppressive art" (and its place in the classroom) as a modern phenomenon. For centuries, women, especially women of color, have struggled against their objectification, have fought for justice, for an end to violence, and have striven to highlight the prevalence and horror of sexual assault. To act as if the #MeToo movement marks the beginning of this consciousness is to allow that these issues have only mattered as long as mainstream culture has been paying attention.

In that Palm Springs motel, with a light-up neon sign of a woman in a 1950s bathing costume, I did the only thing I could do to get through *Lolita*. I took a bright pink highlighter and I marked every instance of Lolita's speech. Anything she said in quotation, I included. Anything Humbert paraphrased, I left out. When I got back to campus, I typed up everything that I had highlighted. It is a ten-page document that I still have. I counted how many words Lolita says, and calculated, roughly, what percentage of the novel is Lolita's speech—what percentage, you might say, Lolita dictates.

A year later, in my college English building, I found a copy of Anne Carson's *The Albertine Workout*. In it, Carson attempts to resurrect the "real" Albertine (Marcel's love object in several volumes of *In Search of Lost Time*) from the narrator's objectifying, biased gaze. At one point, Carson counts up how often Albertine's name appears in the novel: "Albertine herself is present or mentioned on 807 pages of Proust's novel," she writes. And then she calculates what percent of those pages she is asleep: "On a good 19% of these pages she is asleep" (*The Albertine Workout*, 5). It was a strange parallel, between my project and Carson's.

CLASSROOM READING EXPERIENCES

When we returned from break to discuss *Lolita*, a Russian student looked down at the copy of the novel on his desk and said he wished he had never opened the book.

We spent two classes discussing whether our professor should have given us a trigger warning. My professor was worried that knowing about the content of *Lolita* in advance would destroy the effect of the book. It would be less successful in confounding us; it would be politicized too quickly. I was in favor of a trigger warning. Most people who open *Lolita* know what it is about. Most people read the back of books. In my opinion, knowing a girl will be assaulted does not diminish the novel. A trigger warning is no different than saying to your friend "can I tell you something awful?" You would do it naturally, and I believe that teachers would find it easier if they thought of it in different terms. Crucially, I would rather someone get a spoiler for a book than experience extreme duress. No great novel is ruined by a plot point being revealed prematurely.

The final classes devoted to *Lolita*—once we'd gotten past the trigger warning question—were primarily occupied with discussing either the Quilty sub-plot and Nabokovian word games or the morality and effect of the book itself. Effect is the right word, I think. No book is immoral because of its content; if any book is immoral, it is a book that makes the reader *more* misogynistic, *more* racist. We can think of a piece like *The Birth of a Nation*, which escalated and mythologized Klanism in a way that altered reality.

Though all of our classes on *Lolita* were interesting, they seemed to miss something crucial. Instead of looking at the book in front of us, we were reaching around it, politicizing it, avoiding it as literature. Talking about the issues of the text—rape, silencing, degradation—without investigating the text itself is a mistake. The story of *Lolita* does not exist in an abstract way—you cannot recount the plot and then judge the work. The book exists only as a string of words, and it is the language of the book that we must turn to in order to understand it.

LITERARY RESPONSES TO *LOLITA*

Feminist readers of *Lolita* struggle to justify a novel in which rape is so intrinsic that even the relationship between narrator and reader can feel predatory. Many have responded by attempting to resurrect the titular character.

Sarah Weinman's 2018 true crime book, *The Real Lolita,* details a real-life kidnapping that may have partially inspired Nabokov. Weinman's approach is to prioritize fact over fiction; she explains that "Real little girls end up getting lost in the need for artistic license. The abuse that Sally Horner . . .

endured should not be subsumed by dazzling prose" (*The Real Lolita*, 32). To illuminate the true experiences of victimhood, Weinman depicts the kidnapping of eleven-year-old Sally Horner by Frank LaSalle, and their subsequent trip across the country. In a San Jose trailer park, Horner was finally able to call for help. She was rescued, and returned home, where her kidnapping and abuse was almost never spoken of. Not long after, she died in a car crash with a boy she had just met.

Horner never got the chance to speak about what had happened to her during those months she spent with Frank LaSalle. Her family and friends found the events shameful and willed them to be forgotten. When we look for the facts of victimhood, we are often left with a void; abuse silences, just as Humbert's narration seemingly silences Lolita. Weinman—and her readers—study photographs of Sally to intuit glimpses into her personality, state of mind, and experiences. There is no doubt that her story tugs on our heart strings, but eventually we must conclude that we will never know Sally Horner. As Weinman herself says, "absence is as telling as substance. Inference will have to stand in for confidence. Imagination will have to fill in the rest" (87). Weinman introduces extraneous content in order to remedy the damage done by *Lolita*, but she ultimately fails to locate the "real" character of Lolita, the real truth of victimhood.

I understand and empathize with Weinman's preoccupation. With the desire to expose Nabokov as a puppet master, using the story of a real girl's abuse to tell a seductive and lascivious story. But the place to find a counternarrative to Humbert's is not in fact.

Other authors have attempted to offer counternarratives to Humbert's in the form of fiction. Pia Pera's *Lo's Diary* is a version of *Lolita* from Lolita's point of view, which guesses at Lolita's thoughts and feelings. Pera paints Lolita as a perverse, sex-obsessed seductress. In order to salvage Lolita from being relegated to objecthood, Pera casts her as actively as possible. What she misses, however, is that it is possible to be both a victim and an actor, to actively resist victimhood.

Both Pera and Weinman fail, just as my classes on trigger warnings did, because they leave behind the text. The most basic tenet of studying literature is that the text comes first. Faced with the confusion and seduction of *Lolita*, we forget this. But the answers to our questions can only be found in the pages of *Lolita*.

GOING INTO THE TEXT

The great success of my Nabokov class was Professor Anne Dwyer's guidance in firstly helping us understand the multiple layers of meaning across which Nabokov's novels operate, and secondly encouraging and assisting us in doing intensive studies of the work.

For my final essay in the class, I returned to my document of *Lolita*'s collected speech, and wrote an essay which analyzed only her words, citing none of Humbert's. My idea was that I would locate Lolita in the text. Not to prove some abstract point about literature, but because I believed she was there, lurking within the novel. Why else would generations of women have taken up her cause?

Lolita seems to be silenced throughout *Lolita*; even her name is Humbert's refashioning of her—she calls herself Dolly. But reading literature is not about accepting surface meanings; it, like *Lolita*, is about the opposite. A good reader looks deeper, sees past the surface, and often reads against the obvious "truth" of the narrative. *Lolita*, for all that we find disgusting within it, teaches us to read closer, look deeper, and find what lives beyond the façade of the text. And when we do look deeper, we find that the "real" Lolita, exists, buried, within Humbert's narrative.

To locate this "real" Lolita, I followed her language, and her gaze within the novel. This work convinced me that Lolita takes linguistic and imagistic control of the novel, and it turned into my undergraduate thesis. The conclusion of my work was, to me, clear: Nabokov buries the evidence of Lolita's agency, but once excavated, it is undeniable.

Lolita makes explicit that an inequality of power is constructed by the very structure of narrative. Durantaye writes that "though Nabokov . . . say[s] a great writer's world' is a 'magic democracy' the writer himself, as Nabokov sees him, is an absolute monarch" (25). But it is not only the writer who is a monarch. The narrator too, it seems, is placed in a position of privileged power. When the narrator describes his love object, he creates a subject-object relationship with her. Description relegates *something*—a Maserati, an ashtray, or a ballerina—to the role of object. The narrator speaks; the object does not.

Within the novel, the narrator is a dictator. Michael Wood calls this Humbert's "tyranny," but given Humbert's disregard for reality and his predilection toward propaganda, we might go so far as to call it fascism (*The Magician's Doubts*, 116). Rhetorical persuasion bordering on propaganda, the suppression of reality, the enforcement of a personal moral code onto others, violence against a category of people—if we are willing to validate "nymphets" as a category—these are the tenets of Humbert's fascism.

A novel narrated by a child molester highlights the monstrosities made possible by the narrator-object structure. *Lolita* spotlights abuse. "The word is incest," Lolita tells Humbert (141). Twice she says: "you raped me" (119, 202). But while *Lolita*'s very form emphasizes the fascism of the male narrator, the novel actually struggles against this orientation.

The apparent hierarchy of *Lolita*—in which Humbert has agency and Lolita does not—is undercut by Lolita's metafictional objections to the narrative, her attempts to rewrite Humbert's story, and her relationship to the physical objects around her, which at times act in defense of her. Lolita subverts the narrative of *Lolita,* and in doing so she overthrows the fascism of narration, creating a more equal novel-world. Through this subversion *Lolita* becomes, in Nabokov's words, a "magic democracy."

Like in many of Nabokov's novels, an alternate narrative hovers behind the surface narrative of *Lolita*. Books, newspapers, and diaries mentioned in *Lolita* suggest alternate versions of Humbert's narrative. As John Ray Jr. tells us in the introduction, we can find alternate versions of Humbert's story in several local newspapers. Also in the introduction, we learn that Vivian Darkbloom, Clare Quilty's co-playwright, has written her own memoir, a double to Humbert's *Lolita* (4). Charlotte owns a parenting guide full of questionnaires meant to track one's child's development, in which she has filled out her observations of her daughter; this book records Lolita through Charlotte's eyes instead of through Humbert's. These alternate texts imply that there are many *Lolita*s; Humbert's is not the only narrative. Nabokov draws the reader's attention to what exists beyond Humbert's awareness, at the edges of his narrative.

In Humbert's last conversation with her, he records Lolita, saying "if somebody wrote up her life nobody would ever believe it" (273). Lolita herself is explicitly interested in the narration of her life and the communication of that narrative to an audience. Similarly, Lolita sometimes gains a metafictional awareness of her status as character in a novel. After Humbert picks her up from camp, Lolita scolds him by saying, "You talk like a book, dad" (114). The sentence clearly taunts metafiction; Lolita knows that Humbert is writing her into a story.

Mona, Lolita's closest friend, writes to Lo that her letters are being "rigidly controlled," demonstrating that the girls know that their voices are being silenced and that they must find ways to work around the censorship (223). Lolita writes in her schoolbook that talk of boys makes her gag. Later, during their last meeting, she tells Humbert that "this world was just one gag after another" (273). Lolita is gagged by the male-dominated world, and she is aware of this silencing.

The only text over which Lolita has explicit control is her quoted speech, though even here Humbert's record cannot be entirely trusted. Dialogue grants Lolita the greatest access to authorial control. One afternoon at Beardsley, Humbert finds Lolita reading the chapter on "Dialogue" in Baker's *Dramatic Technique*. As if aware of her role within a novel, Lolita studies dialogue in order to better directly represent herself within the text. All of these moments taunt the possibility that Lolita has a, at least partial, metafictional awareness.

In Lolita's school play, written by Clare Quilty, the Young Poet character believes that another character is his poetic invention. Likewise, Humbert believes that Lolita is his invention, the love object of his novel. But he couldn't be more wrong.

One afternoon during their drive across the country, Lolita reads a newspaper column about sex offenders, and kidnapping, aloud:

> "If picked up, mark down the license of the car."
> "... and the brand of the candy," I volunteered ...
> "If you don't have a pencil ... scratch the number somehow on the roadside."
> "With your little claws, Lolita." (166)

And so she does.

Though Humbert's suggestion to mark down candy brands is a joke, Lolita's inclination toward candy bars, junk food, and drugstores throughout the novel provides a map of her culture for the reader. And though the newspaper article mistakenly insinuates that sexual assault perpetrators are primarily strangers lurking in public restrooms, Lolita is able to use the advice provided. She learns to scratch her message in the margins of the novel, however improbable it seems.

She even literally writes a license plate number at one point during the novel. It is not Humbert's license plate that she writes down, but a nonsense number that she uses to obscure his record of Quilty's license plate. Lolita is not looking for rescue like the newspaper advised; she is trying to rewrite Humbert's text.

Lolita's vocabularies enter the text and subvert Humbert and his own language. When he picks her up from camp after Charlotte's death, she uses two sets of language to establish her distance from Humbert. "We washed zillions of dishes," she tells her stepfather, "'Zillions' ... is school-marm's slang for many-many-many-many." While Humbert has previously tried to teach Lolita French, Lolita responds by teaching Humbert her slang, creating an equivalency between his language and hers. Lolita adds a word to Humbert's vocabulary and, since it is recorded in the novel, to the text of his narrative.

Lolita continues describing camp: "Last but not least, *as Mother says* ..." (114, emphasis added). By adopting her mother's language, Lolita invokes Charlotte's presence in the space of the car. She keeps her mother's linguistic predilections alive even after Charlotte's death.

Lolita also vests linguistic control through mispronouncing words. By warping words, Lolita makes them her own. She invents spellings. Humbert attempts to transcribe these mispronunciations by misspelling words like "delickwent" and "dahrling" (113, 119). In recording these words that clearly belong to Lolita, he cedes some control of the text to her. She becomes a kind of co-author. Most explicitly, Lolita uses language to take direct control of her narrative when she tells Humbert that "the word is incest" (141). By supplying her own word, she illuminates his abuse.

Quilty and Dick, Lolita's two lovers, also adopt Lolita's language. Quilty refers to their time together as a "vacation," a word that Lolita has used to refer to her time with Humbert (298, 173). But while Lolita's language becomes a part of the novel, invading Humbert's text and giving her an authorial role, her language also exists as an inaccessible, secret code. Humbert imagines that she and the nurse are conspiring together in a foreign language (243).

Lolita also communicates without direct speech. Leading Humbert to a window display when he asks where she ran off to earlier, she presents both him and the reader with a highly suggestive image, a kind of roadmap for reading *Lolita*. In the shop window, two mannequins have been disturbed by something. One is naked; one wears a wedding dress. The naked figure has no wig and no arms, and seems, from its size, to be a child. The larger mannequin, the one in the wedding dress, is only missing one arm. On the floor, where the missing arms and wig lie, the shopkeeper is attempting to clean up the scene. The arms, lying on the ground, look as if they are begging or praying.

In this scene, Lolita and Charlotte stand, the former naked and armless, the latter in a wedding dress and veil. Humbert crawls around on the floor, attempting to make the show window more beautiful, to aestheticize the traumatic image.

These are not the first fragmented women to whom Lolita has drawn our attention. On the living room davenport, a younger Lolita shows Humbert (plus the reader) a picture in a magazine in which a man relaxes on the beach while beside him lies a replica of the Venus di Milo, famously armless and partially buried in sand (58).

Lolita, like the arms lying on the shop window floor, guides her reader and her narrator to the mutilated female body. Through the linguistic and the imagistic, Lolita traces a story, like all writers must.

Throughout the novel Lolita attaches herself to certain things—physical objects—which, invested with Lolita's love, become talismans for the title character. By tracing these talismans, the reader can discover the generative and artistic world that Lolita creates out of the prison of the novel. Like language, these physical objects are manifestations of Lolita's power within *Lolita*. They provide her at times with a platform for self-expression, at times with protection.

Explaining his reluctance to let Lolita visit gas-station restrooms, Humbert admits that he "[feels] . . . that toilets—as also telephones [are] . . . the points where my destiny [is] liable to catch." He continues: "We all have such fateful objects" (211) Humbert is right about telephones; in his first sexual encounter with Lolita, during which he rubs himself off against her body on the living room davenport, she escapes his grasp with the excuse of a ringing telephone. The telephone saves Lolita from Humbert's grasp.

The telephone saves Lolita from Humbert again in Beardsley. During their most violent fight, Lolita finally confronts Humbert with her narrative of events, accusing Humbert of attempting to molest her while her mother was still alive, and of subsequently murdering her mother (205). Humbert grabs her wrists, hurting her. It is only when Humbert becomes aware that the telephone is ringing that Lolita is able to escape. About this second escape aided by telephone, Humbert says: "with people in movies I seem to share the services of the machina telephonica and its sudden god" (205).

But while the telephone appears as a Nabokovian deus ex machina that sabotages Humbert, there are other material objects and cultural artifacts, such as junk food and cars, which Lolita herself imbues with power and which she actively uses in her subversion of Humbert.

At tense and emotional moments in *Lolita*, our title character frequently turns to food as a way to distract Humbert or soothe herself. Food becomes a talisman that both protects Lolita and serves as one of Humbert's "fateful objects," frequently sabotaging him.

Lolita's love of food is well documented in the novel; Humbert remembers her enamored with a new dessert at the soda fountain (76). He watches her add ice cream to her cherry pie (122). She "follow[s] the scent of rich food ads" (147). Even her language is food-rich. She calls a cop a "fruithead" and says that she learned to "be a cake" at camp (113, 114).

Lolita's predilection for food is put into direct opposition with her rejection of Humbert: "To think that between a Hamburger and a Humburger she would . . . plump for the former" (166). Lolita actively chooses food, in stark contrast to the lack of consent she expresses in her relationship to Humbert.

When Humbert picks Lolita up from camp, he lies to her about Charlotte, saying she is ill and needs a serious operation, to which Lolita's only response is "Stop at that candy bar" (115). Though Humbert might read this non-reaction as proof of Lolita and Charlotte's strained relationship, one which he consistently fails to comprehend, Lolita's candy-bar craving might be a longing for comfort, a way of escaping the painful reality of her (soon to be) loss.

Lolita continues to use food as a diversion, an escape from Humbert. At the hotel, the night after Humbert picks her up from camp, Lolita says, "let's cut out the kissing game and get something to eat" (120). Much later in the novel, when she wants Humbert to leave the hotel room, she says she "crave[s] fresh fruits" and Humbert leaves to find her some. While he is gone, she goes outside, presumably to confer with Quilty.

If food provides Lolita with comfort, diversionary tactics, excuses, escapes, and alibis, it consistently sabotages Humbert. This sabotage is the other facet of its role as Lolita's talisman. If Humbert notices that telephones and toilets are objects that tend to bring about his downfall, food might be added to that list. Lolita's fondness for food manifests a protective layer around her.

This protective layer can most clearly be seen in Humbert's first attempt to rape Lolita, in the hotel room at the Enchanted Hunters Hotel, after he has tried and failed to drug his stepdaughter. Lying next to her, wondering if the sleeping pills have worked, Humbert is plagued by heartburn for which he blames the French fries he ate at dinner (129). Food, particularly fatty foods—one of Lolita's favorite kinds—troubles Humbert to the point of distracting him from her. Later, he describes himself as "burning with desire and dyspepsia," the dyspepsia now having taken an equal footing with his desire (131). The two feelings are mentioned alongside each other, as if the desire on the one hand is balanced out by the indigestion on the other. Lolita's food has parried Humbert's blow; Lolita is momentarily safe.

Also in the realm of food, *Lolita* refers several times to issues of dieting and body image. Charlotte frequently diets. The camp Lolita attends has a dietitian (110). And while scolding her for lying, Humbert advises Lolita to "watch [her] diet," saying, "the tour of your thigh, you know, should not exceed seventeen and a half inches" (209). He then retracts this slightly by saying he was kidding, but, kidding or not, the notion of dieting hovers in the background of *Lolita*, and Humbert's obsession with measuring Lolita provides adequate evidence to suppose that Lolita may feel some pressure to diet, to lose weight, to remain small for her captor who is obsessed with her nymphancy. Lolita's love of food then—of sugary, fatty, junk food—might be a rebellion, a way in which she resists Humbert's control, literally growing beyond his measuring tapes.

On one of their final drives together, Humbert gets a flat tire (228). Quilty pulls up behind Humbert, and Humbert starts to walk toward him. Then, a passing truck honks and he looks back at Charlotte's car to see it "gently creeping away" with "Lo ludicrously at the wheel."

Lolita has transformed from backseat driver—frequently chastising Humbert for his driving (113, 116, 149)—to actual driver, getting behind the wheel of her mother's car. She is about to escape Humbert, and her newfound freedom is crystalized in the realization that she, after watching her captor do it for hundreds upon hundreds of hours, can drive.

Lolita marks roadmaps with lipstick to plan her escape with Quilty; she reaches toward the steering wheel when Humbert threatens to turn the car around; she studies dialogue and makes metafictional jokes that only the reader—not Humbert—can understand. Lolita overthrows the fascism of narration and, ultimately, *Lolita* belongs to her.

CONCLUSION

Lolita is a novel about the tyranny of the male narrator, yet his female subject takes control of the very text Humbert has created. This is a uniquely Nabokovian feat, but one that can teach us about how to read democratically, not to satisfy moral purposes, but to realize art's aesthetic possibilities. In this essay, I have made an argument about how to study and teach *Lolita*, and how that methodology can help us decide what role morality and identity should play in studying literature.

As readers, we engage with complex texts in order to heighten our awareness of multiple strains of meaning. The very act of studying literature then, is, as I see it, one of extreme equality. The reader works to challenge the text, to see past it. To unearth the truth behind the guises of the characters and narrators. Like in life, in literature, there is always another perspective. Feminism asks that we read against the narrative of misogyny, that we challenge it. Literature asks that we read against a different kind of narrative. The skills of one are applied to the other easily.

Lolita says 2,121 words in *Lolita*, a novel which contains 112,473—that is 1.88 percent of the story. Among her most frequently used words are "no" (seventy-four times) and "oh" (twenty-seven times). There are thirty-one dashes, places where her language is cut off, either by her or by Humbert, and then often repeated as she attempts to make herself heard. To read *Lolita* well, to locate Lolita, we must follow her gaze, and listen to her narrative.

WORKS CITED

Carson, Anne. *The Albertine Workout*. New Directions, 2014.

Durantaye, Leland de la. *Style Is Matter: The Moral Art of Vladimir Nabokov*. Cornell University Press, 2010.

Nabokov, Vladimir. *Lectures on Literature*. Houghton Mifflin Harcourt, 2017, *Google Play*, play.google.com/store/books/details?id=P9JBDwAAQBAJ&rdid=book-P9JBDwAAQBAJ&rdot=1&source=gbs_vpt_read&pcampaignid=books_booksearch_viewport.

———. *Lolita*. New York: Vintage, 1989. Print.

Wood, Michael. *The Magician's Doubts: Nabokov and the Risks of Fiction*. Princeton University Press, 1998.

Weinman, Sarah. *The Real Lolita*. HarperLuxe, an Imprint of HarperCollinsPublishers, 2018.

NOTES

1. A note about the canon: my favorite book at fifteen was *The Great Gatsby*. I loved *Nine Stories*. I'd read Ben Lerner. I thought I *was* a male narrator, apathetic and roaming, watching the world as a fully autonomous *I*, never being watched in return, never living the double life of perceiving and being perceived. It wasn't until the following year, when I read *To the Lighthouse*, that I realized I was a woman.

Index

activist, activism, 12, 13, 23, 27n6, 75
androcentric, 15

Blasey Ford, Christine, 5, 109, 110, 120
bodylessness, 52

child sexual abuse, 2, 12, 14, 15, 18, 20, 23, 24, 29n19, 106, 106n4, 167
creative pause, 3, 51
Couturier, Maurice, 86
C. K., Louis, 69, 70n7

emotional intelligence, 110, 111, 115, 120, 122

female gaze turned inward, 52
"feminist killjoys," 15

hashtivism, 13
Herbold, Sara, 25, 40, 86, 122, 147
"helpless bystander" syndrome, 3, 51
Horner, Sally, 7, 18, 26, 27n3, 69, 71n10, 78, 88, 89n29, 111, 122, 159, 170, 171; Sally Horner Case, 27n3

incest, 2, 12, 18, 23, 28n8, 29n18, 75, 172, 174
Iser, Wolfgang, 3, 46, 47, 55. *See* reader-response theory

jouissance, 19, 23

Kavanaugh, Brett, 5, 109, 110
Kubrick, Stanley, 73, 93, 101; *Lolita* (1962), 4, 13, 74, 103, 111

Lolita's body, 17, 18, 19. *See* bodylessness
Lyne, Adrian, 4, 13, 27n5, 80, 85, 93, 103, 149n17

male gaze, 11, 17, 18, 26n1, 52, 66
misogyny, 11, 15, 24, 25, 73, 78, 84, 86, 87, 89n25, 89n28, 122, 178

Nabokov's Women: The Silent Sisterhood of Textual Nomads, 40, 40n10, 52, 55, 56n5, 56n17, 87, 88, 90n37, 90n62, 121, 122
Nabokov: *Bend Sinister*, 34, 47, 56n3, 66, 69, 71n13; *The Enchanter*, 27n3, 54, 94; "Good Readers and Good Writers," 19, 34, 40, 40n5, 54, 55, 56n24, 89n20, 122; *Invitation to a Beheading*, 34, 35, 50, 58, 126, 148; *The Luzhin Defense*, 35; "A Nursery Tale," 6, 128, 135, 137, 138, 148; "On a Book Entitled *Lolita*," 2, 37, 40, 40n4, 40n9, 94, 106, 159, 160; *Strong Opinions*, 22, 31, 35, 38, 40, 40n6, 100, 101, 106, 106n7, 129, 137, 148; "The Vane Sisters," 6, 137, 138

pedophilia, 2, 12, 13, 21, 24, 26, 27n3, 28n15, 29n18, 102, 133, 139
Pera, Pia, 122
prison literature, 3, 57, 59

Rakhimova-Sommers, Eléna, 3, 39, 40n10, 55, 56n17, 66, 71n13, 88, 90n37, 90n62, 110, 121, 148n1
reader-response theory, 3, 46, 47
"resisting reader," 15
re-traumatizing, 2, 14

Scarry, Elaine, 3, 66, 68, 71n12
sexual objectification, 13, 17, 18, 24, 135

sexual agency, 20, 137
sexual assault, 7, 12, 13, 14, 24, 28n16, 33, 38, 54, 140, 143, 154, 159, 164n14, 169, 174
suffering, 18, 47, 53, 57, 63, 64, 66, 67, 109, 140, 161

trigger warnings, 2, 14, 25, 28n10, 29n19, 157, 171

victim blaming, 65

Weinman, Sarah, 7, 27n3, 70n9, 78, 89n29, 159, 170

About the Editor

Eléna Rakhimova-Sommers is principal lecturer in Russian and global literature at the Rochester Institute of Technology. Her previous edited collection, *Nabokov's Women: The Silent Sisterhood of Textual Nomads*, was published in 2017. Rakhimova-Sommers' Nabokov-related publications ("Nabokov's Passportless Wanderer: A Study of Nabokov's Women," "Nabokov's Mermaid: 'Spring in Fialta,'" "The 'Right' Versus 'Wrong' Child: Shades of Pain in *Bend Sinister* and *Pnin*," and "The 'Olgalized' Otherworld of *Bend Sinister*") appeared in *Nabokov Studies*, *Russian Studies in Literature* and in the *Nabokov's Women* volume. Her 2018 study of Russian social ads incentivizing motherhood, "Your Stork Might Disappear Forever!" was published in *Cultural and Political Transformations in Putin's Russia*. Rakhimova-Sommers' next project is a study of the ten most influential Russian female YouTubers titled "When Women Lead Protest Movements."

About the Contributors

Charles Byrd has been teaching *Lolita* to American undergraduates for more than thirty years. He received his PhD in Slavic languages and literatures and comparative literature from Indiana University in 1996. Having taught at Texas Tech University and Washington University in St. Louis, he is currently senior lecturer in Russian at the University of Georgia. His articles on the eighteenth-century Russian writers Vasily Kapnist and Gavriil Derzhavin appeared in *Slavic and East European Journal* and *Russian Literature and the Classics*. Byrd is currently working on a book manuscript, "Faces of Imposture: Popular and Literary Russianization of Napoleon."

Francesca McDonnell Capossela is a writer and poet, currently pursuing a Master's in creative writing at Trinity College Dublin. She graduated cum laude from Pomona College with a BA in English and was awarded the best English thesis prize for her work on Vladimir Nabokov's *Lolita* and Marcel Proust's *In Search of Lost Time*. At Trinity College Dublin, she was awarded the Constantina Maxwell scholarship for her writing. Capossela's essays were published in the *Los Angeles Review of Books* and *The Point Magazine*, and her poetry has appeared in *Hanging Loose Magazine*, *Banshee*, and *The Cormorant Broadsheet*.

Julian W. Connolly is professor emeritus of Slavic languages and literatures at the University of Virginia where he served as chair of the Slavic Department for over fifteen years. He is the author of five books—*Ivan Bunin* (1982), *Nabokov's Early Fiction: Patterns of Self and Other* (1992), *The Intimate Stranger: Meetings with the Devil in Nineteenth-Century Russian Literature* (2001), *A Reader's Guide to Nabokov's* Lolita (2009), and *Dostoevsky's* The Brothers Karamazov (2013). He also edited four volumes of critical essays, including *Nabokov's* Invitation to a Beheading: *A Course Companion* (1997), *Nabokov and His Fiction: New Perspectives* (1999), and *The Cambridge Companion to Nabokov* (2005). He has published over ninety articles on Russian literature and culture. In 2016 he received the Richard Stites Senior Scholar Award from the Southern Conference on Slavic Studies and in 2018 he received the Leonor and Justo Ulloa Award for the best critical essay published in the *MIFLC Review* in 2018.

Anne Dwyer is associate dean and associate professor of German and Russian at Pomona College. She has published on literary treatments of the multiethnic Habsburg, Romanov, and Soviet empires; on life writing; and on the history of literary theory. She is currently writing a book on the Soviet lives of Viktor Shklovsky and Russian Formalism.

Marilyn Edelstein is associate professor of English at Santa Clara University, where she also teaches in the Women's and Gender Studies Department and the Ethnic Studies Department. She teaches contemporary American literature, feminist theory, women and literature, literary and cultural theory, and multicultural literature and theory. She has published two previous essays on *Lolita*: "Before the Beginning: Nabokov and the Rhetoric of the Preface," in *Narrative Beginnings: Theories and Practices*, edited by Brian Richardson (University of Nebraska Press, 2009); and "Teaching *Lolita* in a Course on Ethics and Literature," in *Approaches to Teaching Nabokov's Lolita*, edited by Zoran Kuzmanovich and Galya Diment (MLA Publications, 2008). She has also published book chapters and journal articles on Nabokov's *Pale Fire*, feminist theorist and cultural critic bell hooks, feminist psychoanalytic theorist Julia Kristeva, literature and ethics, feminist theory, and multiculturalism. She is working on a book on race, gender, and empathy in multicultural fiction.

Eric Naiman is professor and Bernie Williams Chair in the Department of Russian and Comparative Literature at the University of California, Berkeley. He is the author of *Sex in Public: The Incarnation of Early Soviet Ideology* (1997) and *Nabokov, Perversely* (2010) and has also written widely on nineteenth- and twentieth-century Russian literature.

Eléna Rakhimova-Sommers is principal lecturer in Russian and global literature at the Rochester Institute of Technology. She is the editor of the current volume, *Teaching Nabokov's* Lolita *in the #MeToo Era*. Her previous edited collection, *Nabokov's Women: The Silent Sisterhood of Textual Nomads*, was published in 2017. Rakhimova-Sommers' Nabokov related publications ("Nabokov's Passportless Wanderer: A Study of Nabokov's Women," "Nabokov's Mermaid: 'Spring in Fialta,'" "The 'Right' Versus 'Wrong'

Child: Shades of Pain in *Bend Sinister* and *Pnin*," and "The 'Olgalized' Otherworld of *Bend Sinister*") appeared in *Nabokov Studies*, *Russian Studies in Literature*, and in the *Nabokov's Women* volume. Her 2018 study of Russian social ads incentivizing motherhood, "Your Stork Might Disappear Forever!" was published in *Cultural and Political Transformations in Putin's Russia*. Rakhimova-Sommers' next project is titled "When Women Lead Protest Movements."

José Vergara is visiting assistant professor of Russian at Swarthmore College, where he teaches courses on Russian language and culture of all eras, including one on Russian prison narratives. He has also taught various literature classes at two correctional institutions in Wisconsin and Pennsylvania. In his research, he specializes in prose of the long twentieth century, with an emphasis on experimental works. Vergara has published articles on writers including Vladimir Nabokov, Mikhail Shishkin, and Sasha Sokolov in *Nabokov Online Journal*, the *Slavic and East European Journal*, the *Slavonic and East European Review*, and *The Russian Review*. His current primary research project examines literary responses to James Joyce.

Lisa Ryoko Wakamiya is associate professor of Slavic in the Department of Modern Languages and Linguistics and courtesy associate professor of English at Florida State University. She writes on transnational literary migration, post-Soviet literature and film, and the intersections between narrative and material culture. Her publications appeared in *Slavonica*, *Novoe literaturnoe obozrenie*, and *Approaches to Teaching Nabokov's* Lolita. She is the author of *Locating Exiled Writers in Contemporary Russian Literature: Exiles at Home* and co-editor of *Late and Post-Soviet Russian Literature: A Reader*.

Alisa Zhulina is assistant professor of theatre studies in the Department of Drama at New York University and affiliated faculty with the Department of Russian and Slavic Studies. Her articles have been published or are forthcoming in *The Journal of the History of Ideas*, *Modernism/Modernity*, *Modern Drama*, *Theatre Survey*, and *Performance Research*. Her writings on Nabokov have appeared in *Nabokov's Women: The Silent Sisterhood of Textual Nomads*, edited by Eléna Rakhimova-Sommers, and in *Vladimir Nabokov et la France*, edited by Yannicke Chupin, Agnès Edel-Roy, Monica Manolescu, and Lara Delage-Toriel. She is currently completing a book titled *Theater of Capital: Money and Modern Drama* that analyzes the works of, among others, Ibsen, Strindberg, and Chekhov.

www.ingramcontent.com/pod-product-compliance
Lightning Source LLC
Chambersburg PA
CBHW061715300426
44115CB00014B/2701